D1498899

NEW FEMINIST ESSAYS ON VIRGINIA WOOLF

NEW FEMINIST ESSAYS ON VIRGINIA WOOLF

Edited by
JANE MARCUS

University of Nebraska Press

Lincoln

© Jane Marcus 1981
All rights reserved. No part of this publication may be
reproduced or transmitted, in any form or by any means,
without permission

First published in the United States of America
by the University of Nebraska Press,
Lincoln, Nebraska 68588

Printed in Hong Kong

Library of Congress Cataloging in Publication Data

Main entry under title:

New feminist essays on Virginia Woolf.

  Includes index.
  1. Woolf, Virginia Stephen, 1882–1941—Criticism
and interpretation—Addresses, essays, lectures.
2. Feminism and literature—Addresses, essays,
lectures. I. Marcus, Jane.
PR604. N4   823'.912   80–51873
ISBN 0–8032–3070–2

For Lisa
a daughter to think forward through

Contents

Acknowledgements

The editor and contributors would like to thank the following for their help with the preparation of this book: the Henry W. and Albert A. Berg Collection, Astor, Lenox and Tilden Foundation, the New York Public Library and its helpful curator, Dr Lola L. Szladits. They also wish to thank the many colleagues, friends and students who have contributed so much to new feminist criticism of Virginia Woolf, and are grateful to those who have provided a forum for their work in the Modern Language Association Woolf Seminar, and the conferences at Santa Cruz, Princeton and Bucknell, where many of these papers were first read. Brenda Silver has been an invaluable help in answering our questions about Virginia Woolf's reading notes, and is a silent contributor to this volume.

The editor wishes to thank the National Endowment for the Humanities for a research fellowship which supported this work, the staff of the Matematisk Institut, Aarhus, Denmark, for their generous help in providing facilities in which to pursue this project, and Michael Marcus, who built her a study in which to finish it.

The editor and publishers wish to thank Angelica Garnett and Quentin Bell, on behalf of the Literary Estate of Virginia Woolf, and The Hogarth Press Ltd and Harcourt Brace Jovanovich Inc., for permission to quote from the following published works: extracts from *Jacob's Room, The Years, Between the Acts, The Common Reader, Monday or Tuesday, A Haunted House and Other Stories, The Moment and Other Essays, A Writer's Diary, Three Guineas, The Letters of Virginia Woolf* (vols 1–5), *Collected Essays* (vols 1–4), *The Second Common Reader, The Waves, A Room of One's Own, To the Lighthouse, The Voyage Out, The Pargiters, Mrs Dalloway, and Orlando* by Virginia Woolf, and *Moments of Being: Unpublished Autobiographical Writings of*

Virginia Woolf, edited by Jeanne Schulkind, © 1920 by George H. Doran Co.; © 1921, 1922, 1925, 1927, 1929, 1931, 1932, 1937, 1938, 1941, 1944, 1948, 1972 by Harcourt Brace Jovanovich Inc.; © 1928 by Virginia Woolf; © 1948, 1949, 1950, 1953, 1954, 1955, 1956, 1957, 1959, 1960, 1965, 1966, 1967, 1969 by Leonard Woolf; © 1976 by Harcourt Brace Jovanovich Inc. and Marjorie T. Parsons; © 1975, 1976, 1977 by Quentin Bell and Angelica Garnett.

Notes on the Contributors

LOUISE DESALVO teaches at Farleigh Dickinson University. She is the editor of the early draft of *The Voyage Out* called *Melymbrosia*, published in a limited edition by the New York Public Library, and of 'The Journal of Mistress Joan Martyn' (with Susan Squier), *Twentieth Century Literature* (Autumn/ Winter 1979).

NORA EISENBERG teaches at the City University of New York (La Guardia) and has completed her first novel. She has contributed to the *Virginia Woolf Miscellany*.

ELLEN HAWKES'S 'The Virgin in the Bell Biography' was the first of the new feminist approaches to Woolf scholarship. She taught women's studies and modern literature at Boston University. Her first novel will appear in 1981.

SUZETTE HENKE is the author of *Joyce's Moraculous Sindbook: a Study of 'Ulysses'* and coeditor of a collection of essays on Joyce's women characters. She teaches at the State University of New York at Binghamton.

JANE LILIENFELD teaches at Boston University and is at work on *Women Writers, their Mothers and their Texts*. Her earlier essay on *To the Lighthouse* appeared in *Twentieth Century Literature*.

JUDY LITTLE is a poet and scholar who teaches at Southern Illinois University at Carbondale. Her essay on *Between the Acts* in *Women and Literature* is an important contribution to Woolf scholarship.

JANE MARCUS edited a special issue of the *Bulletin of the New York Public Library*, a revaluation of *The Years* (Winter 1977). She is at present preparing Dame Ethel Smyth's letters to

Virginia Woolf for the Women's Press, *One's Own Trumpet: Dame Ethel Smyth and Virginia Woolf – a Portrait in Letters.* Volume 2 of *New Feminist Essays on Virginia Woolf* is being prepared.

SELMA MEYEROWITZ is completing a book on Leonard Woolf. She contributed to the *Virginia Woolf Miscellany*.

MADELINE MOORE edited the 1977 *Women Studies* special issue on Virginia Woolf, organised the Santa Cruz Woolf Conference in 1974, and is finishing a book on Virginia Woolf. She teaches at the University of California at Santa Cruz and is at present at Sussex University on an exchange professorship.

SARA RUDDICK, who teaches at the New School for Social Research, is a philosopher. She coedited *Working it Out* and is at work on a book on maternal thinking.

SUSAN SQUIER teaches at the State University of New York at Stony Brook. She recently gave a paper on Virginia Woolf at the Simone de Beauvoir Conference in New York.

J. J. WILSON is an editor of *Virginia Woolf Miscellany*. Her book *Women Artists* (with Karen Petersen) was published by Harper and Row/The Women's Press. She teaches at Sonoma State University in California.

Introduction

JANE MARCUS

'Publishers are capitalists – publishers are cowards' says Miss
Marchmont in *Jacob's Room*, which is why the Miss Marchmonts
and Virginia Woolfs of this world buy their own presses and
publish their own pamphlets on how 'colour is sound – or,
perhaps it has something to do with music', and their novels
without heroes and plots. Nowadays cowardly capitalist publishers (who are sometimes known to do the right thing for
the wrong reason) have discovered that radical and feminist writers have a large audience of radical and feminist
readers.

This book is for those readers. The critical work of the
contributors has often been buried in academic and feminist
journals, their papers read at Virginia Woolf conferences or
the Modern Language Association seminar. Now we should
like to share it, as we have shared our work on the manuscripts, our new readings of the novels, our reinterpretations
of the life, with each other. For feminist criticism of Virginia
Woolf has been a collective effort. Our methodologies differ,
as do our training and our ages and our styles. We are linked
by sex and a sense that something has been missing in Virginia
Woolf scholarship. As a literary critic, Virginia Woolf is the
mother of us all, in precisely the personal and political ways
that Gertrude Stein meant when she claimed this kinship with
Susan B. Anthony. This book is meant as a claim of kinship
with Virginia Woolf. By now, she is saying, from her garret
window in the house of fiction, you should have shaken the
shoddy fetters of class from your feet; you should be able to
speak freely about .sex and the family; academic journals
ought to let you say that Henry James is 'lewd' if you want to,
and that Carlyle should have had a baby and Jane written a

novel. Alas, she also left the legacy to her literary daughters of 'writing beautifully', which (as she told Ethel Smyth) she was too busy to do as she had to say things which had not been said before. We feel those same pressures, and so leave that legacy to our literary daughters and our students.

Our work has been greatly inspired by the publication of Virginia Woolf's diaries, letters and manuscripts by Quentin and Anne Olivier Bell, and Nigel Nicolson and Joanne Trautmann, and by the co-operation of the curators of the Berg Collection at the New York Public Library and of the Monk's House Papers at the University of Sussex.

As a literary critic and novelist, Virginia Woolf thought not only back through her mothers but also sideways through her sisters. It was a collective historical effort and an active political effort of committed socialist feminism. There is no need to rewrite her biography as one of the Lives of the Obscure which so fascinated her. We must simply shine our lights into the musty corners that neither nephews nor professors have ever seen the need to dust off.

Motherhood, even literary 'motherhood', remains a taboo subject, though Ellen Moers has demonstrated brilliantly how women writers influence each other across continents and centuries. And Adrienne Rich has shown the ways in which patriarchal culture has dispossessed us of motherhood and of our own mothers, in literature and in life, frustrating both our instinctual and our intellectual claims to kinship. When Virginia Woolf writes 'women alone stir my imagination', we are bound to consider the power of that influence. She raided the patriarchy and trespassed on male territory, returning to share her spoils with other women: women's words, the feminine sentence, and finally the appropriate female form. Her place in modern European letters, next to the giants of her age, was won by defiance, rebellion and deliberate self-consciousness as an outsider.

As Jacob leaves his 'respectable', 'intelligent' prostitute to work at the British Museum, the narrator comments that 'something was wrong'. Patriarchal culture, here described as 'the whole bag of ordure, with difficulty held together', threatens to spill over the pavement. Why, we women critics ask, has so little attention been paid to the social criticism, the sexual politics, of Woolf's novels? Have the critics' eyes been so riveted on the 'feminine sentence' that their ears have not heard what it says?

'There is in the British Museum an enormous mind', the narrator tells us. 'Consider that Plato is there cheek by jowl with Aristotle; and Shakespeare with Marlowe. This great mind is hoarded beyond the power of any single mind to possess it.' The 'exasperated sensibility' of Julia Hedge, the feminist, is burdened with the 'gigantic labour' of penetrating that mind, while Jacob can work 'composedly, unconcernedly'. Julia Hedge wets her pen in bitterness and leaves her shoelaces untied from the effort of stealing women's history from that closely-guarded hoard. 'Her eye was caught by the final letters in Lord Macaulay's name' (and the feminist reader wonders if this is a reference to Jacob's paid tryst with Laurette on the previous page). 'And she read them all around the dome – the names of great men which remind us – "Oh damn," said Julia Hedge, "why didn't they leave room for an Eliot or a Brontë?" ' No wonder 'death and gall and bitter dust were on her pen-tip'. For the raids on the hoarded culture at the British Museum recorded by Virginia Woolf and her feminist characters, by Elizabeth Robins and Dorothy Richardson, are still necessary. Resting there recently, after a frustrating attempt to find the Millicent Garrett Fawcett Women's Library, which had disappeared without a trace from its old house in Victoria, I was reading one of Virginia Woolf's drafts in the manuscript room. It occurred to me that the Keeper might know where it had gone, that treasure house of British women's history and literature. Yes, he said, it had gone to a polytechnic in the East End. 'Can you imagine', he exclaimed, looking me straight in the eye, 'they wanted *us* to take it, those women's papers!' Did he notice, that like Julia Hedge, my cheeks flushed red, a defensive light lurked in my eye? I did not know at the time that Virginia Woolf had been a major supporter of the Women's Library, that she had contributed money and books and urged her friends to do the same. What I did find there in 1970 was a letter to one of the Strachey sisters asking for a headache remedy to counter a visit from her mother-in-law.

The space around the dome is now blank, as blank as the cheques in *Three Guineas* before the narrator figures out just where her loyalties lie as a female middle-class intellectual. We have spent far too much time as literary critics trying to penetrate the male mind; and Virginia Woolf's mind, her philosophical and political thought, is a subject almost totally ignored by her biographers and critics. It is virgin territory, across which we may make what she called in her draft of *The Years* a 'track of our own'.

Let us imagine, then, a room of our own in the British Museum, one great woman's mind throbbing under its dome. Let the ring of great names read Sappho, Jane Austen, George Eliot . . . Woolf cheek by jowl with Wollstonecraft. We shall leave the 'savage' and 'pedantic' scholarship to the descendants of Jacob. With these mothers to think back through, we ought to be worthy literary daughters of Virginia Woolf.

This point of view demands some revision of the 'canon' of the uncanonised artist. One must look carefully at *The Voyage Out* and see, as Madeline Moore does, a dramatisation of the Demeter and Persephone myth. *A Room of One's Own* and *Three Guineas* must be read for their meaning as well as their style, as is done by all the writers in this book. The classics can be re-examined from this angle, as Jane Lilienfeld is always teaching us new ways to read *To the Lighthouse* and Suzette Henke shows us the way to read *Mrs Dalloway* as a redemptive mystical novel. The revolutions against traditional forms can be explored as J. J. Wilson 'with explanation kind' diminishes the difficulties of *Orlando* and Judy Little reads *Jacob's Room* as comedy, a parody of the *bildungsroman*. The manuscripts yield new insights through this method, as in Nora Eisenberg's examination of 'Anon', and Louise DeSalvo's study of an early short story.

Perhaps the most important revision of the current canon of Woolf's works is our claim that *Night and Day* and *The Years* are two of her greatest novels. In addition to the essay here by Susan Squier, the reader may consult some of our previous collective efforts to analyse these novels: in the Winter 1977 special issue of the *Bulletin of the New York Public Library*, a revaluation of *The Years*; and, on *Night and Day*, Margaret Comstock's essay in the Virginia Woolf issue of *Women's Studies* (1977) and mine in Ralph Freedman's collection *Virginia Woolf: Revaluation and Continuity: A Chorus of Voices* (Berkeley, Calif., 1979). Dismissed by previous critics as dull novels of fact, shrill and boring exceptions to the rule in prizing only the 'poetic' style of an apolitical and anti-social Virginia Woolf, these novels are examined by feminists as being deeply subversive of patriarchal and capitalist British culture. *Night and Day* read in this way is neither merely a modern Meredith novel nor Jane Austen revisited; it shakes the very foundations of the archetypes in reversing the male and female roles and the light and darkness of patriarchy's most glorious celebration of itself as civilisation, Mozart's opera *The Magic Flute*.

Volume 25 of *Twentieth Century Literature* contains editions of unpublished manuscripts by contributors to this book. Louise DeSalvo and Susan Squier have edited the short story 'The Journal of Mistress Joan Martyn'; Ellen Hawkes has edited 'Friendships Gallery'; Madeline Moore provides an edition of *Orlando* and letters from Vita Sackville-West and Harold Nicolson. Brenda Silver has edited 'Anon' and 'The Reader', which are discussed here by Nora Eisenberg.

It is already clear that we do not consider 'Bloomsbury' as an important influence on Virginia Woolf. Ellen Hawkes contributes a study of Woolf's feminist utopian impulses and the influence of her literary sisters and women friends. Ellen Hawkes's work on this subject has been an early and important influence on the development of feminist criticism of Virginia Woolf. The political and feminist themes of the short stories emerge in Selma Meyerowitz's study of the 'politics of deception'.

In view of the attacks on Leonard Woolf and the brutal examination of Virginia Woolf's 'madness' in the recent biographies, one is tempted to read one of these stories, 'The Legacy', as an allegory. The stories are far closer to auto-biographical reality than the novels, less successful artistically but suggestive of some of the problems of her marriage. 'Lapin and Lappinova' is a heartbreaking story of a husband's abrupt refusal to continue playing a fantasy game of love, his abandonment of his wife to walk unreal paths alone without the least attempt to lure her into the real world. And 'The Legacy' may be read as an allegory of Woolf's primary commitment to the struggle of the working class, her suicide as an escape from a husband deeply and daily involved in political work while ignoring the claims of women and their working-class brothers for political freedom. The dead wife's diary reveals to the complacent husband that she was deeply committed to revolution and willing to die to prove her loyalty to her lover and his values. What shocks him most is the revelation that she has killed herself to escape from him, her jailer and keeper, while he with smug self-satisfaction had congratulated himself on being a good husband. A feminist approach to Virginia Woolf's life inspires Sara Ruddick to a study of real and fictional brothers in 'Private Brother, Public World', incisive in its psychological analysis and rewarding in its literary analysis of *The Waves*. Here again, a 'poetic' novel is seen to have a political message. My own interest is expressed in two impulses: the claim that Woolf's thought ought to be examined in the context of the women who influenced its development, and the more insistent claim that her work and life ought to be wrenched out of their provincial English Bloomsbury setting and seen in relation to the work of her real contemporaries: Proust, Kafka, Brecht, Benjamin – the exiles, Jews, homosexuals and radicals, the Europeans with whom she seems most at home in her homelessness.

Something may be said here about the growth of Virginia Woolf's feminism. It is too often lightly assumed that this was a traditional form of rebellion against a Victorian father's oppression. But there are more subtle complications and more severe contradictions. As Noël Annan has pointed out in his biography, Leslie Stephen was thin-skinned and highly sensitive about masculinity. Insecure himself, he pushed his body to the limits of its endurance in mountaineering expeditions and then collapsed with real and fancied illness into the arms of a series of women to be nursed back to physical and mental health. He was obsessed with the idea of chastity in women; the names of his daughters are testimony to his dependence on male literary images of virginity from Dante to Swift to Lowell. His objections to Hardy's sexual women are well known, as is his formation of the taste of an age of readers of the *Cornhill* by the choice and direction of the writing of lady novelists whom he championed as fit for female readers and despised at his ease among men. The double literary standard which he did so much to promote was the cause of many real-life disasters. While the virtues of such a character may be seen in Vernon Whitford in *The Egoist*, the total disaster he wreaks in other people's lives may be seen in

Hardy's re-creation of him as Henry Knight in *A Pair of Blue Eyes*. Knight is so blinded by the need to prove the purity of the owner of those blue eyes that he destroys not only her life but also his own and many others besides. But Virginia Woolf's greatest rebellion was against her mother.

Virginia Woolf was the child of a woman whom the great feminist Meredith adored and tried to change. He sought to stir her conscience against her self-chosen role as 'princess to a patriarch', to teach her sex-loyalty and to encourage her to raise her baby girls to regard their brother Thoby as an equal, not a superior. But Julia Stephen was an anti-feminist, an active and staunch conservative on the question of women's rights. By signing Mrs Humphry Ward's anti-suffrage petition she gave her name and reputation to an infamous historical document which forever proclaims treason to her sex. Julia Stephen was not an ignorant and superstitious woman, and cannot be excused for class snobbery and collaboration on those grounds. She chose, even before her marriage to Leslie Stephen, to accept what her daughter was to 'detest' as 'the male point of view'. Julia Stephen named her daughters in acts of obeisance to this point of view, to suit male images of female propriety and chastity: Stella and Vanessa for the male misogynist literary imagination of Jonathan Swift, and Virginia (though it was a family name), in deference to James Russell Lowell, Leslie Stephen's American literary friend, after the former colony named in honour of Queen Elizabeth. The literary male obsession with chastity in women is here given a maternal authority far more destructive to female identity than any sibling groping in the dark.

But this is to state the problem in intellectual terms, to attempt to understand what Elizabeth Hardwick called 'that great mind working' in Virginia Woolf. That Virginia Stephen grew up to equate virginity with freedom and protected her chastity with a vengeance, that she eventually attempted to argue that virginity was a natural desire of all women, is a result of her mother's intellectual influence. Those portraits of virgin mothers, Mrs Ramsay and Mrs Dalloway, which confuse and excite us, are the product not of Christian piety but of an aggressively godless household where women were worshipped and despised. These contradictions were not lost on Virginia Woolf, nor did she fail to note the price paid by those who collaborate in their own oppression.

'Every mother is a judge who condemns her children for the sins of the father' is the epigraph to Rebecca West's powerful feminist novel *The Judge* (1922). Virginia Woolf could only get through half of it before she gave it to her sister Vanessa as a birthday gift. There is a way, if one works intellectually and politically, of seeing Virginia Woolf's novels as personal acts of expiation to her mother for her father's sins, as well as public acts of expiation, songs of sisterhood to atone for her mother's inability to accept feminism.

JANE MARCUS

1 Thinking Back through Our Mothers

JANE MARCUS

I. THE COLLECTIVE SUBLIME

Writing, for Virginia Woolf, was a revolutionary act. Her alienation from British patriarchal culture and its capitalist and imperialist forms and values, was so intense that she was filled with terror and determination as she wrote. A guerrilla fighter in a Victorian skirt, she trembled with fear as she prepared her attacks, her raids on the enemy. She was so hostile to the patriarchy and felt that her anger was so present in all her efforts that no evidence of literary 'success' was assurance enough of acceptance, and she collapsed after sending her books to the printer. She always feared she would be found out, that the punishment of the fathers for daring to trespass on their territory was 'instant dismemberment by wild horses', as she told Ethel Smyth.[1] The violence of men's imagined retaliation was in direct proportion to the violence of her hatred for their values. Like Kafka she felt that writing was a conspiracy against the state, an act of aggression against the powerful, the wilful breaking of a treaty of silence the oppressed had made with their masters to ensure survival. Language and culture belonged to *them*; to wrest it from them was an act requiring the utmost courage and daring. If language was the private property of the patriarchs, to 'trespass' on it was an act of usurpation. To see herself as untying the Mother Tongue, freeing language from bondage to the fathers and returning it to women and the working classes, was also to cause herself acute anxiety about what *they*

1

would do when they found out. By writing she committed a crime against the fathers, and she expected, like her beloved Antigone, to be buried alive for it. As Antigone's defiance of Creon was not simply that of the individual against the state, or a woman against men, but the assertion of old matriarchal forms against a new male legalistic and revengeful culture, so Virginia Woolf's rebellion sought not only the overthrow of male culture but also a return to the oppressed of their rightful heritage and the historical conditions in which to enjoy it. No wonder she was afraid.

When she published 'A Society', in which she dared to suggest that a sisterhood of philosophical inquiry might be as necessary to women as male secret societies or brotherhoods to men, Desmond MacCarthy, as 'Affable Hawk', showed his claws. She never reprinted the sketch, in which her characters decided that a way must be found for men to bear children to occupy themselves in a useful way and to prevent them from obstructing women's progress towards intellectual freedom. She answered him,

> Can he point to a single one of the great geniuses of history who has sprung from a people stinted of education and held in subjection, as for example the Irish or the Jews? It seems to me indisputable that the conditions which make it possible for a Shakespeare to exist are that he shall have had predecessors in his art, shall make one of a group where art is freely discussed and practised, and shall himself have the utmost freedom of action and experience. Perhaps in Lesbos, but never since, have these conditions been the lot of women.[2]

Virginia Woolf's position as 'daughter of an educated man', a self-styled 'outsider' in British society, may be likened to the position of the Jewish intellectual in Weimar Germany.[3] While the Holocaust provides historical evidence that Kafka and Walter Benjamin were not neurotic in their perception of the hatred of the Germans, British male violence against women took less murderous forms. Nevertheless, Woolf's *feelings* about women's oppression match those of her German Jewish contemporaries. Even as they felt that as Jews they were administering the intellectual property of a people who

denied them the right to do so, Virginia Woolf felt as a woman
literary critic in the same untenable position in relation to
British culture. Rationally they could prove that hatred of
them as Jews or as women was unfounded; in neither case
could that lessen the sting of real and genuine contempt.
Kafka regarded words as stolen property; he strove for
perfection in prose style in High German as Woolf did in
English, to lessen the anxiety of being found out. The products
of bourgeois families, they saw the enemy within as well as
without, in those who pretended that Jews or women were not
the hated objects of society's contempt. For the Jews the way
out lay in Zionism and communism; for Virginia Woolf it was
feminism and socialism.

Walter Benjamin kept notebooks full of quotations; tearing
statements out of context, he felt like a robber making attacks
on history. Virginia Woolf did the same thing, as the
notebooks for *Three Guineas* and *The Pargiters* show us. By
quotation she sought to rob history of its power over women.
The quotations she used in *A Room of One's Own, Three Guineas*
and *The Pargiters*, the scholarly footnotes in which documenta-
tion is a form of possession of the truth and exorcism of evil,
are the intellectual pacifist outsider's only weapons against lies
and injustice. Like Bernard in *The Waves* or the eccentric
Samuel Butler, the Jewish or female notebook-keepers could,
by collecting facts and insults, rob them of their power to hurt.
'All notebook literature', she wrote in 'Mr Kipling's
Notebook', 'produces the same effect of fatigue and obstacle,
as if there dropped across the path of the mind some block of
alien matter which must be removed or assimilated before one
can go on with the true process of reading. The more vivid the
note the greater the obstruction.' It was with this consciousness of creating an obstacle course for the reader that she used
the technique herself. When Virginia Woolf wrote essays on
women writers or collected material for her projected *Lives of
the Obscure*, part of the excitement lay in her role as raider on
received history. She could see herself as a redeemer of lost
lives and described with rapture the feeling of rescuing
stranded ghosts, as their 'deliverer'. Finding *Udolpho* much
better than she had been led to believe, she declared that she
would lead 'a Radcliffe relief party'. The artist of the
oppressed articulates the desire for deliverance of the

stranded ghosts of her ancestresses throughout history. She seems hardly to have lived among her contemporaries but to speak directly to the future, to our generation. Leonard Woolf described his wife's peculiar walk, how people stared at her; it is the same as Hannah Arendt's description of Walter Benjamin's – a mixture of advancing and tarrying, one foot in the past and one in the future. The 'incandescent death' which Bertrand Russell found alight in her novels derives from what Lukács called 'transcendental homelessness' in the modern novelist and from her identity as spokeswoman for the outsiders. She was a redemptress of time, saying to her contemporaries in *Between the Acts*, with Kafka, 'there is an infinite amount of hope, but not for us'.

When Clive Bell compared his sister-in-law's style (in living and writing) to Constantin Guys, the Parisian painter and *flâneur*, he claimed a worldliness and cosmopolitanism which few others have recognised in Virginia Woolf. But a female *flâneur* is almost a contradiction in terms. For a woman who walks the streets of a big city aflame with curiosity can only be a street-walker, a prostitute. A self-defined 'street-haunter', Virginia Woolf knew all the awkwardness of these contradictions. While Benjamin was haunted by all the Berlin streets from which class and race prohibited him, Woolf was inhibited both by sex and by class from following her nose or her eyes wherever they longed to go. She knew not only the fright which followed Rose's experience of the pervert exposing himself on the corner of her own street in *The Years* but also the humiliating crippling of the imagination which forces Rose to give up thinking of herself as the brave, adventuring Pargiter of Pargiter's Horse. Each excursion was dangerous and debilitating, an anti-patriarchal act, a storming of the citadel of male dominance. Whether the men were would-be attackers or would-be protectors, they impeded her halting progress through the streets. And women whose interest was in maintaining the *status quo* were the first to stare and point at the eccentric whose relaxed insistence on being her natural self in the street violated all the taboos by which one can always distinguish a lady from a tramp. Caring so little for class distinction signified, ironically, a lack of sexual discrimination in a person so fundamentally pure.

Imagining herself a woman warrior, Virginia Woolf

stormed the city of London (as she 'stormed' the texts of classical male culture with her Greek teacher, Janet Case). London was simultaneously the citadel of her suffering and the space of her joy. So she enshrined it in memory, while mocking its monuments to patriarchy, imperialism and capitalism. In her London novels, *Night and Day, Mrs Dalloway, Jacob's Room, The Waves* and *The Years*, as well as her essays, all the temples to great men are descrated and denounced, St Paul's, Harley Street, Big Ben and the Houses of Parliament, the British Museum and Westminster Abbey. She felt the pulse of London all the more powerfully because she was an 'outsider'. Like Walter Benjamin's record of a bourgeois Jewish childhood in Berlin, she recorded a ghetto which pretended it was paradise before its members disappeared into the diaspora. Benjamin has captured a whole culture in *Paris: The Capital of the Nineteenth Century*. But Virginia Woolf has memorialised a *London: The Capital of the Patriarchy*. Her own battles for psychic and physical space in that all-male territory which restricted middle-class women to the private house are recorded in *A Room of One's Own*. The woman artist's need for privacy is there declaimed not as a retreat, but rather a place to put on her armour for her assaults on the public world. When one is both a radical and a feminist, one must build a counter-world to that of both the fathers and the mothers. And, while she was at it, Virginia Woolf also built in her fiction a spiritual protest to the self-righteous ethics of her family.

Virginia Woolf, like Walter Benjamin, was both a 'Marxist' and a mystic. It has been far easier for critics to chase the 'rainbow' in her style than to knock their heads against the 'granite'. When forced to recognise the pervasive feminism, they have diagnosed it as a social disease which breaks out in ugly spots, branding her as a bitter ingrate. Will she ever be greeted with the sum of her attributes rather than with the partial acclaim which must exclude the content from the form or the radical message from the luminous matter? Can we see her as a scholar, a fantasist, a historian and a practical joker, a recluse and a *flâneur*, a poet and a propagandist, a mystical dreamer and a hard-working journalist? If she could read Proust for the social criticism as well as the poetry, we can learn to read her in the same way. Like Walter Benjamin she reads the things of the real world, the objects and spaces luminous in her own memory, both as sacred texts and as productions of dialectical historical forces. For both of these refugees from bourgeois reality, dwellers in the diaspora of dreams, memory is the mother of muses. And she demands that, if you dig deep enough (for Benjamin she emodies the archaeologist digging the layers of Troy, while for Woolf she is the fisherwoman letting down her line into the depths of the unconscious) you can draw out of the individual memory the 'illuminations' or 'moments of being' which allow the artist to touch the collective memory. By her spiritual geography in the mapping of places and monuments, time is defeated by space and the remembrance of rooms and rhythms and objects (like her mother's chair in 'A Sketch of the Past'). Remembrance, as in Proust, is a triumph over time, the building of a 'continuing city'. Recall the moment in *Mrs Dalloway* when the aeroplane flies over Greenwich – an intersection of time and space. But here is no hallowed image of time the reaper. Instead a solitary man rolling the lawn observes the scene. As in Marvell's 'The Mower against Gardens', time has been the sower of discord and war, and is demolished and rolled flat. Big Ben in her novels, particularly *Mrs Dalloway* and *The Years*, is a great masculine bully, dominating the lives of the citizens.

Like Benjamin, Woolf works topographically against the patriarchal and geneological imperative, the strength of whose dicta we see in her own remembrance of the inability to step over a puddle (and Rhoda's in *The Waves*). It is with fear and trembling that one crosses the thresholds of street space strictly forbidden by the fathers. In mapping the diaspora the writer takes on an enormous task, the book's last gesture of defiance before the loudspeaker and the film drown out the human voice. In both writers a fierce leftist desire for social change is matched by visionary myths and symbols for order and community. The pacifist's passion for a violent cleansing is only just held in check. The reader trembles in conspiracy with the writer of *Three Guineas*. Will the patriarchs (pictured like police posters of the enemies of society) leap off the page *en masse* and imprison us, who have identified them as the real fascists? Woolf's concept of the collective sublime was Greek, operatic, Brechtian; an anti-authoritarian rational and mystical answer to individualistic, romantic and personal traditions of European thought and action. If we see her with Benjamin and Proust, Brecht and Kafka rather than with Forster and Lawrence, we are doing the right topographical job as critics. With the right maps we may find our way in the city of her novels.

Fascism is what they feared. Both Woolf and Benjamin chose suicide rather than exile before its tyranny. It seems oddly coincidential that they were both tormented by the same dream figure, the little hunchback of German fairy tales, the crippled figure which appears in so many of Woolf's novels. 'We are Jews', she described herself and Leonard – meaning they were outsiders, oppressed critics of oppression. *Three Guineas* was the pacifist's last stand against fascism, whose origins were to be found in the family and private property. Women and the working classes were not responsible; let the capitalists and imperialists fight it out. In the meantime women and their working-class brothers ought to 'trespass' on the private property of language and literature, educate themselves in anti-capitalist colleges and assert their own collective values. This view infuriated her own generation. Its ethical purity appeals to ours, little as we live up to it.

While she lived and wrote and battled against the fathers, she sought relief from anxiety about these attacks in the imagination of a linked history of literary and political mothers. (Her childhood, she told Ethel Smyth, was dominated and depressed by 'those 68 black books', her father's *Dictionary of National Biography*; her *Lives of the Obscure* would slay the patriarchal ghost.) 'Thinking back through our mothers', a necessary act for all women writers, would afford one maternal protection for one's own raids on the patriarchy and simultaneously raise female consciousness. For finding our mothers is no easy task (Woolf was particularly tormented about the gap between Sappho and Jane Austen). She expected that women artists would become feminists through this experience and also that they would make common cause with other oppressed groups. She herself found Joseph Wright, who wrote the *English Dialect Dictionary*, to be a brother; the witty Sydney Smith so 'lovable' a man that she wished she could have married him.

All her life, Woolf sought 'protection' from living women as well as from historical mothers. '... what you give me is protection', she wrote to Ethel Smyth.

> I look up at you and think if Ethel can be so downright + plainspoken . . . I need not fear instant dismemberment by wild horses. It is the child crying for the nurse's hand in the dark – you do it by being so uninhibited – so magnificently unselfconscious. This is what people pay £20 a sitting to get from Psychoanalysts – liberation from their own egotism.

Woolf knew by experience how women influence each other. Far from Harold Bloom's concept of the 'anxiety of influence', it is rather the opposite, affording the woman writer relief from anxiety, acting as a hideout in history where she can lick her wounds between attacks on the patriarchy. Anxious Virginia Woolf was indeed, but not out of the need to appease her ancestresses or outdo her mothers. She did desire to surpass her sister contemporaries, but laughed at Katherine Mansfield calling her the new Jane Austen. Her own portrait of Jane is in fact a self-portrait set a century before ('She, too, in her modest, everyday prose, chose the dangerous art where one slip means death'), and *Mrs Dalloway* is not a new *Clarissa* except in so far as English fiction demands that chastity *is* woman's character.

When Virginia Woolf wrote that 'we think back through our mothers', she had, as usual, a triple point to make, since her roles as artist, feminist and socialist were subtly intertwined in what she called 'the triple ply', and her literary criticism is always a braided narrative with three strands of thought. She meant here, I think, to assert that fiction had long been female territory, but, more than that, that each generation of women writers influences each other, that style evolves historically and is determined by class and sex. She expected her literary 'daughters' to take up where she left off; they would not be so discreet about sex and they would not have 'the shoddy fetters of class on [their] feet'. 'For masterpieces are not single and solitary births', she wrote in *A Room of One's Own*, still using her maternal metaphor, 'they are the outcome of many years of thinking in common, of thinking by the body of the people, so that the experience of the mass is behind the single voice.'[4] And her letters always maintain to her critics that if the

Edwardians had been better writers, the Georgians would have been better still.

Was she trying to establish a female 'canon' of great works by women as an alternative to male critical authority? I think not. She saw herself as a link in a long line of women writers; she knew just where her own work fitted and what heritage she was leaving for the women writers who would come after her. She wrote to Ethel Smyth of her

> ecstasy at your defence of me as a very ugly writer – which is what I am – but an honest one, driven like a gasping whale to the surface in a snort – such is the effort and anguish to me of finding a phrase – and then they say I write beautifully! How could I write beautifully when I am always trying to say something that has not been said, + should be said for the first time, exactly. So I relinquish beauty, leave it as a legacy for the next generation.[5]

It is interesting that Woolf characterises women's protection as liberation from the ego. For the ego is the enemy; even in herself, where she fought fiercely to control it, she saw the ego as male, aggressive and domineering. In the psychic triangle of mother, father, child, it was an attempt to eliminate the father. In Freudian terms, she sought to fuse the id and the superego – in *her* artistic terms, granite and rainbow – leaving the mental, the personal, out altogether. The 'damned egotistical self' must be repressed, and one can even see in Marxist terms that her worship of solid objects and their spiritual reality is a fusion of sub- and superstructure, avoiding as much as possible the middle term of patriarchal society as it exists. What some readers have seen as her incapacity to create character is not an incapacity at all but a feminist attack on the ego as male false consciousness. She will not supply us with characters with whom we may egotistically identify. This would be weakness on her part, encouragement of self-indulgence on the part of the reader. She disarms us. We are forced to lay down our weapons as readers. All our egotism and individuality, the swords and shields of the hated 'I, I, I' must be abandoned outside the doors of her fiction. Not only do her novels advance a collective idea of character, but the common reader is stripped of his/her individual relation-

ship to author and text. We are to see ourselves as part of a
collective audience, as in Brecht's epic theatre, linked to
readers of the past and future as the writer is engaged in
building the structure of 'literature' as a historical effort. In
'How It Strikes a Contemporary' she urges us to see 'writers as
if they were engaged upon some vast building . . . being built
by common effort. . . . Let them scan the horizon; see the past
in relation to the future; and so prepare the way for
masterpieces to come.' (T. S. Eliot uses a similar idea in
'Tradition and the Individual Talent' to enforce reactionary
patriarchal ideas.)

The final apotheosis of this anti-individual 'philosophy' is
expressed in *Moments of Being*

> we – I mean all human beings – are connected with this;
> that the whole world is a work of art, that we are parts of the
> work of art. *Hamlet* or a Beethoven quartet is the truth about
> this vast mass that we call the world. But there is no
> Shakespeare, there is no Beethoven; certainly and emphati-
> cally there is no God; we are the words; we are the music; we
> are the thing itself.

This is the final victory over the ego, the utter identification of
art with human struggle, as Marx and Engels defined history
as *'nothing but* the activity of man pursuing his aims'. The
rapture which the writer feels on perception of the collective
unity of art and life in history is extraordinary. As a
philosophy of art it revives the romantic notion of literary
progress while eliminating the idea of artists as a priesthood of
men of genius. While the poet is still for her the legislator of
morality, his authority is derived not from an individual talent
but from the expression of collective consciousness. The
'egotistical sublime' of the patriarchy has been replaced by a
democratic feminist 'collective sublime'.

Her model is the opera house – Bayreuth, to be specific.
Her 1909 visit had filled her with the desire to make fiction
aspire to the condition of Wagner's opera: a unity of the
audience and the natural world with the words and music, the
nearest approach to the sublime she had experienced. It was
epic theatre for ordinary people, an aspiration fulfilled in *The
Years* and *Between the Acts*. As in Brecht (whose essay on epic

theatre she may have read in Desmond MacCarthy's *Life and Letters* in 1936) there is no Aristotelian catharsis, no empathy with the stirring fate of the hero. We are educated to be astonished at the circumstances in which the characters function and dramatic moments are caused by interruptions of daily life. The reason for the 'plotlessness' of Woolf's novels is that they reverberate to the rhythm of the common life, not of the individual life. She could say with Proust, what is the plot of Ecclesiastes or the *Divine Comedy*? She wants to close the gap, to fill in the abyss which separates the players from the audience, art from life. In an age in which fascism and socialism fought for the allegiance of the masses, she sought to hold history, art and the people in the embrace of a giant 'we'.

We are to play the role of the chorus in a Greek play: we share her risk – 'how dangerous this poetry, this lapse from the particular to the general must of necessity be'; 'the intolerable restrictions of the drama could be loosened' by the comments of the chorus, 'the undifferentiated voices who sing like birds in the pauses of the wind' to capture 'those ecstasies, those wild and apparently irrelevant utterances'[6] which characterise her novels from *Jacob's Room* onward. Participating in the collective sublime of Woolf's narrative voice, we share her dangerous mission, become co-conspirators against culture. In redeeming our own past we become our own redeemers.

II.   REDEMPTION AND RESURRECTION

Virginia Woolf first learned to say 'we' as a woman. It was not so much a liberation from her own ego, as she explained to Ethel Smyth, as a liberation from the loneliness of individual anxiety. Thinking back through her mothers gave her her first collective identity and strengthened her creative ability. Her whole career was an exercise in the elimination of the ego from fiction in author, characters and readers. It was the expansion of the word 'we' in a world of women writers past and future which grew eventually to speak for all the alienated and oppressed, as Mary Datchet's feminism expands in *Night and Day* to international socialism.

Virginia Woolf's 'mothers' and aunts and women friends brought her into being as a writer, encouraging her efforts, publishing her work in the *Guardian* (a church weekly).[7] In this circle of female friendship the members collected the letters and diaries of their mothers and aunts, wrote their biographies, shared faded photos and anecdotes of ancestresses. The first lives of the obscure which attracted Virginia Woolf's romantic vision of herself as 'deliverer' were women's. She would untie their tongues – 'the divine relief of communication will soon again be theirs'. Her essays provide an example and a methodology for feminist critics and biographers, extending the literary and political rescue and redemption to obscure and working-class men (such as Joseph Wright) and to 'the eccentrics'. 'Sometimes, though it happens far too seldom, lives have been written of these singular men and women, as, after they are dead, someone half-shamefacedly has put together their papers.' Coming to their rescue she found them

> often so dishevelled, in such dishabille from their long obscurity and fantastic behaviour that we are not certain of remembering even their names. Without names and so strangely inspired, leaving behind them now one line, now one word, and now nothing at all, what whim is it that bids us go seeking them round the corners and just beneath the horizons of so many good books devoted to good men? Surely the world has been right in conferring biographies where biographies are due? Surely the shower of titles and honours has not always descended on the wrong heads? That the world's estimate has been perverse from the start, and half her great men geese, are themes too vast to be disposed of in one short article.[8]

If our mothers provide us with protection, camouflage and courage, the duties of daughters include not only redemption of their lives and works but resurrection as well. In the 'heart of the woman's republic' – a place Virginia Woolf felt had a reality in the company of Margaret Llewelyn Davies and her companion Lilian Harris, Janet Case, her Greek teacher, and her sister Emphie – the lives of women would be brought to light and life. In the woman's republic all our sainted mothers are present only by our efforts in raising them from obscurity and reprinting their works.[9]

What Virginia Woolf sought in her intense personal and artistic relationships with women may best be explained in mythological rather than psychological terms. The work of the great classical scholar Jane Harrison had a powerful influence on Virginia Woolf's imagery and metaphors.[10] Harrison's work on mothers and daughters in pre-classical Greece, her study of the transition of the powerful myths of mother-goddess worship into patriarchal Greek thought as we know it, was very important to Virginia Woolf's writing and thinking. The 'Hymn to Demeter' and the story of Persephone were especially moving for a writer who always thought of herself as a 'motherless daughter'. It may help us to understand what she meant by 'thinking back through our mothers'. She sought in her friendships with women both freedom and protection. The Demeter–Persephone myth affirms eternal refuge and redemption as well as resurrection. The mother will never abandon her daughter. She will weep and wail and search the underworld, bring her out of the darkness of sexual experience, childbirth, madness, back into the world of light and freedom. She will restore her virginity.

Woolf's mother died just as her daughter reached puberty, linking sexuality and death forever in her mind. Marrying, she added a note of savagery to the chastity of her name and self-image. In 'A Sketch of the Past' she recalled the intense pleasure she felt when her mother praised a story she had written: 'it was like being a violin and being played upon'. Her mother's praise unleashed all the dormant creative forces within her, untied her tongue, gave her freedom and speech. Did she relive the experience when her women friends approved her manuscripts? 'It is true', she wrote to Ethel Smyth in 1930, 'that I only want to show off to women. Women alone stir my imagination.'

She sought out people who remembered her mother, cherishing Elizabeth Robins's description of Julia Stephen as 'half madonna, half woman of the world'. She and her friends discussed their mothers. Early in her relationship with Ethel Smyth she wrote, 'Yes, I think your mother adorable. So was mine.' 'Odd as it may seem to you', Ethel Smyth wrote on 2 May 1930, 'I did love you before I saw you, wholly and solely because of *A Room of One's Own*.'[11] Woolf's feelings confirm Smyth's theory that

> with me and I think many women the root of love is in the imaginative part of one – its violence, its tenderness, its hunger . . . the most violent feeling I am conscious of is . . . [her dots] for my mother. She died thirty-eight years ago and I never can think of her without a stab of real passion; amusement, tenderness, pity, admiration are in it and pain that I can't tell her how I love her (but I think she knows). Now you can imagine how much sexual feeling has to do with an emotion for one's mother!

(About as much sexual feeling as Woolf dramatises in Lily Briscoe's love for Mrs Ramsay, one imagines.)

There is a poignant irony in the situation, given the real Julia Stephen's actual opposition to women's emancipation. She signed the ardent anti-suffragist Mrs Humphry Ward's petition in the *Nineteenth Century*, joining the ranks of middle-class mothers who were the worst foes of women's freedom in the eyes of radical feminists from Mary Wollstonecraft to Olive Schreiner, George Meredith to Virginia Woolf. Meredith mocked his friend, 'Enough for me that my Leslie should vote, should think. Beautiful posture of the Britannic wife! But the world is a moving one and will pass her by.' Julia Stephen remained his 'stout Angel', but he never ceased to criticise her for playing the reactionary role of 'princess to a patriarch'. For he knew that it was the daughters of such mothers who suffered, and he asked to see the children before their father had convinced Thoby that he was superior to his sisters, and before Julia had insisted that they accept the role of inferiors. 'Courage is proper to women', he told her, 'if it is properly trained.' Meredith was having a difficult pregnancy with his great feminist novel *Diana of the Crossways* as she was bringing to birth her daughter Virginia. The feminist novelist wrote to the mother of his successor as feminist novelist, worried mother to worried mother. But Julia Stephen had no sympathy whatever with Diana, the fictional motherless daughter who wants both a political and an artistic career.[12]

Virginia Woolf kept her mother's copy of *Diana of the Crossways*, inscribed by Meredith, 'An Emma might this Julia

have been,/To love at least forgive, the heroine.'[13] She did not
live to love or forgive her own Diana-like daughter. And other
women – Margaret Llewelyn Davies, Madge Vaughan, Violet
Dickinson, Vita Sackville-West, Ethel Smyth – were able and
willing to play the role of Emma. The most important
relationship in Meredith's novel is between Diana and her
friend Emma. The two intellectual women belong to the
'sisterhood of sensibility'. They play the roles of mother and
daughter and of lovers to each other. In an extraordinary
scene which makes 'George Verimyth' worthy of his nickname
and echoing with the power of the Demeter and Persephone
myth, Emma brings Diana back to life by feeding her from the
same spoon and sleeping with her. Diana's suicide attempt was
to starve herself to death. Emma brings her back to life and
into marriage with a 'radical', warning her in the end of the
dangers of childbirth and the terrors of the journey.

Life, of course, often imitates fiction, but seldom as accurately as Virginia Woolf lived the life of her fictional step-
sister, Diana. As we know from the *Letters*, her relationship
with Violet Dickinson exactly paralleled that of Diana and
Emma, even down to the details of Violet nurturing the
post-suicidal Virginia back to life after her disappointing
sexual experiences with a man. Diana's 'betrayal' of the Corn
Law repeal as an anti-patriarchal act is like Virginia Woolf's
involvement in the Dreadnought Hoax.

Violet Dickinson's wedding gift of a cradle to Virginia
Woolf seems explicable in the same terms. After an apprenticeship (both literary and human) as daughter, then as lover,
the young woman is sent into the world of men by the childless
older woman to become a mother and an artist. But, as
Persephone comes back to the woman's world of sunlight and
freedom for half the year, so the daughter fears separation
but hopes for protection. Their shared ideal is an ideal of
freedom and freedom is symbolised by virginity. The fear of
marriage (in fiction and in life) is the fear of loss of freedom
with loss of virginity. Maternal love makes one both chaste and
free. In Woolf's female utopia (in the Berg collection) written
for Violet Dickinson, freedom is the theme in a world much
like Carroll Smith-Rosenberg's 'female world of love and
ritual'. Liberty is eroticised by the idea of the power of
maternal love to redeem and rescue the daughter, who can

enter the male world but return for rebirth into light and
freedom, back in her mother's arms, a virgin.

Woolf sought from many 'mothers', including her husband,
maternal protection from her own suicidal impulses. The
letters, early and late, refer to the 'ethical' aspects of suicide.
She demands from her sister Vanessa, and from Ethel Smyth,
philosophical arguments on the ethics of suicide. That
Leonard agreed to a suicide pact in case of Nazi invasion was
enough 'maternal' approval for her to sink herself forever in
mother water.

She had demanded to know how her friends wrote, painted,
composed music, thought – and she shared with them her
own deepest analysis of writing. She also flirted outrageously,
courted affection and then withdrew, wanting love letters
more than love scenes, for words to her had as much potency
as acts to other people. She explained that words, like women
artists, need privacy. 'Why?', she asked in *A Writer's Diary*, and
answered herself, 'for their embraces, to continue the race'. In
'Craftsmanship' she claimed, 'Our unconsciousness is their
privacy; our darkness is their light.' Words, she wrote, 'are
much less bound by ceremony and convention than we are.
Royal words mate with commoners. English words marry
Irish words, German words, Indian words, Negro words, if
they have a fancy. Indeed, the less we enquire into the past of
our dear Mother English the better it will be for that lady's
reputation. For she has gone a-roving, a-roving.' Language
can mean liberation, Woolf believed, and her image here of
Mother English as promiscuous is another of those forays
against patriarchal culture. Not only has she changed the sex
of language and culture; she has robbed them of respect-
ability.

In 'Royalty' she wrote of Queen Victoria,

> between the old Queen and the English language lay an
> abyss which no depth of passion and no strength of
> character could cross. . . . When she feels strongly and tries
> to say so, it is like hearing an old savage beating with a
> wooden spoon on a drum. . . . But probably she owed much
> of her prestige to her inability to express herself. The
> majority of her subjects, knowing her through her writing,
> came to feel that only a woman immune from the usual

frailties and passions of human nature could write as Queen Victoria wrote. It added to her royalty.

Here she has completely turned the tables of history: the Queen is a savage because she misuses language; commoners who can express themselves are the real aristocracy of culture. The woman who was the symbol of an age's repression of women, symbolic of their loss of freedom in politics and art, is reduced to a stone-age caricature, a primitive animal. 'We begin to wish that the Zoo should be abolished; that the royal animals should be given the run of some wider pasturage – a royal Whipsnade . . .'; then she attacks: 'Words are dangerous things let us remember. A republic might be brought into being by a poem.' Certainly she believed that the 'woman's republic' might be brought into being by the extension of the literary franchise to 'the feminine sentence' – that is, as she wrote in the original 'Professions for Women', if men could be educated to stand free speech in women.

The fertile and promiscuous mother tongue is the first mother we think back through in Virginia Woolf's theory of how collective history and the collective unconscious collaborate in the female artist's mind. In 'English Prose' she has robbed culture not only of its male origins but also of its princely pretensions, for she sees prose as Cinderella, occupied with 'menial tasks'. She has to do all the work of the house; to make the beds, dust the china, boil the kettle, sweep the floors.' And in *The Years* she has accomplished the final revolution, the creation of the artist as charwoman to the world. This is a startling concept and as radical as the New York playwright who makes God a Puerto Rican janitor. In 'Men and Women' she wrote, 'For the first time for many ages the bent figure with the knobbed hands and the bleared eyes, who, in spite of the poets, is the true figure of womanhood, rose from her wash-tub, took a stroll out of doors, and went into the factory. That was the first painful step on the way to freedom', but 'it will not be in this generation or the next that she will have adjusted her position or given a clear account of her powers'. She quotes Bathsheba in *Far From the Madding Crowd* on having the feelings of a woman but 'only the language of men' in which to express them. 'From that dilemma', wrote Woolf, arise infinite confusions and complications. Energy has been liberated, but into what form is it to flow? To try the accepted forms, to discard the unfit, to create others which are more fitting, is a task that must be accomplished before there is freedom or achievement. Further, it is well to remember that woman was not created for the first time in the year 1860. A large part of her energy is already fully employed and highly developed. To pour such surplus energy as there may be into new forms without wasting a drop is a difficult problem which can only be solved by the simultaneous evolution and emancipation of man.

Each of her novels is an experiment in the evolution of these new forms; they are to be forms 'appropriate', as she says in another essay, to women; the role of the chorus and of the reader as collaborator grows greater and greater. The gap is bridged as the prose imitates music more than human speech and the form of fiction dissolves in epic operatic theatre for ordinary people. The woman artist has evolved from anonymity through egotism and female identity back to anonymity. She wrote to Ethel Smyth in 1933,

> I didn't write 'A Room' without considerable feeling even you will admit; I'm not cool on the subject. And I forced myself to keep my own figure fictitious, legendary. If I had said, 'Look here, I am uneducated because my brothers used all the family funds' – which is the fact – 'Well', they'd have said, 'she has an axe to grind'; and no one would have taken me seriously, though I agree I should have had many more of the wrong kind of reader, who will read you + go away + rejoice in the personalities, not because they are lively and easy reading; but because they prove once more how vain, how personal, so they will say, rubbing their hands with glee, women always are; I can hear them as I write.[14]

While she herself was pushing the literary she-condition further and further towards the objective universal condition, she nevertheless valued very highly women writers who told the truth about their personal feelings. In February 1940, Woolf wrote to Ethel Smyth:

I was thinking the other night that there's never been a woman's autobiography. Nothing to compare with Rousseau. Chastity and modesty I suppose has been the reason. Now why shouldn't you be not only the first woman to write an opera, but equally the first to tell the truth about herself? But the great artist is the only person to tell the truth. I should like an analysis of your sex life as Rousseau did his. More introspection. More intimacy.

Ethel Smyth had written in her diary that after meeting Virginia Woolf in 1930 she thought of little else for eighteen months. 'I think this proves what I have always held – that for many women, anyhow for me, passion is independent of the sex machine.'
I have written elsewhere of the important influence in Virginia Woolf's life of two contemporary 'mothers', Margaret Llewelyn Davies and Ethel Smyth.[15] Here let me suggest that the social worker and the musician embodied the dual characteristics which fascinated her in her own mother. One might see Margaret Llewelyn Davies as the Mrs Ramsay who goes off to visit the sick and worries about how sanitary the milk is and Ethel Smyth as the Mrs Ramsay who gives a glorious dinner and draws people together. Woolf once told her friend that she had given a party as classical as Jane Austen's Box Hill party and tried to describe its effect (July 1930). She had mastered 'the difficulty of keeping one's atmosphere unbroken . . . rolling and warbling from melody to melody like some divine quartet, no, octet. I say, Ethel, what a party! What a triumph.'
Remembering her mother in 'A Sketch of the Past' she uses similar musical imagery. Julia Stephen brought people together, made life musical and whole. Leslie Stephen was deaf to music, interrupted and destroyed the family harmony.
The first raiders on the patriarchy have untied the mother tongue and come back with words. Then we must have music, and that too is marked 'female' and associated with the harmony and rhythm of daily life with her mother, before the interruptions of the aggressive male ego of her father. She wrote to Ethel Smyth, 'writing is nothing but putting words on the backs of rhythm. If they fall off the rhythm, one's done'. Earlier she had written to Vita Sackville-West, 'Style is a very

simple matter; it is all rhythm. Once you get that, you can't use the wrong words.' In 'Professions for Women' words are fish caught by letting down one's line in the collective unconscious of mother water. The rhythm then rides the back of that dolphin of *The Waves* whose fin shows above the waste of waters. All this activity of the artist is 'dangerous'; 'one slip' means death for Jane Austen, 'instant dismemberment by wild horses' for herself. It is as if the generations of women artists are marching single file across the 'narrow bridge of art', crossing the 'abyss' or 'chasm', as she called the male mind, 'to find a sentence that could hold its own against the male flood'. The path has been cleared by 'some mute inglorious Ethel Smyth', for men have always obstructed the way. (Woolf wrote that a history of male opposition to women's emancipation might be more interesting than the story of women's struggle.) Of the fact that it was a battlefield, she had no doubt.

With all the violence of her pacifist conviction she described Ethel Smyth's work for women artists:

> She is of the race of the pioneers: She is among the ice-breakers, the window-smashers, the indomitable and irresistible armoured tanks who climbed the rough ground; went first; drew the enemy's fire; and left a pathway for those who came after her. I never knew whether to be angry that such heroic pertinacity was called for, or glad that it had the chance of showing itself.[16]

Ethel Smyth, who only wanted to write symphonies, was forced into being 'a blaster of rocks and the maker of bridges', and in literature 'I owe a great deal to some mute and inglorious Ethel Smyth'. 'All that we have ought to be expressed – mind and body – a process of incredible difficulty and danger.' It is indeed 'dangerous' to say, as she said, 'I detest the masculine point of view', but worse to compromise one's moral feminism as in her fight with Bruce Richmond of *The Times Literary Supplement*. She wanted to describe Henry James's fiction as 'lewd'; it was not allowed to criticise 'poor, dear Henry James'.

But the full force of Woolf's violence in this speech/essay is reserved for her description of the murder of the 'Angel in the

House', throttled and bombarded by inkpots. This creature is the ladylike self, the pride of Victorian parents, who prevents the artist from telling the truth. Despite the romantic tone of her memories of her mother, Woolf dared in *To the Lighthouse* to express her ambivalence as well as her love. That indeed is one source of the novel's greatness. For Mrs Ramsay demands that all women be angels, and as readers we lay at her door the deaths of a son in battle and of a daughter in childbirth, for she has demanded that men and women play their Victorian roles. Not only is Lily freed for art at her death, but Mr Ramsay has an identity crisis in old age and grows up. Thus James can identify with him and come to manhood and Cam can vaguely fish in imaginative streams. While Julia Stephen is not the angel in any neat equation, the psychic difficulties of coming to terms with one's own mother in personal as well as historical ways is given dramatic form by Virginia Woolf.

Are we then to murder in our minds our own mothers (and all the messages they gave us about how to live in the patriarchal world) in order to think back through the mothers of literature and history? Is mental matricide necessary for the woman artist? No, Woolf tells us. Abandoned, motherless daughters must find new mothers, real and historical, a linked chain of sisterhood over past time in present space, and rescue and redeem their own mothers' lives from their compromises with the patriarchy. She set us a good example, a Persephone who rescues herself from the underworld, forgiving and understanding why Demeter died.

III.   THE IRRESISTIBLE ARMOURED TANK

In her 1931 speech to professional women, Virginia Woolf followed Ethel Smyth onto the platform, publicly giving her praise in Dame Ethel's presence. (She had also praised Margaret Llewelyn Davies at a Working Women's Co-operative Guild meeting.) After attending her concerts Woolf had always wanted to meet Ethel Smyth, and had praised her memoirs in print as well as arguing with 'Affable Hawk' in *The Nation* that there were few such women composers not because of 'intellectual inferiority', but because men refused to train women except to sing and play for their amusement. Their meeting and their intense relationship was very important for Virginia Woolf as an artist, for she had worked all her life to give her fiction musical form and operatic structure. To be loved by the great composer of English opera was a trying but thrilling experience. *The Waves* owes some of its beauty to the intensity of its author's relationship with the composer, and Ethel Smyth's memoir *As Time Went On* is dedicated to Virginia Woolf. Finishing *The Waves* while writing 'Professions for Women', Woolf wrote that 'the mind bobs like a cork on the sea', and imagines Ethel (who had tried conducting) 'waving your hand over that chaos'. *The Prison*, which Ethel was composing at the same time as *The Waves*, is set to a poem by Henry Brewster on Plotinus's lines about individual death as merging with the universal sublime – surely a source for Bernard's brave and beautiful challenge.

She told Ethel that her own speech was 'clotted up and clogged', that she would not print it as it stood, but it might make 'a small book, about the size of A Room'. 'Your speech, meanwhile, was divine and entirely expressive', she praised Ethel. 'Leonard says about the best of its kind he ever heard, and done, he says, with supreme skill, which I interpret to mean that you liquidated your whole personality in speaking and threw in something never yet written by being yourself there in the flesh – anyhow we must print your speech, by itself entire.'

Hogarth Press did not publish Dame Ethel's speech, but she published several amusing lectures on women and music in *Female Pipings in Eden*.[17] Chapter 4, 'The Difficulties of Women Musicians', must have been at least part of her speech because it contains a funny story about the Woking Golf Course which Vera Brittain reported in her column in *The Nation* (31 January 1931, p. 571).

Dame Ethel begins with the legend of Eve 'picking out a tune' in a hollow reed in which she has bored holes. Adam tells her to stop that horrible noise and, 'if anyone's going to make it, it's not you but me'. She is tired of being asked the same question for the millionth time and her answer is 'there are no great women composers for the same reason there are no female Nelsons . . . it is absolutely impossible in this country for a woman composer to get and to keep her head above water; to go on from strength to strength, and develop such powers as she may possess.' Nowadays Adam silences the hollow reed with cotton wool and the music dies down. Dame Ethel explains the determination with which men have kept women out of orchestras and confined them to singing in choruses and teaching children their scales. 'I burned with curiosity as to whither woman's wings will carry her once she is free to soar.... Few deny that the Brontës and Jane Austen brought a new note into our literature. Why then should not our musical contribution be equally individual and pregnant?' She describes the slow process of infiltration in to the second violins only to find the taboos against women enforced again after the war – 'a metamorphosis such as we read of in V. Sackville-West's *Orlando* took place [Woolf pointed out the error but Ethel let it stand] only the other way around. By degrees these female back-benchers turned into men and as in the "Orlando" business it seemed impossible to learn how and when and why the change had come about.' Men's 'vicarious sense of modesty' has kept women from playing the cello but allowed her to play the 'unlucrative' harp, cherishing her 'white-armed presence in their midst, much as the men in the Welch [sic] regiment cherish the regimental goat'. Not a single woman alive has had the musical training necessary to compose, so it is no surprise that 'no advancing army of eminent women composers is to be descried on the horizon'.

Ethel Smyth then contrasts literary and musical careers, agreeing with Virginia Woolf that since Jane Austen's time women have been allowed to write 'on the sly'. It is not expensive, there is only a publisher between a writer and her public and she stands in no one else's way. But musical engraving is very costly; conductors add little to the standard repertory and less that is controversial because of the composer's sex or difficulty. In an appendix Dame Ethel lists sixteen performances of her important choral works in England in forty years, despite rave reviews from isolated critics, such as Shaw's for her Mass in 1892, when he prophesied the conquest of musical composition by women. As did Virginia Woolf in her speech, Ethel Smyth cautions against 'natural bitterness' and for patience. She tells the story of the fourteenth hole at Cromer Golf Course falling into the North Sea. Several generations of committees had seen the erosion but wanted it to remain a purely seaside links and so they waited a century to lay out new holes. A man disapproved of Amy Johnson's flight over Africa.

> 'Well,' I said, 'speaking for myself, at any age [she was in her seventies] I would willingly risk all that happened to that lady, and worse, rather than have men settling for me what I might and might not do! If one came to grief among these savages it would be a bit of bad luck, but to be deprived of one's freedom would be a bit of bad luck that would go on all the time!'

She tells how disappointed she was to read that Albert Einstein was opposed to women in science. 'Are then even the greatest men half-witted?' she asked herself, on the subject of women. She wrote to inquire, and he replied denying that he had said such things and insisting on women's right to participate in 'all branches of intellectual endeavour'. She says, 'Surely there are enough rocks, papyri, flowers, insects, stars and corpses to go round?'.

Man will not '*see* a woman's work until the psychological moment has arrived' and 'the male eye has been broken in'; 'that is, as eventually happened in literature, prejudice has been broken down, twig after twig'. Like Virginia Woolf, Ethel Smyth believed that the development of genius takes generations of moderate exercise:

> you cannot get giants like Mont Blanc and Mt Everest without the mass of moderate-sized mountains on whose shoulders they stand. It is the upbuilding of this platform that is impossible so long as full musical life is denied to women, and I suppose it is unnecessary to say that conductors and Committees are generally of one mind about keeping us out of Parnassus. . . . We know what 'Candide' said about the duty of cultivating your garden; but what if the authorities keep all the agricultural instruments under lock and key?

Like Woolf, she could go on composing because of a small independent income and the money she earned by writing memoirs. This was the only way to eternal fame for a composer whose operas were not staged, as it has been for women painters whose pictures were not hung, and for actresses before film and tape could record their gestures and voices. Their memoirs sometimes save them from total oblivion.

'So far,' Ethel Smyth wrote in the 1930s, 'admission to the house of music on equal terms with men is unthinkable for a composer of my sex.' But taboos can be broken 'though a future chain of great women composers may seem as improbable even today as the arrival in the channel of a battleship full of incipient female Nelsons'. She complained that it was nonsense to insist on all-male orchestras in the interests of 'unity of style', 'Art is bi-sexual'. Keeping women out is like Nazi propaganda about racial superiority, 'bullying the Jews', she argues here (though her private letters contain antisemitic remarks about Leonard Woolf).

The situation for women in music has been so bad for so long that some women have accepted male values in order to survive. All good voice teachers are women, she asserts, but to get ahead the woman student may ask for a singing master: 'I hope she gets a bad one and that he ruins her voice!' Once women have 'slipped the slave's collar' they will show 'mental independence' and 'directness'. The directness she illustrates with a story of the substitution in Spain of cows for bulls in the ring, unsuccessful because the cows paid no attention to the red flags but went straight for the toreadors and killed them all. She urges her audience to form local branches of the SPCWM, the Society for the Prevention of Cruelty to Women Musicians. 'That men have been on top of the wave since time was, whereas we are still fighting our way upwards from the bottom of the sea, is a fact that will surely set an eternal stamp on our destiny as does the difference of sex.'

She wants women to be original and say with James Fitzjames Stephen exactly what they think and feel:

perhaps it lies at the bottom of the sea, where we are at home; and perhaps our fate, not an ignoble one, is to bring it up to the surface . . . non-creative women, listening to the song of their sisters, be it literature, painting, or music, will say: 'O what is this that knows the way I came?' . . . then would my girl student pause a moment, contemplate her half-finished serenade for eight harps, eight trumpets, ten trombones, twelve percussion instruments, and two dozen explosive bombs, and murmur: 'But this is imitative rubbish', tear up her MS. and throw it into the wastepaper basket.

The peroration of the speech Virginia and Leonard Woolf admired so much is worth quoting in full, for, despite its unfortunate title, *Female Pipings in Eden* does for women in music what Virginia Woolf did for women in literature; it gives women artists a myth of their own creative origins and urges them to struggle for possession of the past in order to forge the future. Ethel Smyth's Eve is the mother of music:

> let her once more take up her hollow reed and start afresh. And if Adam should again awake and bid her stop that horrible noise, Eve need not be rude. Let her merely say *dolce senza expressione*: 'My dear Adam, if you don't admire my tunes I don't always admire yours. But don't threaten as you once did to make this particular horrible noise yourself, for it's my own composition and I hold the copyright. Besides which you couldn't make it yourself if you tried. Some other tune, yes. But not this.' . . .

> Ah me! if Act I Scene I of the human drama had only been more carefully thought out, what happy days might have been spent in Eden! No hunting poor Eve into the marsh; no ramming cotton wool up the little reed she had fashioned for her own fingers! She and Adam would each have constructed a sound-proof hut in different corners of the garden (as far apart as possible), and towards evening they would have been heard piping peaceful pastorals in two parts, later on taking it in turns to conduct the family orchestra . . . . if from the very first Eve had been granted a chance of self-development, there would have been no furtive hanging about the Tree of Knowledge, no illicit truck with serpents and apples, and of course – this would have been rather sad – no Militant Suffragettes.

There were thirty years between Dame Ethel and Virginia Woolf, great differences in temperament and political ideas.

Ethel Smyth (who appears as Rose in *The Years* and contributes to Miss Latrobe in *Between the Acts*) was as thoroughly British as Virginia Woolf was internationalist. She was as fiercely militant, patriotic and egotistical as Woolf was pacifist, socialist and 'anonymous'. Yet on the question of women and art their answers and actions were a united feminist front. Ethel Smyth drove a tank across the narrow bridge of art; danger and struggle were her element and her music reaches sublime heights after ferocious skirmishes in the field. Virginia Woolf was a sniper in the ranks of women writers, leading the unknown female foot-soldiers across less difficult territory.

While the composer was in the position of Jane Austen with a gap unfilled by those necessary 'second rankers' between her and the Greeks, the novelist claimed many good mothers. Conscious of being women warriors, they were struggling towards a 'woman's republic' in art in which their 'daughters' would be free. The word, the sentence, the appropriate female form would be found; the serenade for explosive bombs would go off, and all the flutes, cleared of cotton wool, could play any tune they wished. But the battles are not all won; some daughters are still skirmishing on the bridge and some men still need education in tolerating free speech in women. It is still 'dangerous' for a woman to say what she really thinks and feels, but we are almost over the abyss and we can see the other side. Because of women like Virginia Woolf and Ethel Smyth, we know our own voices when we hear them; they sing in Ethel Smyth's and Virginia Woolf's choruses and the 'we' expands to include others whose tongues have been tied, whose flutes have been silenced. The 'heart of the woman's republic' will be reached by thinking back through our mothers. As Woolf wrote to Ethel Smyth in 1930 while writing *The Waves*, 'though the rhythmical is more natural to me than the narrative, it is completely opposed to the tradition of fiction and I am casting about all the time for some rope to throw the reader'. Catch.

NOTES

A version of this paper was read at the Bucknell Virginia Woolf Conference, April 1977 and I am grateful to Catherine Smith and the participants for their comments and encouragement. The first draft was written on a

Newberry Library Fellowship, the final version while on a National Endowment for the Humanities Research Fellowship using the facilities of the Matematisk Institut, Aarhus Universitet, Denmark.

1. Letter of Virginia Woolf to Ethel Smyth, 29 Mar 1931, with permission of Nigel Nicolson, Quentin Bell and The Berg Collection, Astor, Lenox and Tilden Foundation, New York Public Library, for this and subsequent letters to Ethel Smyth.
2. *New Statesman*, 16 Oct 1920.
3. See Walter Benjamin, *Illuminations*, Fontana edn, ed. Hannah Arendt (London: Collins, 1973), and *Reflections*, ed. Peter Demetz (New York: Harcourt, Brace, Jovanovich, 1978). Ralph Freedman in *The Lyrical Novel* (Princeton, N. J.: Princeton University Press, 1963; Oxford: Oxford University Press, 1963) is the only critic to see Woolf in a European context.
4. For a discussion of *A Room of One's Own* and *Three Guineas* as 'the propaganda of hope and the propaganda of despair', see my 'No More Horses: Virginia Woolf on Art and Propaganda', *Women's Studies*, IV, nos 2–3 (1977) 264–90.
5. Letter of Virginia Woolf to Ethel Smyth, Berg Collection.
6. Virginia Woolf, 'On Not Knowing Greek', *Collected Essays*, vol. I (London: Hogarth Press, 1966).
7. Virginia Woolf's obituary for her aunt Caroline Stephen, the Quaker visionary whom she called 'Nun', is reprinted here in full from the *Guardian* (church weekly), 21 Apr 1909, with permission of Quentin Bell. While it makes a rather long note, it is unlikely to be collected elsewhere and will provide the student with hints for the sources of Woolf's spiritual vision, the ascetic, moral, practical and political 'religion' which informs her writing. Woolf's 'communion of saints' was a conspiracy against the aggressive godlessness of Leslie Stephen and Leonard Woolf – it was a political and anti-patriarchal piety in which the materialist worship of solid objects and solid flesh could be combined with the visionary rhapsodies of a Greek chorus demanding justice from the gods. Caroline Stephen left her niece a larger legacy than the money for a room of her own; she gave her an English feminist religious context and history in which to extend the rhapsodic single voice into a chorus of voices. (Another aunt whose influence is worth studying is Lady Henry Somerset, whose impetuous marriage to a homosexual lord who soon left her to chase boys in Italy, brought disastrous scandal on her head, not his – an example which may have saved her niece from marrying Lytton Strachey. Lady Henry Somerset then devoted herself to social work and became the active leader of the Temperance Movement in Britain, an important sphere for women's expression of political ideas and organisation.)

The death of Caroline Emelia Stephen will grieve many who knew her only from her writing. Her life had for years been that of an invalid, but she was wonderfully active in certain directions – she wrote, she saw her friends, she was able occasionally to read a paper to a religious Society, until her final illness began some six weeks ago. Her books are known to a great number of readers, and it is not necessary here to dwell upon their contents. The *Service of the Poor* was published in 1871, *Quaker Strongholds* in 1890, *The First Sir James Stephen* in 1906 and *Light Arising* in 1908. A few words as to her life and character may interest those who had not the happiness of knowing her personally. She was born in 1834, and was the daughter of Sir James Stephen, Under-Secretary for the Colonies, and of his wife, Jane Catherine Venn, daughter of the Rector of Clapham. She was educated, after the fashion of the time, by masters and governesses, but the influence which affected her most, no doubt, was that of her father, always revered by her, and of her home, with its strong Evangelical traditions. Attendance upon her mother during her last long illness injured her health so seriously that she never fully recovered. From that date (1875) she was often on the sofa, and was never again able to lead a perfectly active life. But those who have read her *Quaker Strongholds* will remember that the great change of her life took place at about this time, when, after feeling that she 'could not conscientiously join in the Church of England Service' she found herself 'one never-to-be-forgotten Sunday morning . . . one of a small company of silent worshippers'. In the Preface to that book she has described something of what the change meant to her; her written and spoken words, her entire life in after-years, were testimony to the complete satisfaction it brought her.

Her life was marked by little outward change. She lived at Malvern for some time, but moved in 1895 to Cambridge, where she spent the last years of her life in a little cottage surrounded by a garden. But the secret of her influence and of the deep impression she made even upon those who did not think as she did was that her faith inspired all that she did and said. One could not be with her without feeling that after suffering and thought she had come to dwell apart, among the 'things which are unseen and eternal' and that it was her perpetual wish to make others share her peace. But she was no solitary mystic. She was one of the few to whom the gift of expression is given together with the need of it, and in addition to a wonderful command of language she had a scrupulous wish to use it accurately. Thus her effect upon people is scarcely yet to be decided, and must have reached many to whom her books are unknown. Together with her profound belief she had a robust common sense and a practical ability which seemed to show that with health and opportunity she might have ruled and organised. She had all her life enjoyed many intimate friendships, and the dignity and charm of her presence, the quaint humour which played over her talk, drew to her during her last years many to whom her relationship was almost maternal. Indeed, many of those who mourn her to-day will remember her in that aspect, remembering the long hours of talk in her room with the windows opening on to the garden, her interest in their lives and in her own; remembering, too, something tender and almost pathetic about her which drew their love as well as their respect. The last years of her life among her flowers and with young people round her seemed to end fittingly a life which had about it the harmony of a large design.

8. Virginia Woolf, 'The Eccentrics', *Athenaeum*, 25 Apr 1919, pp. 230–1.
9. Readers will perhaps recognise what the woman Co-operator was like from D. H. Lawrence's portrait of Mrs Morel in *Sons and Lovers*. In 1927 Margaret Llewelyn Davies wrote an introduction to Catherine Webb's *The Woman with the Basket: The Story of the Women's Co-operative Guild* published by the Manchester Co-operative Guild. Here Margaret Llewelyn Davies uses the same terms, calling the Co-operators 'this republic of women', and 'individual heroines of the home'. She quotes a letter from a middle-class visitor to the 1916 conference, and from its style we may well assume that visitor was Virginia Woolf: 'It seemed as if the working women of England were gathered together and become articulate. Working women were addressing working women about the questions which interest them, and not to have shared their experiences seemed, for the first time, perhaps, to set a woman, or even a man, apart in a way that was curiously humiliating. Certainly no middle-class woman could speak with anything like the knowledge and conviction with which these women spoke on one subject after another.'
10. See my 'The Years as Greek Drama, Domestic Novel and Götterdämmerung', *Bulletin of the New York Public Library*, Winter 1977, pp. 276–301, and 'Pargeting the Pargiters', ibid., Spring 1977, pp. 416–35.
11. This and subsequent letters from Ethel Smyth to Virginia Woolf quoted by permission of Letcher and Sons for the Smyth Estate, and the Berg Collection, Astor, Lenox and Tilden Foundation, New York Public Library.
12. See J. Marcus, 'Clio in Calliope: History and Myth in *Diana of the Crossways*', *Bulletin of the New York Public Library*, Winter 1976, pp. 167–92.
13. In Washington State University at Pullman library containing the collection of Leonard and Virginia Woolf's books.
14. Christopher St John, *Ethel Smyth* (London: Longmans Green, 1959) pp. 229–30. The next quotation is from p. 232.
15. See 'No More Horses', the two essays on *The Years* and 'The Snow Queen and the Old Bucanneer', *Virginia Woolf Miscellany*, Winter 1977, pp. 4–6.
16. See Virginia Woolf, 'Professions for Women', in '*The Pargiters*': The *Novel–Essay Portion of 'The Years'*, ed. Mitchell A. Leaska (New York: New York Public Library and Readex Books, 1977).
17. Ethel Smyth, *Female Pipings in Eden* (London: Peter Davies, 1934).

2 Woolf's 'Magical Garden of Women'[1]

ELLEN HAWKES

Biographies of women writers are sometimes more like funhouse mirrors than true reflections of the subject's life. Pulled out of shape here, lengthened there, one side diminished, the other grossly exaggerated, even a familiar figure becomes unrecognisable. The source of these distortions is complex, as complex as any culture whose assumptions and attitudes, mythic beliefs and economic requirements necessarily result in stereotyped images of women. Instead of reciting causes or miring myself in defects of society, however, I would rather take the leap into a different kind of biographical study, invoking from the outset Virginia Woolf's cautionary remark that 'it is the masculine values that prevail'[2] in both life and literature.

In biographical and literary studies of Woolf, the accent has often fallen on the men in her life. Father, brothers, husband, brother-in-law, male Bloomsbury friends, not to mention the familiar list of male writers and philosophers, have carried more weight, as if masculine physical strength can simply be translated into dominant forces in her personal and artistic development. But the Woolf who speaks for herself in her diaries, letters, essays and fiction sinks beneath these interpretations. Still, she did plead her own cause in her caustic dismissal of masculine influence on women writers: 'The ape is too distant to be sedulous' (ROO, p. 79).

A new story emerges from different assumptions: first, the fact of Woolf's sex matters; and, secondly, she plays an active role in her own biography. Here I take my cue from Simone de Beauvoir's classic restatement of female destiny: 'I shall place woman in a world of values and give her behavior a dimension of liberty. . . . She is not the plaything of contradictory drives; she devises solutions of diverse values in the ethical scale.'[3] In this frame, Woolf's personality seems neither as malleable nor as passive as other assessments would have it. She is not the traditional heroine, acted upon, given life, rescued by the 'heroes' of her biography; rather, she makes choices, finds solutions, in short, shapes her own life and creates for herself her own dimension of liberty. And the source for her sense of personal and artistic possibilities she found in other women.

This is the story not of the 'anxiety of influence' but of its reassurance. Throughout her diaries and letters, in her essays and fiction as well, she insists upon a *hortus conclusus* – an enclosed garden where women can tell their tales, laugh and even get angry. This is her utopia, what she called her 'magical garden of women', a safe surrounding in which women preserve and sanction their shared values derived from their special experiences as 'outsiders'. And it was in this refuge from the patriarchal world that Woolf confronted the plaguing question 'Who am I?' and found answers in the mirrors of identity held up by women friends and women writers.

I

Woolf first mapped a special female world in reaction to the stifling atmosphere of 22, Hyde Park Gate after the deaths of her mother and her half-sister, Stella Duckworth. While the gloomy despair of the home was depressing enough, she also rebelled against the firm patriarchal rule established not only by her father but also by the Duckworth brothers, George and Gerald. Against Sir Leslie's endless demands and unquenchable need for sympathy and attention from his daughters, against George's imperious rules of decorum and dress, against George and Gerald's sexual expression of power and manipulation, she and Vanessa would stand united. They were, as Woolf later exclaimed, 'in league together against the world'.[4]

Such defiance! But absolutely necessary as Woolf insisted in her 1939 'Sketch of the Past'. She and Vanessa formed 'a very close conspiracy', 'a private nucleus', 'a small world inside the big world' 'of many men, coming and going'. It was to each other she and Vanessa turned for respite, refuge and confirmation for what they were seeing and feeling:

> We had an alliance that was so knit together that everything
> . . . was seen from the same angle; and took its shape from
> our own vantage point. Very soon after Stella's death we saw
> life as a struggle to get some kind of standing place for
> ourselves in this [illegible]. We were always battling for that
> which was always being interfered with, muffled up,
> snatched away.[5]

They were fighting for their own identities in a Victorian world; they were looking ahead to *their* futures while the men were imprisoning them in the past, in a 'framework with all kinds of minutely teethed saws' (*MB*, p. 131).

The deaths of Julia Stephen and Stella Duckworth had made the father and brothers adamant in their expectations and rules of dress, behaviour and conversation. Even the more 'conspiratorial' brothers, Thoby and Adrian Stephen, were in no position to intervene: Adrian too young; Thoby, in his 'remote station, as . . . an undergraduate' 'aloof, judicial, conventional' and complacently certain that the sisters 'should accept [their] place' (*MB*, p. 123). It befell Vanessa to play the roles bequeathed by Julia and Stella, to live up to the image so revered by the Victorian family, 'part slave, part angel of sympathy' (*MB*, p. 125). Earlier Woolf had elaborated the burden placed on Vanessa, explaining in her 1907–8 memoir, 'Reminiscences,' that 'so many demands were made on her; it was, in a sense, so easy to be what was expected, with such models before her, but also it was so hard to be herself' (*MB*, p. 54).

While the ghosts of Julia and Stella hovered over, indeed sanctioned, the rules of dress, manners and propriety, Woolf also believed that her mother might have been more sympathetic to the glimmers of nonconformity in her daughters; she might have appreciated in some small measure the fact that Vanessa and Virginia 'were explorers, revolutionists, reformers' (*MB*, pp. 126–7). In 'Reminiscences' Woolf is more explicit about the loss of her mother's watchful eye over their developing personalities and styles of life:

> If her mother had lived it is easy to imagine how Vanessa, questing about her, like some active dog, would have tried one experiment after another, arguing, painting, making friends, disproving fallacies, much to her mother's amusement; she would have delighted in her daughter's spirit and adventures, mourned her lack of practical wisdom, and laughed at her failures, and rejoiced in her sense. But that is one of the things, which though they must have happened, yet, incredible though it seems, never did happen, death making an end of all these exquisite preparations.
>
> (*MB*, p. 55)

In Woolf's poignant summary of what her sister (and by implication she herself) missed because of their mother's death we hear an echo of Mary Datchet's exclamation in *Night and Day*: 'What was the good, after all, of being a woman if one didn't keep fresh, and cram one's life with all sorts of views and experiments.'[6] But one needs a source of strength and support for these explorations, and that source for young women is very often the mother. As Woolf herself acknowledged, 'we think back through our mothers if we are women' (*ROO*, p. 79).

Without their mother, Vanessa was on her own, trying to catch glimpses of her identity in the mirror, Woolf remembers:

> ... perhaps once or twice she looked steadily in the glass when no one was by and saw a face that excited her strangely; her being began to have a definite shape, a place in the world – what was it like? But her natural development, in which the artistic gift, so sensitive and yet so vigorous, would have asserted itself, was checked; the effect of death upon those that live is always strange, and often terrible in the havoc it makes with innocent desires. (*MB*, pp. 31–2)

Written for Julian Bell, Woolf's reminiscence of her sister says a great deal about her own situation. If Vanessa tried to define her new being in the mirror, Woolf sought reflections of herself in her sister. Vanessa provided for Woolf the absent maternal love for which she yearned throughout most of her life; equally, she was the woman to whom Woolf often compared herself, puzzling out answers to her own questions of identity and reinforcing her sense of not only being different from the family's expectations but also of being justified in her rebellion. In 'their league together against the world', Woolf recalled, she first came to understand and to value women's status as 'outsiders' and 'spectators' (*MB*, p. 132).

Throughout Woolf's life, her relationship with her sister was extremely close, sometimes difficult, but always central to her feelings about herself and her women friends. Too complex for a full study in this essay (and deserving further exploration and reinterpretation elsewhere), it stands, nevertheless, as the basis for Woolf's appreciation and need for women friends. She acknowledged this herself in a 1927 letter to Vanessa. As usual taunting her about her own love for women and her affair with Vita Sackville-West, Woolf traces her feelings back to Vanessa and significantly selects the metaphor of the garden to make her point: 'You will never succumb to the charms of any of your sex – what an arid garden the world must be for you! What avenues of stone pavements and iron railings. . . . I see that you will attribute all this to your own charms in which I daresay you're not far wrong.'[7]

On the basis of the sisters' conspiracy, Woolf continued to insist on the importance of women's friendship as she tremulously emerged from the shell of Hyde Park Gate. Rebelling against her father's and her brothers' 'patriarchal machinery' would not have been enough in and of itself. She needed her sister and other women to give back to her a sense of confidence and self-esteem as both a woman and a writer. Acutely aware of this need, she seems to invest her reading of literature with her own personal situation. In her 1909–11 reading notes, she remarks that Desdemona is perplexed by the behaviour of Othello and other men around her. And, since she has no confirmation for her perceptions from other women, Desdemona, Woolf claims, has no alternative to her confusion. Here Woolf's voice merges with an imagined cry

from Shakespeare's heroine: 'These men! These men!
... One's belief in one's own sex corresponds to one's belief in
oneself.'[8]

II

In 1902, at the age of twenty, Woolf met another woman who
helped her believe in herself. Violet Dickinson was then
thirty-seven, an imposing, forthright person, with aristocratic
connections, a Quaker's moral certitude, and a witty intelligence. Quentin Bell includes in his biography Woolf's first
description of her new friend:

> She came down to dinner in flowing picturesque garments.
> For all her height, and a certain comicality of face, she treats
> her body with dignity.... Indeed, she was singularly unre-
> served in many ways.... It was only after a time that one
> came to a true estimate of her character – one saw that all
> was not cheerfulness and high spirits by any means – She
> had her times of depression and her sudden reserves.
> ... To a casual observer, she would appear, I think, a very
> high spirited, rather crazy, harum-scarum sort of per-
> son.... Such an observer would be superficial indeed.[9]

Like Vanessa, perhaps even more than Vanessa because of
her age and her immunity from Stephen family pressures,
Dickinson provided the maternal comfort and affection that
Woolf had missed as an adolescent. It is clear from her letters
that Woolf fell in love with the older woman. The rather
regressive tone of her early letters, as well as her pose of the
shy little animal, 'the sparroy' needing to be petted and loved,
the baby kangaroo seeking protection from the world in the
'mother's' pouch, are symptomatic of Woolf's adoption of
Dickinson as a surrogate mother.

Dickinson acceded to these terms of the relationship, becoming not only a mother, but also a teacher and confidante.
Woolf articulated the nature of such 'apprentice' relationships
between a young woman and an older female teacher when
she described Kitty Malone in her 1932 draft of 'a novel essay',

The Pargiters. Kitty is in love with her tutor Lucy Craddock because, as Woolf explains in the fifth essay, she was not sent to school and had no friends her own age (facts reminiscent of Woolf's own life). Her love is undoubtedly mixed with other loves, but, most importantly, she 'was falling in love with something which seemed to her wonderful, new, exciting – the disinterested passion for things in themselves'.[10] On the one hand, the new disinterested passion takes Kitty beyond the narrow confines of her home; on the other, it is all directed towards her teacher: 'She treasured every word of praise that Miss Craddock gave her; she invested all Miss Craddock's relations with glamour; kept every note she had from her; and left a pot of white azaleas at her lodgings once when she was ill' (*P*, p. 112).[11] Woolf also realised, surveying not only her own life but also the lives of many women in the past, that a young woman's infatuation with an older woman teacher was cultural as well as psychological, citing as confirmation in the same essay Mrs Humphrey Ward's tribute to her women tutors: 'What I learnt during those years was learnt from personalities' (ibid.).

While Woolf was undoubtedly recalling, in these remarks, her youthful affection for her own tutor, Janet Case, she also turned to Violet Dickinson for similar guidance, for instruction in ideals and values. It as as much from this 'idealisation' of her older friend as from her search for a missing mother that Woolf's romantic tone derives.

Further, what some readers of the Woolf–Dickinson correspondence have dismissed as neurotic, aberrant or simply silly takes on a different meaning when set in a cultural context. Carroll Smith-Rosenberg's significant study of friendships among women in Victorian America casts a different light on Woolf's passionate devotion to Dickinson. Exploring why 'the social structure and the world view . . . made intense and sometimes sensual female love both a possible and an acceptable emotional option', Smith-Rosenberg concludes that 'rigid gender-role differentiation' and 'emotional segregation of women and men' lie behind the 'closeness, freedom of emotional expression, and uninhibited physical contact which characterized women's relationships with each other, while the opposite was frequently true of male–female relationships'.[12] Fully aware of the rigid sex segregation in her family and the strictly defined rules of 'feminine' behaviour, Woolf found in her friendship with Dickinson a similarly refreshing freedom. In his introduction to the first volume of Woolf's letters, Nigel Nicolson claims that the ones to Dickinson are so fatiguingly sentimental that the later ones to Clive Bell and other men 'come as a relief' because she 'honed her wit upon their rougher texture, and gave her letters more sinew' (*L*, I, p. xx). I, however, see the friendship with Dickinson and the intense, sometimes exaggerated outpouring of affection in the letters to her, as a necessary emotional apprenticeship – a common characteristic, Smith-Rosenberg notes, of relationships between mothers and daughters and between female friends. By retracing emotional patterns with a surrogate mother, by expressing and testing her feelings with a friend, Woolf began to gain self-confidence, establishing for herself an equal footing not only with Dickinson but with her male contemporaries as well.

As the letters reveal, the friendship gradually changed from one of filial attachment to one of reciprocal understanding and love for each other's individuality. Quentin Bell explains that Violet Dickinson's 'breezy masculine assurance' attracted Woolf (*VWB*, I, p. 83). True, her strength and candour appealed to the younger woman. Significantly, however, Woolf did not mark these as 'masculine' traits. Instead, she insisted on her friend's femininity and specific aspects of female personality, as if to emphasise a special world of women, to define, as she had with Vanessa, their conspiratorial alliance. She often remarks upon Dickinson's 'womanliness', her 'feminine sympathy'; 'be a woman', she exhorts, beginning letters and individual sentences with 'my woman' or simply 'woman'. Conventional Victorian forms of address, they are repeatedly used by Woolf as though she were reminding herself and her friend of an important fact: they are women together, it is their womanly qualities that unite them. From these aspects of 'womanly sympathy' she seems to create a positive image of femaleness that will help her in her own search for an authentic identity. As she announces in a 1903 letter to Dickinson, 'I am susceptible to female charms', then taking the opportunity to compare conversations with men to those with women, those with Violet in particular: 'Gerald [Duckworth] is giving us his views upon Florence. You are the only person I ever do feel the least inclined to talk to – poor intimate. You dont talk damned theories or expect sentiments' (*L*, I, p. 75).

Exploring her sense of herself as both a woman and a writer, Woolf was irritated when Dickinson, like so many of her family and acquaintances, urged her to marry. At the same time, though, she worried out loud, not about her virginity *per se*, but about its effect on her writing. When her friend Madge Vaughan had criticised her writing for being cold and heartless, she turned to Dickinson: 'really I begin to get alarmed. If marriage is necessary to one's style, I shall have to think about it' (*L*, I, p. 228). At the same time she enclosed samples of her writing for Dickinson's criticism, obliquely requesting a counter-opinion, some validation for her own decision that her artistic ambition took priority over a search for a husband. A 1909 letter reveals a similar need; Woolf wants her friend to confirm her writing and personality by insisting on the depth of their emotional attachment: 'They say my creatures are all cold-blooded. . . . But you dont, my Violet, do you? Ever since we trod the groves together you have seen that my passion was for love and humanity; though it had to kindle through depths of green water' (*L*, I, p. 379).[13]

Most importantly, Dickinson did encourage Woolf as a writer, a fact too overlooked in most accounts of her literary development. After reading some of her early essays, Dickinson introduced her to Margaret Lyttleton, the editor of the Women's Supplement of the *Guardian*, who then published Woolf's earliest reviews and sketches. While Woolf and Dickinson sometimes violently disagreed about fiction, Woolf acknowledged that her friend was the one person from whom she wanted or could take criticism. Still defensive, still fearful of others' reactions to her writing, she was much more forthright when she enclosed '2 delightful manuscripts' with a note to her friend: 'I'm not sure whether they're worth sending to Mrs. L[yttleton] or not; only I took quite a lot of trouble over the New Forest one. . . . You shall have heaps more when you come back. You are the person I can best stand criticism from – which aint saying much' (*L*, I, p. 173). That Woolf found support and encouragement is evident in a later letter. Even in 1912, when the intensity of the friendship had begun to wane, she worried about her friend's reaction to

The Voyage Out: 'The worst of it is, you wont like it; you'll tell me I'm a failure as a writer, as well as a failure as a woman. Then I shall take a dive into the Serpentine which, I see, is 6 feet deep in malodorous mud. By the way, *Are* you fond of me?' (*L*, I, p. 499).[14]

In other versions of Woolf's life, we hear about her new freedom in Bloomsbury, where she could banter with Clive Bell, Lytton Strachey and the other Cambridge friends of her brother Thoby. Actually she was still very shy and, somewhat defensively, did not find the conversation of these young men terribly appealing. With Dickinson, however, she could be herself. She credited her friend with 'saving her life' during her serious breakdown after her father's death in 1904 when she stayed at Dickinson's home in Burnham Wood. Thus, during those early Bloomsbury years, Woolf derived as much from this friendship as from those daring Thursday evening conversations, finding still in their 'league together' sources of her feelings about herself and her ambitions. It was in the heat of this affection that Woolf kindled so many of her ideas about people, art and politics.

Through her friendship with Dickinson, Woolf began to discover a form of understanding based on empathy between the self and others. Even as her ideas about this way of perceiving the world became more complex over the years, she felt it was more inherent in women's experience because they had their private world within the larger public sphere. This form of communication was possible among both sexes only if identities were not screened or walled off by what she called 'masculine egotism'. As she wrote to Dickinson in 1903, 'Life would be so much simpler if we could flay the outside skin all the talk and pretences and sentiments one doesn't feel etc. etc. etc. – Thats why I get on with you isn't it?' (*L*, I, p. 97). Continuing, she explains why women seem better able to break through convention and to communicate without pretences: 'You remember there is a very fine instinct wireless telepathy nothing to it – in women – the darlings – which fizzles up pretences, and I know what you mean though you dont say it, and I hope its the same with you' (*L*, I, p. 98). We can look ahead from this image of wireless telepathy between women to the metaphorical filaments that connect characters in *Mrs Dalloway* or to the intuitive understanding of others by

Mrs Ramsay in *To the Lighthouse* or to Orlando's revelation, 'When communication is established there is nothing more to be said.'[15]

Woolf returned the gift of identity to Dickinson in the form of a spoof biography. Written in 1907, 'Friendships Gallery' is bound in violet leather and is typed with a violet typewriter ribbon. A comic version of Dickinson's unique personality and a tribute to the friendship, it prefigures the longer, more elaborate panegyric to Vita Sackville-West in *Orlando*. Also beginning in play and ending in love, 'Friendships Gallery' shows Dickinson and Woolf changing the society in which they live. In the first of three parts, Dickinson disrupts her coming-out party by acting outrageously. Dressed unconventionally, with hardly a thought to fashion, she reels around the party and her wit and slapstick behaviour create anarchic disarray, bringing the party to an end. Woolf announces her own role at the end of this section; she establishes herself as a modernist author who will explore the labyrinths of the mind.[16]

In the second section, Woolf imagines her magical garden of women, a utopian community inspired and led by Dickinson. Woolf gives a mock chronicle of the revolutionary changes: women start to eat off plain crockery, fling off their stays and corsets, develop muscles from working in the fields and are called comrade by their husbands. Again, she places herself within this community, but, while Dickinson is the activist leader, she is the artist, model for other women writers, and the recorder of the community's progress.

The third section is a kind of mythic tale. Both Dickinson and Woolf are towering goddesses who combat little evil creatures who threaten destruction. Instead of prayers or exorcism, however, these goddesses require laughter from their worshippers as their special form of devotional prayer. Dickinson has supreme powers of strength, while Woolf is an etherial princess who by virtue of distilled magic in her veins can cast spells in a private language of symbolic transformation. Under their influence, the world becomes so anarchic – systems of organisation and hierarchies tumble – that their shrines are closed and they are banished as subversives. Still in league together, they continue to prod the evil monsters back into the sea with their umbrellas. This conclusion reads as a comic foreshadowing of Bernard's serious challenge to death in *The Waves*. There death advances as well, and he flings himself 'unvanquished and unyielding' against it. One might also see this as Woolf's tribute to Dickinson's care during her breakdown when she combated the forces of depression that threatened to overwhelm her 'patient'.[17]

Woolf never forgot the importance of this early friendship and its effect on her during such difficult years. When Dickinson praised *Night and Day*, Woolf replied with gratitude for what the other had done to make her literary career possible. And in a very late diary entry, when Woolf had been rereading their correspondence, she says how difficult it is to put into words why their friendship had brought her to the point at which she could confidently say, 'I am a writer.'[18]

III

During these early years Woolf also turned to other women writers and to women characters in literature to retrieve from the past affirmation for her sense of herself as a writer. Her essays and remarks are backward glances at choices made, her accents fall on those aspects of a woman's life about which the literary woman has to make courageous decisions. An artist, Woolf believed, needs a sense of shared goals, tradition and community. As she summarises in *A Room of One's Own*, 'masterpieces are not single and solitary births; they are the outcome of many years of thinking in common, of thinking by the body of the people, so that the experience of the mass is behind the single voice' (*ROO*, pp. 68–9). But Woolf knew from experience that women writers could not simply rely on the established male tradition. Instead, she created for herself and other women a female tradition in *A Room of One's Own*, which was the culmination of her many years of 'thinking back through [her] mothers'.

I prefer to call these forerunners Woolf's 'literary sisters', to stress that she made the facts of their lives present to herself; giving their experiences a contemporary emphasis, she found support for her own decision to replace the angel in the house with the artist.

Woolf's literary interest in women, in their biographies and in their roles in society was evident at an early age. As she recalled in her diary, she read *Three Generations of English Women* in 1897, when she was fifteen, and began to write her own 'history of women'.[19] Some of her earliest reviews in 1903–5 focused on women: 'Famous Women of Wit and Beauty', 'Women in America' and 'Feminine Fiction'.[20] At the bottom of her reading list for 1904–5, she has taken notes from Dicey's *Law and Opinion* which mark significant historical changes in women's status, including the Married Women's Property Act, Mill's publication of *The Subjection of Women* and the founding of Girton and Newnham Colleges.

Her reading notes from 1909–11 show her concentration on women as well, particularly on women characters in Shakespeare's plays. In all her remarks, she is acutely aware of fathers' domination of daughters in the name of patriarchal authority. For example, her discussion of the plays are not the clear-sighted summaries her own father might have expected. Instead, she gives emotional descriptions of the plight of the women characters. She considers only briefly the central issue of Hamlet's failure to act; rather, she designates Polonius and Laertes as typical overbearing masculine types and criticises their tyranny of Ophelia. She is angry that they are more worried about their reputations than about her feelings. Woolf also reacts to Goneril and Regan with surprising leniency. She holds King Lear responsible for their self-consuming passion without attributing to them any malice or evil: 'Lear has always been storming. His daughters have suffered from it. This is done partly I suppose to excuse or account for his extraordinary actions . . . – an arbitrary, imperious old man.'[21] The connections she seems to be making to her own father are confirmed by a passage from *To the Lighthouse* in which Lily Briscoe realises that the death of Mrs Ramsay has allowed Mr Ramsay to tyrannise his children: 'Had they dared say No . . . he would have flung himself tragically backwards into the bitter waters of despair. . . . He looked like a king in exile.'[22]

Woolf loved her father, but she hated his tyrannical imposition of roles and expectations on his daughters' lives. Discovering in both her friends' lives and in the biographies of women writers that most women had to confront patriarchal dominance allowed her eventually (and not without ambivalence) to transform her psychological anger into political analysis. She was aware that rebellion against the father often changed the way women saw themselves in their society. For example, she called attention to Mary Wollstonecraft's childhood experiences as a motivating force behind her revolutionary ideas and actions by comparing her to a woman whose family life was not as extreme: 'If Jane Austen had lain as a child on the landing to prevent her father from thrashing her mother, her soul might have burnt with such a passion against tyranny that all her novels might have been consumed in one cry for justice.'[23]

Woolf also found in Elizabeth Barrett Browning's work another example of the way women translate into literature their resentment of the father's dominance. In her essay about *Aurora Leigh*, Woolf insists that because 'the connection between a woman's art and a woman's life was unnaturally close', a reader of the poem should be aware that the author 'had been immured by the tyranny of her father in almost conventual seclusion in a bedroom in Wimpole Street' (*SCR*, pp. 185–6).

Never underestimating either the difficulty of rebelling against the father or the ensuing guilt, Woolf knew from her own experiences that the problem was compounded if the father was old and sick. Her remarks about George Eliot have the authentic ring of a personal reminiscence fused with the literary 'mother's' life: Eliot's arduous work of translating Strauss could 'scarcely have been made less so by the usual feminine tasks of ordering a household and nursing a dying father'.[24] Woolf also noted the pain of choosing a life and holding ideas which went against the family's expectations. Eliot, she writes, had to face the 'distressing conviction, to one so dependent upon affection, that by becoming a bluestocking she was forfeiting her brother's respect' (*CE*, I, p. 198).

These are just a few examples of Woolf's many comments about fathers and their power. Certainly, her general remarks in *A Room of One's Own, Three Guineas, The Years* and *The Pargiters* derive not only from her feelings about her own father but also from her persistent attention to patriarchal attitudes controlling other women's lives. She does, indeed, find fathers in the most surprising places. Complaining about the stifling, genteel atmosphere in a biography of Mary Russell Mitford ('ladies sigh . . . and smile things off, but never . . . dash the teacups on the floor'), Woolf soon discovers that the biographer, a Miss Hill, has inadvertently pressed a secret spring. 'Out topples a stout old gentleman', exclaims Woolf. 'In plain English Miss Mitford had a father . . . he was not a nice father.' The beautiful teapot, pictured at the bottom of the page as emblematic of the family's aristocratic refinement, is suddenly, Woolf rejoices, 'smashed . . . to smithereens. That is the worst of writing about ladies; they have fathers as well as teapots' ('Outlines', part I: 'Miss Mitford', *CE*, IV, pp. 105–6; appropriately titled 'An Imperfect Lady' in the original 1920 version).

Since Woolf knew that if her father had lived longer, 'his life would have entirely ended [hers]' (*WD*, p. 138), she realised as well that she had to kill that part of herself which acquiesced to her father, even to his ghost. What concerns her is the internalised image of the mother – the perfect lady – to which the father and the conventions of society could so easily appeal. As she explained in *Three Guineas*, 'It was the woman, the human being whose sex made it her sacred duty to sacrifice herself to the father, whom Charlotte Brontë and Elizabeth Barrett had to kill.'[25]

Woolf was again looking for examples in the lives of other women writers as if to justify her own act of homicide – what she called 'killing the angel in the house' in her well-known essay 'Professions for Women'. In her description of the angel, we all recognise a partial portrait of her own mother, or at least Leslie Stephen's idealised image of her. But, as Woolf admitted, every house has its own angel, and every woman writer has had to kill some version of this phantom. In many of her essays she singles out the tension between the angel and the artist in the house – a tension which she dramatised in the characters of Mrs Ramsay and Lily Briscoe. Elizabeth Barrett Browning's *Aurora Leigh* explores, according to Woolf, 'the conflict between the woman and the artist' (*SCR*, p. 186). George Eliot pushed herself beyond 'the sanctuary of womanhood to pluck for herself the strange bright fruits of art and knowledge' (*CE*, I, p. 204). In example after example, Woolf discovered that 'killing the angel in the house was part of the occupation of a woman writer' (*CE*, II, p. 286).

Killing the angel was a necessary but not a sufficient step toward becoming an artist. Women were still left with the basic questions of female identity which confronted Woolf, as she reiterated in 'Professions for Women': 'In other words, now that she had rid herself of falsehood that young woman had only to be herself. Ah, but what is "herself"? I mean, what is a woman?' (*CE*, II, p. 286). Woolf went on to assure her audience that she did not know, that no one could possibly know until that young woman 'has expressed herself in all the arts and professions open to human skill' (*CE*, II, p. 286).

Nevertheless, despite her own uncertainty, Woolf continued to look for answers in the lives of other women writers, in their self-proclamations of identity and in their rebellion against convention. Reviewing studies of Christina Rossetti, she is struck by the fact that even as a child Rossetti 'had her own way of life fixed in her head – she was to write' (*CE*, IV, p. 55). Woolf then isolates in the biography what seems to her a momentous act. At a tea-party whose idle patter annoyed the young poet, she rose from a chair, stood in the centre of the room and solemnly proclaimed, 'I am Christina Rossetti!' Woolf's pleasure in this act is obvious: 'Had I been present I should certainly have committed some indiscretion – have broken a paper knife or smashed a tea-cup in the awkward ardour of my admiration when she said, "I am Christina Rossetti!" ' (*CE*, IV, p. 60).

Thus, in Woolf's version of female history, rebellion against feminine stereotypes requires some rather violent acts. Not only acts of homicide but also smashed crockery litters the path towards becoming an artist.

And many of these acts of rebellion, of women's courageous flaunting of convention, took on the status of myths, living in the minds of all women. Mary Wollstonecraft was one of Woolf's favourite examples:

> Independence . . . energy . . . courage . . . and the power to put her will into effect, were her necessary qualities. . . . The revolution thus was not merely an event that had happened outside her; it was an active agent in her own blood. . . . She argues and experiments, we hear her voice and trace her influence even now among the living.
>
> (*CE*, III, pp. 194–5)

Again, I am reminded of Woolf's insistence, in her memoir of Vanessa and in her characterisation of Mary Datchet in *Night and Day*, on the importance of adventure and experimentation in young women's lives. Over and over again Woolf reacted to the plight of women trapped in conventional roles. For example, she mourned the waste of Jane Carlyle's talents in her marriage. While reviewing two novels by Carlyle's friend, Geraldine Jewsbury, Woolf was less concerned with the literary accomplishment than with Jewsbury's efforts to persuade Jane Carlyle to write. 'The bold woman proceeded' to advise Carlyle, Woolf explains: ' "do not go to Mr. Carlyle for sympathy, do not let him dash you with cold water. You must respect your own work, and your own motives" – a piece of advice that Jane . . . would have done well to follow.' And, while Jewsbury boldly speculated that women in the future would become better and stronger and have many more possibilities open to them, Jane Carlyle, Woolf laments, too often was not listening, worried as she was that her husband would hear her friend's declarations – and, after all, 'if there was one creature [he] hated it was a strong-minded woman of the George Sand species' (*CE*, IV, p. 38).[26] Again, Woolf dramatises the story of the woman's life, retelling it as a myth so that it 'reaches us from where she lies . . . in the Bromptom cemetery' (*CE*, IV, p. 39).

Woolf also looked at the domestic details of women's lives, at specifically female decisions, to see how they affected women's identities and work as artists. Particularly, she worried about the effects of marriage and its daily domestic pressures. She notices whether the woman's life with a man has helped or hindered her. Equally important was whether a woman had children. Sara Coleridge, Woolf sympathises, 'wished that she could be given three years respite from childbearing' (*CE*, III, p. 225), but she wished in vain, and for many years the children wore down her health and interrupted her writing. Woolf's ambivalence about her own childlessness not-withstanding,[27] she found that, though literary women differed in many respects, 'it may be a possibly relevant fact that not one of them had children' (*ROO*, p. 69).

While Woolf admitted that we still do not know 'What food . . . we feed women as artists upon' (*ROO*, p. 54), she thought it terribly important to create a literary past out of these details of women's lives both for herself and for other women artists. Of course, she acknowledged, the sense of a shared tradition was crucial to any writer, and she often imagined a universal and common mind which bound great writers and thinkers, from Plato to Shakespeare to the present generation. Nevertheless, she and women writers were often excluded, as she once, in an early diary, complained. Reading and writing, as usual with an eye towards becoming a writer, she records throwing down a book by a great man and sighing that he would only laugh at her ambition.

Even if the forms of their art radically differed from one another, Woolf believed that she and all women artists needed 'literary sisters' who had, against all odds, in the face of laughter and derision, in the midst of what Woolf explicitly condemned as patriarchal society, maintained their integrity and insisted upon their own identities. Taken with *A Room of One's Own*, Woolf's reading notes and essays are tributes to those women who had struggled with the question, 'How does one come to think of oneself as a woman and as an artist?' Each woman writer, she said, should lay a wreath on the tombs of her predecessors. From her own experience she realised that literary sisters provided what Gertrude Stein called 'the sounding board to send back the sound that they are to make inside'.

IV

Woolf had several close women friends, each of whom provided a sounding board for an aspect of her personality. Certainly, Margaret Llewelyn Davies, President of the National Women's Co-operative Guild, and Janet Case, her former tutor, were central to the development of Woolf's politics. Ethel Smyth, a later friend, was a model of a stalwart woman who pursued her artistic goals and valiantly struggled for the feminist cause. Woolf's 1931 version of 'Professions for Women' (prepared as a speech for the National Society for Women's Service and now published in *The Pargiters*, thanks to Jane Marcus's extensive research) restores her praise for this woman, remarks which Leonard Woolf excluded from the posthumously published essay. The tone and the images of Woolf's comment, in fact, give a stronger picture of her feminist commitment:

> we honour [Ethel Smyth] not merely as a musician and a writer, but also as a blaster of rocks and the maker of bridges. It seems sometimes a pity that a woman who only wished to write music should have been forced also to make bridges, but that was part of her job and she did it.
>
> (*P*, p. xxciii)

Woolf was indeed grateful for the political work carried on by her friends. Going to tea with Margaret Llewelyn Davies in 1918, she felt that the Hampstead Centre of the Women's Co-operative Guild was 'the heart of the woman's republic'.[28] During these years she recognised the political importance of a 'magical garden of women'; it was women who might change the society's values, and, in fact, might save it from its self-destruction. As she once wrote to Margaret in 1916, in the face of the war: 'I become steadily more feminist . . . and wonder how this preposterous masculine fiction keeps going a day longer – without some vigorous young woman pulling us together and marching through it' (*L*, II, p. 76).

While each of these women deserves a longer study (and such studies are an integral part of feminist critics' reassessment of Woolf), I want to concentrate here on the major friendship of Woolf's life, one which parallels and accentuates the 'gift of self' which she found in her earlier friendship with Violet Dickinson. I mean, of course, her friendship with Vita Sackville-West.

I want to say from the outset that I am not interested in what Quentin Bell once called the 'coarse physiological facts' of their sexual affair. Their love, like most deep relationships, encompasses so much more than the simple fact that they went to bed together. Rather, I find the friendship significant in its complexity and in its confirmation of what Woolf found in her identification with other women.

Woolf met Sackville-West in 1922. Just as she had appreciated Dickinson's maternal affection, so she enjoyed Sackville-West's: 'she . . . so lavishes on me the maternal protection which for some reason is what I have always wished

from everyone' (quoted in *VWB*, ii, p. 118). Woolf asked her
advice about domestic, cosmetic and fashion questions, as if
she were a daughter or an older sister. She knew that her
friend had found her dowdy and poorly dressed and relished
her subsequent attention to improvements in her appearance.
Woolf also told her friend about the significant events of
growing up, both to draw her closer and to have her share the
meaning of her past. Travelling in Greece in 1932, she wrote
about her memories of those early difficult years: 'There was
my own ghost coming down from the Acropolis, aged 23; and
how I pitied her.'[29] She told her about the women she had
loved when she was young, about Violet Dickinson in particular. As she explained to Dickinson in a 1926 letter, 'So I ..
spent last night describing you to Vita, and how we went to
Greece together 20 years ago . . . , and I behaved so badly and
you behaved so well. There are few people I am fonder of
than Violet Dickinson, I said – or have more cause to be grateful to' (*L*, iii, p. 306).

During the height of their friendship, Woolf and
Sackville-West were as infatuated with the nature of their
relationship as with each other. They commonly teased and
scolded each other about their personalities – both lived by
the head and not by the heart. Woolf had heard this criticism
often enough, and she was particularly sensitive when
Sackville-West levelled the charge: 'But really and truly you
did say – I cant remember exactly what, but to the effect that I
made copy out of all my friends, and cared with the head, not
with the heart' (*L*, iii, p. 127). Not only did Woolf later quote
the letter in which Sackville-West had made this statement;
she eventually retaliated by noticing a corresponding reticence in her friend, in both her personality and her writing; in
passing she defends her own coldness, but admits that
Sackville-West has changed that as well:

> But you dont see, donkey West, that you'll be tired of me
> one of these days (I'm so much older) and so I have to take
> my little precautions. Thats why I put the emphasis on
> 'recording' rather than feeling. But donkey West knows she
> has broken down more ramparts than anyone. And isnt
> there something obscure in you? There's something that
> doesn't vibrate in you: It may be purposely – you dont let it

but I see it with other people, as well as with me: something
reserved, muted – God knows what. Still, still, compare this
19th Nov – with last, and you'll admit there's a difference.
It's in your writing too, by the bye. The thing I call central
transparency – sometimes fails you there too.

(*L*, III, p. 302)

Vita Sackville-West took this criticism seriously, as she
explained in a letter to her husband, Harold Nicolson:

I got a letter from Virginia, which contains one of her
devilish, shrewd, psychological pounces. She asks if there is
something in me which does not vibrate, 'something reserved, muted. . . . The thing I call "central transparency"
sometimes fails you in your writing.' Damn the woman, she
has put her finger on it. There *is* something muted.[30]

If Woolf and Sackville-West worried that their personalities,
and, perhaps more importantly, their writings were cold,
muted or overintellectualised, they also felt that their love
countered these tendencies. And Woolf still believed that such
friendships between women retained a special meaning. As
she wrote in *Mrs Dalloway*:

The strange thing, on looking back, was the purity, the
integrity of her feeling for Sally. It was not like one's feeling
for a man. It was completely disinterested, and besides, it
had a quality which could only exist between women, between women just grown up. It was protective, on her side;
sprang from a sense of being in league together.[31]

Written during the first two years of Woolf's affair with
Sackville-West, the novel is a palimpsest of her relations with
women. In the preceding passage, she uses the phrase which
initially described Vanessa and herself. She also introduces
the maternal aspect of the friendship with Dickinson made
explicit in her appraisal of Sackville-West's affection. And,
while Sally Seton in *Mrs Dalloway* resembles Woolf's 'first love',
Madge Vaughan, one sees hints of Violet Dickinson in her
character. Finally, Woolf blends in her more mature love for
Sackville-West when she describes the erotic feelings that exist

between women, when they 'did undoubtedly feel what men felt' (*MD*, p. 47):

> It was a sudden revelation, a tinge like a blush which one tried to check and then, as it spread, one yielded to its expansion, and rushed to the farthest verge and there quivered and felt the world come closer, swollen with some astonishing significance, some pressure of rapture, which split its thin skin and gushed and poured with an extraordinary alleviation over the cracks and sores! Then, for that moment, she had seen an illumination; a match burning in a crocus; an inner meaning almost expressed.   (*MD*, p. 47)

Woolf is confirming those moments of revelation in women's friendships. In addition to sharing a commitment to writing, Woolf and Sackville-West often discussed in their letters the meaning of their art to their lives, the importance of solitude and the intensity of working toward a vision. And very often each writer's vision was connected to the other's.

In Woolf's tribute to Sackville-West in *Orlando*, she not only gave Orlando some of her own writing problems (a preponderance of present participles and sibilants), but she also grants Orlando a vision of reality which had been a persistent question throughout her life and which became the germinal idea for *The Waves*:

> One sees a fin passing far out. What image can I reach to convey what I mean? Really there is none, I thing. . . . Life is soberly and accurately, the oddest affair; has in it the essence of reality. I used to feel this as a child – couldn't step across puddle once, I remember, for thinking how strange – what am I? etc. . . . All I mean to make is a note of a curious state of mind. I hazard the guess that it may be the impulse behind another book.   (*WD*, pp. 102–3)

In 1926 Woolf had experienced a similar revelation, but in this case her feeling was connected to her thoughts about Sackville-West, then away in Persia:

> Then (as I was walking through Russell Square last night) I see the mountains in the sky: the great clouds; and the

moon which is risen over Persia; I have a great and astonishing sense of something there, which is 'it'. It is not exactly beauty that I mean. It is the thing is in itself enough: satisfactory; achieved. . . . Who am I, what am I, and so on: these questions are always floating about in me: and then I bump against some exact fact – a letter, a person, and come to them again with a great sense of freshness.   (*WD*, p. 86)

Woolf had just received a letter from Sackville-West. The connection spun out between them, even at such distance, gives them a sense of their own existence. It is the source for the astonishing revelation of 'who am I'.

Woolf reciprocally offered her friend the gift of self in *Orlando*. As Joanne Trautmann notes in her fine essay about *Orlando*, the line from *The Waves*, 'Let me then create you. (You have done as much for me.)'[32] captures the theme of the playful biography. Recreating each other's personalities had been an essential part of their correspondence – as Woolf once remarked, 'if you'll make me up, I'll make you' (*L*, III, p. 214) – and often she asked her friend, 'What I am; I want you to tell me' (*L*, III, p. 233). *Orlando* was Woolf's attempt to do as much for Sackville-West.

At first Woolf had planned a spoof of their friendship, much like the last section of 'Friendships Gallery', in which she and Dickinson are twin goddesses. In 1927 she sketched 'The Jessamy Brides' in her diary: 'Two women, poor, solitary at the top of a house' are having a wild adventure in Constantinople; 'Satire and wildness' and 'Sapphism' are 'to be suggested' (*WD*, p. 105). But in the much more elaborate and complex final version, Woolf has removed herself from the action and has become the *deus ex machina*. Thus she can retrieve for her friend the family estate which had been denied her because of her sex; she can also give her a true sexual identity: by order of law, she is female. And finally, at the close of the book, she presents her friend with an astonishing revelation of self.

Woolf admitted from the very beginning that what she most enjoyed in writing *Orlando* was the opportunity to come to understand her friend by 'creating her'. As she wrote in a létter to Sackville-West, 'it's all about you and the lust of your flesh and the lure of your mind. . . . I should like to untwine and twist again some very odd, incongruous strands in you' (*L*, III, p. 429). And, when she was composing the final pages of the book, she again wrote to Sackville-West, 'By the way, do you think I know you? Intimately? A question that I shall ask myself tomorrow morning – you are driving down to Knole [in *Orlando*] and as you go, you exhibit the most profound and secret side of your character' (*L*, III, p. 469).

Orlando was composed of many different and dispersed selves, but when she called Orlando, 'Orlando did not come', only variations, not what Woolf calls 'the true self'. As Woolf elaborates, 'It is, they say, compact of all the selves we have it in us to be; commanded and locked up by the Captain self, the key self, which amalgamates and controls them all.'[33]

Orlando's true self is revealed only through Woolf's own vision which she presents to her friend at this moment – the sense of reality which Orlando perceives in 'the wild goose', the vision which one must pursue. Of course, Woolf plays with the phrase, 'wild goose', as a self-parodic reference to her chases after a vision. Nevertheless, in the course of the narrative the vision of the wild goose is transformed into Woolf's initial and emblematic image of the fin in the water: '"Haunted!" she cried " . . . ever since I was a child. There flies the wild goose. . . . Always it flies fast out to sea and always I fling after it words like nets. . . . And sometimes there's an inch of silver – six words – in the bottom of the net. But never the great fish who lives in the coral groves"' (*O*, p. 313).

It is at this moment when Orlando is immersed in her vision that she has her revelation of self. It is as if Woolf chose to end the book with this gift so that their friendship and their shared vision together bring an answer to the question 'who am I?':

> The whole of her darkened and settled, as when some foil whose addition makes the rounds and solidity of a surface is added to it, and the shallow becomes deep and the near is distant; and all is contained as water is contained by the sides of a well. So she was now darkened, stilled, and become, with the addition of this Orlando, what is called, rightly or wrongly, a single self, a real self. . . . When communication is established there is nothing more tò be said. (*O*, p. 314)

In *Mrs Dalloway*, Woolf describes a similar instance of the gift of self in friendships between two women. Clarissa, in middle age, remembers 'the most exquisite moment of her whole life'. She summons back all the ideas and beliefs and feelings that she and Sally Seton had shared as young women. Then, she recalls, Sally had kissed her, as if to seal their affection and to acknowledge their special attachment:

> [Clarissa] felt that she had been given a present, wrapped up and told just to keep it, not to look at it – a diamond, something infinitely precious, wrapped, which, as they walked . . . she uncovered, or the radiance burnt through, the revelation, the religious feeling!   (*MD*, pp. 52–3)

Woolf's metaphor for identity is the gift which Sally's affection had given Clarissa – the diamond. In later years, when Clarissa looks at herself in the mirror, she realises,

> That was her self – pointed; dartlike; definite. That was her self when some effort, some call on her to be her self, drew the parts together, she alone knew how different, how incompatible and composed so for the world only into one centre, one diamond, . . . a radiancy. . . .   (*MD*, p. 55)

From these experiences Woolf spun out the sense of what women share in their friendships. She had sensed in her own life an unspoken understanding, a conspiratorial allegiance between her sister and herself. What seemed to be a kind of telepathic communication surprised and delighted her when she and Violet Dickinson were close friends. She travelled back into the literary past along threads of identification linking her life with those of other women writers. And she and Vita Sackville-West experienced sudden and astonishing revelations of self through each other – a sense of reality flaring up out of their deep and intimate friendship. Summarising her recognition of this special quality in women's friendships, she once wrote that she found 'the relationship so secret and private compared with relations with men. . . . Why not write about it? Truthfully?' (*WD*, p. 69). And indeed she did, not only in *Mrs Dalloway*, on which she was working at the time of this diary entry, but also throughout her fiction, non-fiction and letters.

Woolf believed that, in the current state of society, patriarchal attitudes tended to isolate individuals behind defensive walls of egotism. If individualism was the watchword, then those who refused to act only out of egotistical motives were often exploited for their sympathy. So women found themselves in the predicament of being controlled and manipulated precisely because they relinquished, or refused to adhere to, those characteristics which would have protected them from emotional exploitation.

In her diary Woolf commented that there were sometimes dangerous consequences when one gave up the screens of egotism. But she also realised that the prisoner behind these ramparts never developed an authentic identity. To escape from this form of alienation so prevalent in modern society, she called for a recognition of what she had first seen in her friendships with women – that special form of communication between the self and other which required no screens or outer pretences. She urged all to relinquish their screens and to develop sympathy – that trait which she had so often discovered in her women friends:

> Have no screens, for screens are made out of our own integument; and get at the thing itself, which has nothing whatever in common with a screen. The screen-making habit, though, is so universal that probably it preserves our sanity. If we had not this device for shutting people off from our sympathies we might perhaps dissolve utterly; separateness would be impossible. But the screens are in the excess; not the sympathy.   (*WD*, p. 97)

Whenever Woolf imagined a world in which sympathy, not screens, would be in the excess, she returned to her dream of the magical garden of women. Remembering those values inherent in friendships among women, she created in her writing societies formed by women, much like the utopian community of women in 'Friendships Gallery'. Her short story 'A Society', written in 1920, is about a group of women who join together to investigate the masculine world. Although the story is sketchy and ends with no specific conclusions, Woolf stresses the most important lesson to be learned by women, not from men but from each other. As the narrator of the story tells one of the members of the society, 'Once [your daughter] knows how to read there's only one thing you can teach her to believe in – and that is herself.' And the friend replies, 'Well, that would be a change.'[34]

As the Second World War rapidly approached, as fascism dragged everyone to the edge of a precipice, Woolf again turned to the society of women as an alternative to patriarchal structures and the seeds of authoritarianism. In *Three Guineas*, while she pretends at first to be addressing a man, she is, in fact, bidding women to believe in themselves – to maintain the integrity of their values, to preserve their status of outsiders and to exclude from their society all masculine values of hierarchy, competition, dominance and power.

Just as she had expressed her own anger in her letters to women friends, so in this book, tacitly surrounded by her society of outsiders, she allows herself her full rage. Women had taught her to believe in herself, to say, 'I am I'. In *Three Guineas* she gives women their own history, their own cultural identities, and sets them apart from the patriarchal world, as if this polemic was the culmination of what it meant to be 'sisters' in the face of masculine power and control. Her connections to literary sisters and to her women friends thus give her the basis for her developed aesthetic and political beliefs. Her psychological need to discover 'Who am I?' was answered by these women. And then she turned her answer – the reciprocal relation between the self and the other to be found in women's sympathy – into a political stand. If women can say, 'I am I', they can also say, 'We are we.' In *Three Guineas* women must be 'in league together against the world' for the survival of humanity.

NOTES

1. This essay was first presented as a lecture at the 1976 Princeton University Conference on Woolf and Her Cultural Setting, organised by Joanna Lipking.
2. Virginia Woolf, *A Room of One's Own*, Harvest edn (New York: Harcourt, Brace and World, 1957) p. 77. Further references are to this edition cited as *ROO*.
3. Simone de Beauvoir, *The Second Sex* (New York: Bantam, 1970) p. 45.
4. Woolf used this phrase about Vanessa and herself in a 1927 diary entry:

A Writer's Diary, ed. Leonard Woolf (London: Hogarth Press, 1965) p. 120. (Further references are to this edition, cited as *WD*.) This became a favourite phrase and reoccurs not only in *Mrs Dalloway* but also in *The Pargiters*. In the latter, however, Woolf is describing a brother–sister relationship in which there is a similar conspiratorial attachment within the family. It is significant that the pact between the brother and sister is never as longlasting as that between sister and sister. It is torn asunder when the brother enters the public world of men.

5. Virginia Woolf, *Moments of Being, Unpublished Autobiographical Writings of Virginia Woolf*, ed. Jeanne Schulkind (New York: Harcourt, Brace, Jovanovich, 1976) pp. 123–4. Further references are to this edition, cited as *MB*.

6. Virginia Woolf, *Night and Day*, Harvest edn (New York: Harcourt, Brace and World, 1948) p. 79.

7. Virginia Woolf, *The Letters of Virginia Woolf*, ed. Nigel Nicolson and Joanne Trautmann (New York: Harcourt, Brace, Jovanovich, 1975) vol. I, p. xx. Further references to the three volumes of *Letters*, published 1975, 1976 and 1977 respectively, are given as *L*, followed by volume and page numbers.

8. Virginia Woolf, 'Reading Notes', Jan 1909–Mar 1911, unpublished notebooks in the Berg Collection of the New York Public Library, p. 10. I am grateful to Dr Lola Szladits, curator of the collection, and to the Berg Collection, Astor, Lenox and Tilden Foundation, as well as to Quentin Bell, for their kind permission to quote from these reading notes.

9. Quoted in Quentin Bell, *Virginia Woolf: A Biography*, 2 vols (London: Hogarth Press, 1972) I, pp. 82–3. Further references are to this edition, cited as *VWB*, followed by volume and page numbers.

10. Virginia Woolf, '*The Pargiters': The Novel–Essay Portion of 'The Years'*, ed. Mitchell A. Leaska (New York: New York Public Library, and Reader Books, 1977) p. 112. Hereafter cited as *P*.

11. It is important to point out that the relationship between Kitty and Miss Craddock is different from that between Elizabeth, Clarissa's daughter, and her tutor Doris Kilman in *Mrs Dalloway*. Miss Kilman wants to control and possess the young woman, and her love is much more similar to the romantic love of men for women than to the impersonal, non-possessive love between women that Woolf describes elsewhere in the same novel.

12. Carroll Smith-Rosenberg, 'The Female World of Love and Ritual: Relations between Women in Nineteenth Century America', *Signs*, I, no. 1, Fall 1975, pp. 8, 9, 27–8.

13. Woolf's use of the image of 'green water' is perhaps subconsciously related to her description of the gloomy atmosphere in her home after her mother's death. In 'A Sketch of the Past', she portrays Leslie Stephen sitting in the back drawing room, 'with the Virginia Creeper hanging a curtain of green over the window, so that the room was like a green cave' (*MB*, p. 94).

14. It is poignantly ironic to find Woolf teasing not only about suicide but about drowning herself. She may also have had in mind the story of a

woman's suicide in the Serpentine, about which she wrote at great length in her 1903 diary.

15. Virginia Woolf, *Orlando: A Biography*, Harvest edn (New York: Harcourt, Brace and World, 1956) p. 314. Further references are to this edition, cited as *O*.

16. Paraphrased from Virginia Woolf, 'Friendships Gallery', in the Berg Collection of the New York Public Library. The text of 'Friendships Gallery' is now available in *Twentieth Century Literature*, vol. 25, no. 3/4, Autumn/Winter 1979, pp. 270–302.

17. Woolf may also have associated Violet Dickinson's care for her with Rhoda's reaction to Percival's death in *The Waves*. [References are to the Harvest edition (New York: Harcourt, Brace and World, 1959), hereafter cited as *W*.] Rhoda's tribute to Percival is a bouquet of violets thrown into the waves (*W*, p. 289), but, unlike Bernard, she is neither 'unvanquished' nor 'unyielding'. Rather, her sense of isolation and her lack of identity (significantly, she never sees herself in a mirror), cause her violets to wither and blacken (*W*, p. 287), and she finally gives in to death.

18. Paraphrased from Woolf's unpublished diary (1936) in the Berg Collection of the New York Public Library.

19. *WD*, 151.

20. B. J. Kirkpatrick, *A Bibliography of Virginia Woolf*, rev. edn (London: Rupert Hart Davis, 1956) pp. 138–9: 'Doubt arises in the following due to the interval between date of dispatch and publication.' Woolf's review 'Women in America', was submitted to the *Guardian* on 15 Jan 1905, but a review called 'The American Woman' was not published until 31 May 1905. Similarly, while Woolf listed 'Feminine Fiction' as completed before Christmas 1904, a review called 'Conventional Heroines' was not published in the *Guardian* until 22 Feb 1905.

21. Virginia Woolf, 'Reading Notes' (unpublished; see above, n. 8).

22. Virginia Woolf, *To the Lighthouse*, Harvest edn (Harcourt, Brace and World, 1955) p. 222.

23. Virginia Woolf, 'Four Figures', *Second Common Reader*, Harvest edn (New York: Harcourt, Brace and World, 1960) p. 142. Further references are to this edition, cited as *SCR*.

24. Virginia Woolf, 'George Eliot', *Collected Essays*, Paperback edn, 4 vols, ed. Leonard Woolf (London: Chatto & Windus, 1966–7) vol. i, p. 198. Further references are to this edition, cited as *CE*, followed by volume and page numbers.

25. Virginia Woolf, *Three Guineas*, Harbinger edn (New York: Harcourt, Brace and World, 1963) p. 134.

26. Woolf thought that her mother resembled Mrs Carlyle in gestures and manners of speech. Leslie Stephen, according to Woolf, also asked over and over again after his wife's death, 'I was not as bad as Carlyle, was I?' (*MB*, pp. 36n., 41).

27. Woolf's disappointment at not having children should not be underestimated, despite the fact that she knew that having children had often impeded women's writing. It was a constant and painful basis for comparison between Vanessa and herself. Perhaps the problem would

not have loomed so large throughout her life if she had not felt that the decision had been taken out of her hands by Leonard and the doctors whom he consulted. See, for example, a 1927 letter to Ethel Sands: 'I'm always angry with myself for not having forced Leonard to take the risk in spite of doctors; he was afraid for me and wouldn't; but if I'd had rather more self-control no doubt it would have been all right' – *L* III, p. 329).

28. Virginia Woolf, *The Diary of Virginia Woolf*, 1915–1919, ed. Anne Olivier Bell with Introduction by Quentin Bell (New York: Harcourt, Brace, Jovanovich, 1977) p. 146.
29. *L*, v, p. 62.
30. Quoted in Nigel Nicolson, *Portrait of a Marriage* (New York: Atheneum, 1973) p. 212.
31. Virginia Woolf, *Mrs Dalloway* Harvest edn (New York: Harcourt, Brace and World, 1953) p. 50. Further references are to this edition, cited as *MD*.
32. *W*, 233, as quoted in Joanne Trautmann, 'The Jessamy Brides: The Friendship of Virginia Woolf and Vita Sackville-West', *Penn State Studies*, no. 36 (1973).
33. *O*, 310.
34. Virginia Woolf, 'A Society', *Monday or Tuesday* (New York: Harcourt, Brace, 1921) p. 25.

3 Shakespeare's *Other* Sister

LOUISE A. DeSALVO

In that meditation upon the relationship between women and the writing of fiction called *A Room of One's Own*, Virginia Woolf wondered why, during, say, Elizabeth's time, 'no woman wrote a word of that extraordinary literature when every other man, it seemed, was capable of song or sonnet'.[1] To answer this 'perennial puzzle', as she called it, she imagined, 'since facts are so hard to come by, what would have happened had Shakespeare had a wonderfully gifted sister, called Judith, let us say' (*ROO*, p. 48):

> She was as adventurous, as imaginative, as agog to see the world as he [Shakespeare] was. But she was not sent to school.... She picked up a book now and then, one of her brother's perhaps, and read a few pages. But then her parents came in and told her to mend the stockings or mind the stew and not moon about with books and papers.... Perhaps she scribbled some pages up in an apple loft on the sly, but was careful to hide them or set fire to them. Soon, however, before she was out of her teens, she was to be betrothed to the son of a neighbouring wool-stapler. She cried out that marriage was hateful to her, and for that she was severely beaten by her father. (*ROO*, p. 49)

She will not concede, however, but takes to the road to London, like her brother, driven by the gift for pen and ink that she knows she possesses. Her end, however, is ignominious simply because she is a woman and not a man:

> at last ... Nick Greene the actor–manager took pity on her; she found herself with child by that gentleman and so – who

shall measure the heat and violence of the poet's heart when caught and tangled in a woman's body? – killed herself one winter's night and lies buried at some cross-roads where the omnibuses now stop outside the Elephant and Castle.

(*ROO*, p. 50)

In *A Room*, Shakespeare's sister, who kills herself both because she has not been allowed to develop those powers that lie within her as surely as they lie within her brother, and because she was forced to flee a household where her marriage had been arranged for her, while becoming embroiled in a relationship with Nick Greene, becomes the emblem of *all* women who have been denied the circumstances in which to cultivate their gift for pen and ink and have become, instead, commodities in the market-place of marriage.

Woolf had been thinking of Shakespeare's sister well before 1928, when she was composing those papers read to the Arts Society at Newnham and the Odtaa at Girton which became transformed into *A Room*. She had, in fact, written an extended fiction based upon the very same idea many, many years before, probably as early as 1906, when she was still Virginia Stephen, although the setting of that early fiction was fifteenth-century and not Elizabethan England.[2]

In August 1906, Virginia and Vanessa Stephen had leased Blo' Norton Hall in East Harling, Norfolk–a moated Elizabethan manor house on the Norfolk–Suffolk border, between Thetford and Diss.[3] On 4 August, she wrote to Violet Dickinson,

The difficulties of writing in this place are many. . . . If only I had chosen a better moment to write to you, I would describe this place. Which now I shant do. It is 300 years old, striped with oak bars inside, old staircases, ancestral vats, and portraits; there is a garden; and a moat. . . . Nessa paints windmills in the afternoon, and I tramp the country for miles with a map, leap ditches, scale walls and desecrate churches, making out beautiful brilliant stories every step of the way. One is actually being – as we geniuses say – transferred to paper at this moment. That might mean that this letter was it: but it isn't. (*L*, I, pp. 233–4)

And on 24 August, she again wrote to Dickinson about that work in progress: 'I have written 40 pages of manuscript since I came here; that is about 3 a day, or rather more; because, of course, one must leave out Sundays' (*L*, I, p. 235).What Woolf had probably been working on was a forty-four-page untitled story in holograph which has recently been published, now in the Berg Collection of English and American Literature.[4] The Untitled Story is set in Norfolk, just a few miles from the location of Blo' Norton Hall, and Woolf transformed the setting of her August 1906 holiday into the Martyn Hall of her fiction.

The tale describes the researches of a character by the name of Rosamond Merridew into the land-tenure system of medieval England, and how, on a June morning some two years before, she saw an old manor house while driving down the Thetford Road between Norwich and East Harling after having tried and failed to recover documents from the ruins of Caistor Abbey. She stops and is given a tour of Martyn Hall, as it is called. While there, she is shown the manuscript of a diary which has been in the family for centuries, the Journal of Mistress Joan Martyn, kept by her when she was twenty-five years old, during the fifteenth century.[5]

This Untitled Story is an extremely significant work in the Woolf canon because it presages many of the central concerns of Woolf's later works: the role of women in the process of history; the opportunities denied women in centuries past; the institution of marriage; the inadequacy of histories as they are traditionally written; the necessity of seeing history in terms of individuals; the necessity for women to discover myths about themselves – to name but a few. It is also significant because it precedes by one or two years the earliest extant version of *The Voyage Out*, and therefore provides a valuable link between Woolf's juvenilia and the earliest drafts of her first novel.[6]

Rosamond Merridew is crusty and irascible – she is what Harriet of *A Cockney's Farming Experiences* might have been like had she become an historian instead of a termagant wife. She has maintained her views about the role of the historian, despite opposition and censure, bowing to no one, neither in her pursuit of historical truth as seen through the eyes of a woman, nor in her protrayal of the *real* stuff of history, the lived life of ordinary human beings as they gathered about the fire in the evenings or as they went about the work of the everyday world during the thirteenth, fourteenth and fifteenth centuries.

Merridew is not modest. She introduces herself as one who has 'won considerable fame among my profession for the researches I have made into the system of Land tenure in mediaeval England . . . & I am not absolutely unknown in one or two secluded rooms in Oxford & in Cambridge' (p. 1). But she has had to exchange 'a husband & a family & a house in which I may grow old for certain fragments of yellow parchment; wh. only a few people can read & still fewer would care to read if they could' (ibid.). This is one of many ironies in Merridew's story – a woman historian, pledged to tell the truth about family life, about the interrelationships between women and men, about the realities of motherhood, as no man has, must *herself* give up the joys of the very things which she cherishes most in order to pursue her career. Indeed, Woolf understood then what she articulated again later – that a woman is forced to make choices which no man must ever make. But Merridew's pieces of parchment have become her children; she does not complain or chafe at the course she has chosen: 'But as a mother . . . a kind of maternal passion has sprung up in my breast for these shrivelled & colourless little gnomes; in real life I see them as cripples with fretful faces, but all the same, with the fire of genius in their eyes'(ibid.).

As an historian, Merridew reflects proudly upon her unique contributions:

> A sudden light upon the legs of Dame Elizabeth Partridge sends its beams over the whole state of England, to the king upon his throne; she wanted stockings! & no other need impresses you in quite the same way with the reality of mediaeval legs; & therefore with the reality of mediaeval bodies, & so, proceeding upward step by step, with the reality of mediaeval brains; & there you stand at the centre of all ages . . . . (p. 2)

This is no woman who rarefies and abstracts history, discoursing upon ideas and movements as if they operated separately from the lived life of real human beings. *This* historian, this

Rosamond Merridew, illuminates the meaning of the ages through women who want and who desire and who make their needs felt – this is an historian who would weld truth and personality into one seamless whole.[7] Merridew's greatest gift, as she sees it, is her

> remarkable gift... for presenting them [her researches into land tenure] in relation to the life of the time.
> ... I have made all these enquiries subsidiary to certain pictures of the family life which I have introduced into my text; as the flower of all these intricate roots; the flesh of all this scraping of flint. (ibid.)

Her major work has been a book called *The Manor Roll*, which, she allows, will either please or disgust the reader because of those digressions which, she insists, are central and not peripheral to her story, those digressions which describe the rabbits being poached, the serf in his cottage, the Lord of the Manor setting off on a journey or calling his dogs for a walk in the fields. 'In another room I show you Dame Elinor, at work with her needle; & by her on a lower stool sits her daughter, stitching too, but less assiduously' (p. 3).

As proud as Merridew has been of her contributions, there are those who do not appreciate her humanistic insights into history; there are those who continue to deride her and to scorn her:

> The critics have always threatened me with two rods; first, they say, such digressions are all very well in a history of the time, but they have nothing to do with the system [of] mediaeval land tenure; secondly, they complain that I have no materials at my side. ... It is well known that the period I have chosen is more bare than any other of private records: unless you choose to draw all your inspiration from the Paston Letters you must be content to imagine merely, like any story teller. And that, I am told, is a useful art in its place; but it should be allowed to claim no relationship with the sterner nobler art of the Historian. (ibid.)

And we know from reading Woolf's later 'The Pastons and Chaucer', that even the Paston Letters are inadequate because

Mrs Paston herself does not tell us what we want to know:

> Indeed, had Mrs. Paston chosen, she could have told her
> children how when she was a young woman a thousand men
> with bows and arrows and pans of burning fire had
> marched upon Gresham and broken the gates and mined
> the walls of the room where she sat alone. . . . She neither
> bewailed her lot nor thought herself a heroine. The long,
> long letters which she wrote so laboriously in her clear
> cramped hand to her husband, who was (as usual) away,
> *make no mention of herself.*[8]

What Merridew understands, however, is that the place of
women in history has not been re-examined primarily because
governmental officials have chosen not to re-examine it: 'If we
were to spend a tithe of the sums that we spend yearly upon
excavating Greek cities in excavating our own ruins what a
different tale the Historian would have to tell!'(p. 4).[9]

Merridew is one heroine in this 1906 meditation upon the
relationship between the woman as historian and history and
upon the need of women such as Merridew to write women
into history. Another woman, Mrs Betty Martyn, is soon
introduced, and it is *her* story counterpointed against the
toughness and honesty and success of Merridew's that forms
another of the continuing series of ironic contrasts upon
which this work is structured. Merridew's drive to discover
manuscripts and her persistence in searching for evidence
that will confirm her views is finally rewarded on that June day
she is recalling. She sees an old house, 'the kind of place, I
thought, as I stood with my hand on the bell, where the owners
are likely to possess exquisite manuscripts, & sell them' (p. 5).
A Mr Martyn answers the bell. He brings her in to meet a rosy
woman, about her own age, who looks like a housekeeper.
This is Mrs Betty Martyn, the analogue of Mrs Martin in *A
Room*, that 'queer, composite being', the ordinary woman.[10]
This is the ordinary woman who forms the stuff of Merridew's
history; but, paradoxically, this is the ordinary woman without
a history:

> The Hall had been in her husbands family for many a year,
> she remarked with some slight pride; she did not know how

long, but people said the Martyns had once been great
people in the neighbourhood. She drew my attention to the
y in their name. Still she spoke with the very chastened &
clear sighted pride of one who knows by hard personal
experience how little nobility of birth avails, against certain
material drawbacks, the poverty of the land, for instance,
the holes in the roof, & the rapacity of rats.   (p. 6)

Mr Martyn knows who *his* ancestors are and what *their*
connections with history have been, as does his wife: there are
portraits of his ancestors hanging round the Hall, and he
points to one, 'painted perhaps in the time of Charles the First'
(p. 8), and tells Merridew his life story:

> [']His name's Willoughby,['] he went on speaking to me, as
> though he wished me to understand the matter thorough-
> ly . . .
>   'Willoughby Martyn: born 1625 died 1685: he fought at
> Marston Moor[11] as Captain of a Troop of Norfolk men.
> We were always royalists. He was exiled, in the Protectorate,
> went to Amsterdam; bought a bay horse off the Duke of
> Newcastle there; we have the breed still; he came back here
> at the Restoration, married Sally Hampton – of the Manor,
> but they died out last generation, & had six children, four
> sons & two daughters.[']   (p. 9)

Mrs Martyn has no such stories to tell, but Merridew keeps
probing, for what she understands is that women need
histories about women. They need myths about their mothers
and facts about their grandmothers,[12] which is why Merridew
has continued to search for that document which will indicate
what it was like to be a woman in the thirteenth, fourteenth
and fifteenth centuries in England. Rosamond must give the
Mrs Martyns of the world the stories of their mothers.
   Although Mr Martyn wonders at her 'queer liking for these
old fathers of mine' (p. 9), at Mrs Martyn's urging, he shows
Merridew all the old things they possess. She makes ready to
leave, but he tells her they are not finished yet. They go into
his office and he shows her some unbound yellow papers tied
with a green silk cord: 'While he bent down before a book case,
I hastily looked at the first inscription on the parchment. "The
Journal of Mistress Joan Martyn["], I spelt out, ["]kept by her

at Martyn's Hall, in the county of Norfolk the year of our Lord 1480.["]' (p. 12)[13]

Mr Martyn does not understand the significance of the document although he has read it and he tries to persuade her of the greater historical significance of 'the stud book of Willoughby' (p. 13). Merridew learns from him that Joan was the only daughter of Giles Martyn, who also had three sons: 'She wrote this Diary when she was 25: she lived here all her life – never married. Indeed she died at the age of 30. I daresay you might see her tomb down there with the rest of them' (p. 13).

Although Mr Martyn values these reminders of his forebears above all things, in an act of utter selflessness, he gives Merridew, not only Joan's journal, but also the story she has been waiting a lifetime for, a story that will provide her and Mrs Martyn with a symbolic maternal figure: ' "If these old papers please you, I'm sure your welcome to 'em." ... I walked off with Grandmother Joan beneath my arm; Betty insisted upon wrapping her in brown paper' (p. 17).

This Grandmother Joan Martyn is the fifteenth-century analogue of both Merridew and Mrs Betty Martyn. She is the third woman whose story Woolf presents and it contrasts with that of Merridew's and the modern Mrs Martyn's.

Rosamond Merridew soon steps aside completely, and the contents of Joan Martyn's Journal are presented directly, without interference, as if Rosamond were reading it or as if we are reading it for ourselves. It is an excellent device for rendering the past as if it were taking place in the present. We learn, from the outset, that these are unsafe times, that women must keep within their lands, that women need stout gates to keep out men and marauders. But Joan rebels against this hemmed-in existence even though she realises why it is necessary:

> I am very bold & impatient sometimes, when the moon rises, over a land gleaming with frost; & I think I feel the pressure of all this free & beautiful place – all England & the sea, & the lands beyond – rolling like sea waves, against our iron gates, breaking, & withdrawing – & breaking again – all through the long black night. Once I leapt from my bed, & ran to my mothers room, crying 'Let them

in![']...But I could not explain what it was that I heard; and she bade me sleep, & be thankful that there were stout gates between me & the world. But on other nights, when the wind is wild & the moon is sunk beneath hurrying clouds, I am glad to draw close to the fire, & to think that all those bad men who prowl in the lanes & lie hidden in the woods at this hour cannot break through our great gates. Last night was such a night; they come often in the winter when my father is away in London, my brothers are with the army, save my little brother Jeremy, & my mother has to manage the farm, & order the people, & see that all our nights are looked to. (p. 18)

The contrast between Rosamond's freedom and Joan's imprisonment is striking, as is the similarity between Joan's imprisonment and Mrs Martyn's self-imposed (or socially imposed) solitude.

But Joan learns that the only way for a woman to be powerful within her society is for her to rule her home:

We may not burn the tapers after the church bell has struck 8 times, & so we sit round the logs, with the priest, John Sandys, & one or two of the servants who sleep with us in the stall. Then my mother, who cannot be idle even by fire light, winds her wool for her knitting, sitting in the great Chair which stands by the cheek of the hearth. When her wool gets tangled she strikes a great blow with the iron rod, & sends the flames & the sparks spurting in showers; she stoops her head into the tawny light, & you see what a noble woman she is; in spite of age – she is more than forty, & the hard lines which much thought & watching have cut in her brow. She wears a fine linen cap, close fitting to the shape of her head, & her eyes are deep & stern, & her cheek is coloured like a healthy winter apple. It is a great thing to be the daughter of such a woman, & to hope that one day the same power may be mine. She rules us all. (pp. 18–19)

Joan learns about the world that exists outside those stout gates and about history through the stories her mother tells her and through some manuscripts that her father sends her from London and through the songs of a traveller by the name of Richard. She learns how to be the kind of woman she is supposed to be largely from these sources, written by and delivered to her largely by men. Her father sends her a manuscript of John Lydgate's *Temple of Glas* and perhaps, also, his *Troy Story*,[14] a poem 'written about Helen & the siege of Troy' (p. 20).

> Last night I read of Helen, & her beauty & her suitors . . . [;] we see very well what they must have been like; & we can weep for the sufferings of the soldier, & picture to ourselves the stately woman herself; who must have been, I think, something like my mother. My mother heals with her foot & sees the whole procession pass I know, from the way her eyes gleam, & her head tosses.   (ibid.)

The young woman, kept behind stout gates in Norfolk, is sent a manuscript by her father who is free to go to London, which reinforces why men needed to keep their women safely locked away during the fifteenth century: like Helen, simply because they are women, they possess within them not only the power to heal (as Joan's mother does), but also the power to unleash the lusts of men, the power, simply by being themselves, to begin wars. And Helen's story reminds Joan, too, that even the choice of a suitor for her might bring ruin upon their house for it might cause those who have been excluded to unite against Joan's father. Joan understands the analogy well: 'We in Norfolk today are much the same as we were in the days of Helen, wherever she may have lived' (ibid.). She perceives the analogy between Helen's being carried off to Troy by Paris, and her neighbour Jane Moryson's being carried off: 'Was not Jane Moryson carried off on the eve of her wedding only last year?' (pp. 20–1).

It is a time, therefore, marked by fear, especially by the fear that women have for the highwaymen who might carry them off. And from her reading she learns that it has been this way throughout the ages: attractive women have been the cause of wars since the time of the Greeks. Indeed, Joan's own nights are filled with fear 'when the time for bed comes' (p. 21): 'The window in my room is broken, & stuffed with straw, but gusts come in & lift the tapestry on the wall, till I think that horses & men in armour are charging down upon me. My prayer last night was, that the great gates might hold fast, & all robbers & murderers might pass us by' (ibid.). Joan cannot help transferring this terror of highwaymen, reinforced through her reading, to men in general. And although she lives in the age of chivalry, the eros of the poetry of her own time has nothing to do with her life and her feelings about men and the way she is treated as a woman. The code of chivalry, Woolf understands, is the stuff of poetry and of romance, not the fact of history.

Joan Martyn's Journal, then, explores the historical and societal causes of the tension between the sexes. In Joan's Journal, the fear that women have of men is rooted in a landholding system that has caused a significant portion of the male population to have no means to sustain themselves and in a society which waged war and then in its peaceful interludes allowed its unoccupied warriors to roam at large, terrorising the countryside, or which employed them to fight in internal skirmishes. (We can understand why Rosamond Merridew has decided that the land-tenure system of medieval England was perhaps its most significant institution for understanding the lived life of the populace.) These men not only took up a life of crime; they also vented their rage against the system upon the bodies of women – upon the daughters and wives of the landholders.

None the less, she would like to travel, despite the perils, as Shakespeare's sister had, to London, even though she knows that she will probably never get there: 'It is a fearful ride, but, truly, I think I should like to go that way once, & pass over the land, like a ship at sea' (pp. 23–4). Joan's Journal illustrates that, because property was valued above all other things, marriage had become an instrument to ensure the continuance of the landholding system. Joan's marriage, like that of Shakespeare's sister, would be arranged for her:

> 'Marriage, you must know my daughter['], went on my mother, [']is a great honour & a great burden. If you marry such a man as Sir Amyas you become not only the head of his household, & that is much, but the head of his race for ever & ever, & that is more. We will not talk of love – as that song writer of yours talks of love, as a passion & a fire & a madness.['] (p. 26)

And, she has adjusted herself to the necessity of such a system: 'Since I was a child, I have always heard my parents talk of my marriage; & saving the last two or three years there have been several contracts almost made I know, that come to nothing in the end. I lose my youth however, & it is high time that a bargain were struck' (ibid.). Marriage might even have its rewards, conferring a status upon her that she now does not possess: 'No other event in the life of a woman can mean so great a change; for from flitting shadow like & unconsidered in her father's house, marriage suddenly passes her to a substantial body, with weight which people must see & make way for' (p. 27). And,

> if I marry well, the burden of a great name & of great lands will be on me; many servants will call me mistress; I shall be the mother of sons; in my husband's absence I shall rule his people,... & within doors I shall store up fine linens & my chests shall be laden with spices & preserves.... And when I lie dead, the people from the countryside shall pass for three days before my body, praying & speaking good of me.... (ibid.)

But she does not always speak so bravely of marriage. Later she thinks,

> O how blessed it would be never to marry or grow old; but to spend ones life innocently & indifferently among the trees & rivers which alone can keep one cool & child like in the midst of the troubles of the world!... Marriage or any other great joy would confuse the clean vision which is still mine. And at the thought of losing that, I cried in my heart, 'No, I will never leave you – for a husband or a lover' & straight way I started chasing rabbits across the heath with Jeremy & the dogs. (p. 28)

One day when Joan ventures beyond the stout gates, she learns why she is kept behind them and why she must soon marry. On this day, she loses her innocence and she learns of the perils in the world outside her protected environment. While she is on the heath with Jeremy and the dogs, she sees 'a Sanctuary man ... prowling out of bounds in search of food.

He had robbed or murdered, or perchance he was only a debtor. Jeremy swore he saw blood on his hands: but then Jeremy is a boy, & would like to defend us all with his bow & arrows' (p. 29).

Later, she visits the cottages of peasants:

> These are the people we must rule; & tread under foot, & scourge them to do the only work they are fitted to do; or they will tear us to pieces with their fangs. . . . Still the sight of that ugly face spoilt the rest of the walk; since it seemed that even my dear country bred pests like these. I saw such eyes staring at me from the . . . bushes, & the tangles of the undergrowth.
>
> It was like waking from a nightmare to enter our own clean hall, where the logs burnt tidily in the great chimney, . . . & my mother came down the staircase in her rich gown, with spotless linen on her head. But some of the lines on her face, & some of the sternness of her voice, had come there, I thought suddenly, because she always saw not far from her such sights as I had seen today.   (p. 30)

One day a man called Richard comes to them from Cornwall. He has a bag stuffed with books and he begins to tell her about several of them:

> Here for instance – in this little volume, are all the stories of the knights of the round Table; written out by the hand of Master Anthony himself. . . . I value this more than my wife or children; for I have none; it is meat & drink to me, because I am given supper & lodging for singing the tales in it; . . . it is horse & staff to me, for it has lifted me over many miles of weary road . . . .   (p. 32)

He begins telling the story of Sir Tristram and the Lady Iseult:

> And as the story grew passionate his voice rose, & his fists clenched, & he raised his foot & stretched forth his arms; & then, when the lovers part, he seemed to see the Lady sink away from him, & his eye sought farther & farther till the vision was faded away; & his arms were empty. (p. 33)

Joan is transfixed: 'And when I opened my eyes, the man, & the gray wall, & the people by the gate, slowly swam up, as from some depths, & settled on the surface, & stayed there clear & cold' (p. 34).

It is stories such as this which reinforce her sense that loving is fraught with danger and which diminish her sense of her own importance as a human being. For how can her dull, circumscribed life compete with the terror and the danger and the allure of those passionate legendary beings? Yet one of her greatest difficulties is in reconciling her family's desire for her to wed with all the frightening consequences of loving inherent in the stories she reads and hears.

Soon it is midsummer, and Joan's fortunes are beginning to change:

> There comes a week, or may be it is only a day, when the year seems poised consciously on its topmost peak; it stays there motionless for a long or a short time, as though in majestic contemplation, & then slowly sinks like a monarch descending from his throne, & wraps itself round in darkness.   (p. 36)

It is a suitable time for her to make a pilgrimage to the shrine of Our Lady, and walking outside is more freedom than she has known in a long while:

> In sober truth, & without metaphor, the mind drives clearly through all the mazes of a stagnant spirit when a . . . pair of legs impells it; & the creature grows nimbler, with its exercise. Thus I suppose I may have thought enough for a whole week lived indoors during these three hours that I spent striding along the road . . . .   (p. 38)

When she gets there, she again becomes submissive, however: 'For one moment I submitted myself to her as I have never submitted to man or woman, & bruised my lips on the rough stone of her garment' (ibid.). In a society with so little regard for the needs or the wishes of women, the cult of the Virgin is irony indeed.

In the autumn, Joan recounts that her marriage to Sir Amyas is not far off. She does not expect much:

Sir Amyas is a good gentleman, who treats me with great courtesy, & hopes to make me happy. No poet could sing of our courtship; &, I must confess that since I have taken to reading of Princesses, I have sometimes grieved that my own lot was so little like theirs. But then they did not live in Norfolk, at the time of the Civil Wars; & my mother tells me that the truth is always finest.   (p. 39)

Her discontent with her impending marriage and with her life is fanned by her literacy: the romances written by men and recited by men stand in ironic contrast to the unimportance of her life and remind her of the potential lack of splendour of her marriage. She remains discontented:

But I confess that deeply though I honour my mother & respect her words, I cannot accept their wisdom without a sigh. She seems to look forward to nothing better . . . ; & the fairest prospect in her mind is, I believe, a broad road running through the land, on which she sees long strings of horsemen, riding at their ease. . . . She would dream of certain great houses, lying open to the sight, with their moats filled up & their towers pulled down. . . .
But at the same time, when I imagine such a picture, . . . I cannot think it pleasant to look upon; & I fancy that I should find it hard to draw my breath upon those smooth bright ways. Yet what it is that I want, I cannot tell; although I crave for it, &, in some secret way, expect it.   (p. 40)

There is something about the look of the earth that is foreboding: she is taken aback by 'a strange new look upon the surface of the land which I know so well' (ibid.) and yet she is fascinated by it:

It hints at something; but it is gone before I know what it means. If you saw such a look upon a living face, your mother or your brother, you would feel half guilty to have surprised a secret; & you would be frightened at the same time to think that one so familiar could have something lurking within them, unknown to you. It is as though a new smile crept out of a well known face; it is strange to think

that something unknown lurked there . . .; & it is omnious;
it half frightens you, & yet it beckons.   (p. 41)[15]

Soon Joan's father finds out about her Journal. He is
envious and realises that he is too lazy for such a task. He
encourages her to continue keeping it; she has learned to read
and write from him. He asks her to walk with him to care for
his father's tomb:

> As I walked with him, I thought of his words & of the many
> sheets that lie written in my oaken desk. Winter had come
> round again since I made my first flourish so proudly,
> thinking that there were few women in Norfolk who could
> do the like; & were it not that some such pride stayed with
> me I think that my writing would have ceased long before
> this. For, truly, there is nothing in the pale of my days that
> needs telling: & the record grows wearisome. And I thought
> as I went along in the sharp air of the winter morning, that if
> I ever write again it shall not be of Norfolk & myself, but of
> knights & ladies & of adventures in strange lands. The
> clouds even, which roll up from the west & advance across
> the sky like the likeness of Captains & of soldiery & I can
> scarcely cease from fashioning helmets & swords as well as
> fair faces & high headdresses from those waves of coloured
> mist.   (pp. 43–4)

What Rosamond Merridew values most, the recital of the
progression of a woman's ordinary days, Joan Martyn comes
to value least, largely because she compares her journal with
the legends she has read and heard. Literacy has brought with
it its own curse: the devaluation of her own experience. When
one ponders, in light of Joan's story, that perennial puzzle of
why women did not write during these times past, one must
conclude that they were taught by the literature written by
men that their own ordinary and humble experiences were
not worth recording.

But Joan still never relinquishes her desire to be a story-
teller, and she hopes that she can be the kind of old woman
who can keep an entire household quiet with her stories.
Before she can write romantic adventures or marry, however,
she dies in her thirtieth year. Her last entry indicates that her

desire to write her story is a wish on her part to please her ancestors:

> As a child I knew the stark white figures used to frighten me; especially when I could read that they bore my name; but now that they never move ... & keep their hands crossed always, I pity them; & would fain do some small act that would give them pleasure. It must be something secret & unthought of – a kiss or a stroke, such as you give a living person. (p. 43)

Writing is the ultimate homage that one can pay the dead: it is an act of love.

One of the most significant features of this early effort is its structure, a structure that is as carefully and meticulously and as subtly organised as *Night and Day* or *The Years*, yet it deceives with its surface simplicity. Like *The Years*, it is both a dirge and a dithyramb:[16] one mourns Joan Martyn's death while one celebrates in ecstasy Rosamond Merridew's resurrection of her spirit. The work is divided into two sections: Rosamond's story is set in present time and Joan's Journal takes one back to the fifteenth century. But these two major time frames contain as complex a sense of time past, present and passing as *Orlando* or *To the Lighthouse*. First, Rosamond is seen reflecting back after two years have passed upon that June morning when she discovered the Journal; one sees Rosamond reflecting upon herself and her historian's task both before and after she discovered her mythical mother. Rosamond, moreover, is fascinated by the ethos of the fifteenth century as Joan is fascinated by the eros of the Greeks. As Rosamond tries to discover a history for herself through Joan's Journal, so Joan tries to discover a history for herself through the legends of Sir Tristram and Iseult and Lydgate's *Troy Story* and *Temple of Glas* and the story of the Virgin Mary. In finding out about Joan and her relationship to *her* own times, Rosamond is discovering the relationship of woman to the ages – from the Greek through the Christian era to the present day. This ostensibly simple structure, therefore, contains within itself the notion that every moment is imbued with the significance of the ages.

Rosamond Merridew is both a historian and a kind of epic

quester as well: she seeks and finds a mythic mother in Joan Martyn. But Rosamond is a kind of mother to Joan in that her perseverance in searching for her enables her to deliver her knowledge of Joan to the world. And Rosamond is aptly named – the first part of her name referring to the 'Rose' and flowering and rebirth and perhaps also to the symbolic medieval associations with that flower and the 'mound' of the second part to death and to pregnancy as well as to the rites of 'calling up' from the mound the spirit of a woman.[17] Rosamond, as historian, seeks, finds and delivers her mythic mother, Joan Martyn, to the world.

Joan, moreover, is the true ancestress of Rosamond: they both have the same drive, the same verve, the same ambition, the same talent, the same desire to become famous and to penetrate the chambers of the scholastic world, the same wish to make an impact upon learning, the same reluctance to wed, the same reverence for the past, the same fascination with women who have lived their lives in ages past and whose lives have been recorded in myths and legends.

Each of the literary allusions also contributes to this complex time scheme and to the complex of mother-and-daughter relationships established within the tale, and there are analogies to Rosamond's and Joan's story in each of them. But perhaps the most important is John Lydgate's *Temple of Glas*, which her father sends her from London. The work begins with the poet dreaming of entering the temple of Venus and finding it filled with lovers complaining of absence, disdain, poverty, and every other grief that lovers can endure. He hears groups of ladies complaining about having been forced into marriages for wealth or as children. Similarly, Rosamond enters Martyn Hall and carries away a Journal describing the feelings of a young woman whose marriage to Sir Amyas will soon be arranged for her. In the temple of Venus, the poet learns that love is an opportunity for suffering and for learning the virtues that come from endurance or from separation just as Rosamond learns about Joan's resignation and Joan learns of Helen's and Sir Tristram's and Iseult's suffering.

Just before the poet approaches the temple of glass, he is so dazzled by the light shining in his face that he can perceive nothing. When some dark clouds pass by the sun, he sees the vision of the sufferers appealing to Venus: the light and dark refer, paradoxically, to the process of his deepening insights into the sufferings of others. Just before Joan sees the suffering Sanctuary man and is initiated into the knowledge of *his* suffering, she, too, is temporarily blinded: 'It was a cold afternoon, but a bright one; as though the sun were made of gleaming ice & not of fire; and its rays were long icicles that reached from sky to earth' (p. 29). And in the temple the poet discovers the fairest woman of all, as the rose is the fairest of flowers, a woman who will be *every* woman.

> An exemplarie, & mirrour eke was she
> Of secrenes, of trouth, of faythfulnes ....[18]

This 'exemplarie' in Woolf's story is both Rosamond and Joan, and they both are given what they ultimately desire as the woman is given what she wants after having to endure suffering in the *Temple of Glas*: Rosamond gets her journal; Joan keeps her diary; the woman in the *Temple* gets her lover. They all suffer; they all endure.

The Untitled Story, then, is a meditation upon Rosamond Merridew's quest for a female past and upon Virginia Woolf's own epic quest for a mythic mother as muse. Because there were none available to her, Woolf simply created one for herself in the person of Joan Martyn. And, after Woolf had first conceived her, and then safely buried her, she was able to begin to set about the business of writing those explorations of the female sensibility which were her later novels.

For Joan Martyn, in a very important sense, is *not* Shakespeare's sister, not the one who died without writing a word and who lies buried where the omnibuses now stop, opposite the Elephant and Castle.[19] She is the one who kept her journal for more than a year and who has been the historian of her own times through those seasons just as Rosamond Merridew has through hers. Born with a great gift, she did not hide her work or set fire to it, she did not become crazed, she did not shoot herself, nor end her days in a lonely cottage outside the village.[20] She held firm to that same driving force that propelled Rosamond Merridew over the Thetford Road to find her on that warm June day. She is Shakespeare's *other* sister, who had another sister called Virginia Woolf.

NOTES

1. Virginia Woolf, *A Room of One's Own* (New York: Harcourt, Brace and World, 1957) p. 43. Further references are to this edition, cited as *ROO*. I should like to thank Jane Marcus for suggesting that I expand an earlier inquiry into this area and for suggesting the title.
2. Virginia Woolf, unsigned and undated holograph of untitled story (? 1906) 44 pp., in the Henry W. and Albert A. Berg Collection of English and American Literature of the New York Public Library, Astor, Lenox and Tilden Foundations. Selections are quoted with the permission of the Berg Collection and the Author's Literary Estate, whom I should like to thank. I should also like to express my thanks to Dr Lola L. Szladits, Curator, for her encouragement. In an earlier and less complete study, I had thought that this manuscript (hereafter referred to as 'Untitled Story') was composed later than 1906. See 'From *Melymbrosia* to *The Voyage Out*: A Description and Interpretation of Virginia Woolf's Revisions' (PhD dissertation, New York, 1977).
   The story has been published as 'Virginia Woolf's *The Journal of Mistress Joan Martyn*', edited, with an Introduction by Susan M. Squier and Louise A. DeSalvo, *Twentieth Century Literature*, vol. 25, no. 3/4, Autumn/Winter 1979, pp. 237–69.
3. *The Flight of the Mind: The Letters of Virginia Woolf*, vol. I *1888–1912*, ed. Nigel Nicolson and Joanne Trautmann (London: Hogarth Press, 1975) p. 233. Further references to the letters are to this volume and edition, cited as *L*, I.
4. See n. 2. References to this manuscript are by page number only. Quotations are from the corrected version of the text, unless otherwise indicated.
5. There is some internal inconsistency with the dates of the tale. On p. 12, Rosamond looks at the inscription in the Journal and it reads '1480'. But on p. 13 Joan is reported as having been born in 1495 and as having started the Journal when she was twenty-five.
6. See Suzanne Henig's edition of two of Woolf's juvenile fictions, *A Cockney's Farming Experiences* and *Experiences of a Pater-familias*, which recount the exploits of Harriet and her husband (San Diego, Calif.: San Diego State University Press, 1972).
7. Virginia Woolf, 'The New Biography', *Granite and Rainbow*, Harvest edn (New York: Harcourt, Brace, Jovanovich, 1958) p. 149.
8. Virginia Woolf, 'The Pastons and Chaucer', *The Common Reader* (New York: Harcourt, Brace and World, 1953) pp. 6–7. Italics added.
9. She wrote to Dickinson on 22 July 1906 (*L*, I, p. 232) that she had been reading S. H. Butcher, *Some Aspects of the Greek Genius*. In another letter to Dickinson, from Norfolk (*L*, I, p. 234), she wrote, 'We read Greek – Greek – Greek – all day long'. She was preparing for her impending trip to Greece.
10. *ROO*, pp. 45–6.
11. Marston Moor is underscored in the original, and there is a question mark after Moor. Note the correspondence between the name of this

Willoughby and Rachel Vinrace's father's name.
12. See Jane Marcus, '*The Years* as Greek Drama, Domestic Novel, and Götterdämmerung', *Bulletin of the New York Public Library*, Winter 1977, pp. 276–301.
13. Elsewhere, however, Jane is reported as having been born in 1495.
14. There is some confusion about the text sent Jane by her father. The manuscript reads that her father sent her 'The Towe Palace of Glass, by Mr. John Lydgate', with Towe cancelled. But, immediately after that, the description of the poem as recounting Helen's story is presented. Woolf is certainly referring to the *Temple of Glas*, although she seems to have forgotten the exact title, but she might have transposed the subject of the *Troy Story* with the title of *Temple*. There is a brief reference to Helen of Troy in *Temple of Glas*, and this may have been the reason for the confusion.
15. 'If you saw' and following has been cancelled.
16. See Marcus, in *Bulletin of the New York Public Library*, Winter 1977.
17. See Jane Ellen Harrison, *Ancient Art and Ritual* (New York: Greenwood Press, 1969) p. 79.
18. John Lydgate, *Lydgate's Temple of Glas*, ed. J. Schick (London: Oxford University Press, 1891) p. 12, ll. 294–5.
19. *ROO*, p. 50.
20. *ROO*, p. 51.

4 Some Female Versions of Pastoral: *The Voyage Out* and Matriarchal Mythologies[1]

MADELINE MOORE

The relationship of creation to survival is a constant focus in Virginia Woolf's novels. And in *The Voyage Out*, she tries, though largely unsuccessfully, to transform the psychological complexities of her relationship with Clive and Vanessa Bell into the central core of her fiction. Her unresolved fear about her mother's love is also an important biographical referent in the novel. None the less, *The Voyage Out* is the novel in which Woolf is least able to transform her own material, and Rachel Vinrace is her most unsuccessful creator figure. In a sense, Woolf, like Rachel, her most romantic heroine, was a victim of her own sensations. And she was tortured by her maiden voyage out into fiction because that voyage failed to give her the distance she needed.

This is not surprising if one understands the social concerns of the novel: the education of a motherless daughter who rigidly distrusts marriage was also Woolf's personal concern. For Woolf had never exorcised her obsessive love–hate feelings for her mother. Nor had she ever truly grieved for her. Throughout her life she tried to reincarnate her in Vanessa, in Violet Dickinson, Vita Sackville-West – even her doctor, Octavia Wilberforce. But, because Vanessa had actually assumed the maternal duties after Julia Stephen's death, Woolf's affection for her never disappeared. Once, in a letter to Vanessa, Virginia cried out, 'Why did you bring me into this world?'.

Certainly her need of Vanessa was most intense after Leslie Stephen's death in 1904 and before her own marriage in 1912 – the years when she was writing *The Voyage Out*. Clive Bell, in fact, recognised Vanessa as Helen Ambrose in *The Voyage Out* and wrote to Virginia, 'I suppose you will make Vanessa believe in herself.'[2]

During Woolf's seven-year apprenticeship towards *The Voyage Out*, she was also tormented about her commitments to men in general. And her apprenticeship was buttressed by four proposals, an adulterous relationship with her brother-in-law, Thoby Stephen's death, and loneliness. At twenty-nine, she was still unmarried, still debating, and Leonard was grimly persistent, frighteningly so. In her affair with Clive Bell was she simply going back to her lost sister? Her letters suggest this.

In the year following her sister's marriage, Virginia would travel with the Bells to Rye, St Ives, Bath, Paris and Florence. Once she wrote to Clive following one of these expeditions, 'When I am with you, I realize my limitations distinctly. Nessa had all that I should like to have, and you, besides your own charms and exquisite fine sweetness (which I always appreciate somehow) have her. Thus I seem often to be only an erratic external force, capable of shocks, but without any lodging in your lives.'[3]

Only two years had elapsed when Woolf wrote to Clive from Manorbrier, 'Kiss Dolphin's nose – if it isn't too wet – and tap pony smartly on the snout. Whisper into your wife's ear that I love her. I expect she will scold you for tickling her (when she hears the message).'[4] If their intimate triad seemed innocent to outsiders, one need only listen to Clive's version in order to fully understand its intensity: 'I dreamt last night that you were come, and that you had read me a volume of short stories; then, waking, I knew that Walter Lamb slept below. . . . Downstairs the beautiful grey manuscript was awaiting me, but not, alas! the authoress by whom we are forsaken.'[5]

In 1909, four years after Sir Leslie Stephen's death and three years after the tragic death of Thoby, Clive Bell became the only male member of the family Virginia could love. Like her own father, he spent hours talking to her about art and literature. More important, however, was the fact that Virginia felt that only through Clive could she re-enter the chamber of her sister's love.

The biographical referents between Clive Bell and Terence Hewet are numerous and exact. First, simply in terms of appearance, photographs show Clive Bell as overweight and blond. Woolf introduces Terence Hewet as being clean shaven with a 'complexion rosy'[6] and then describes him as 'the young man who was inclined to be stout' (p. 21). Quentin Bell says of Clive that 'he had a good seat on a horse and was an excellent wing shot; for while all the rest were pretty obviously intellectual, he came from a society which hunted birds, animals, and in his case, girls. His family had made its way by means of coal to a sham gothic country house and a decent position in the County of Wiltshire.'[7] Woolf calls Hewet's father 'a fox-hunting squire who died in the hunting field' (p. 167). And in their first conversation St John Hirst pegs Hewet as a womaniser. Hewet replies, 'I wonder whether that isn't really what matters most?'

But if Clive and Vanessa Bell were the models for Terence Hewet and Helen Ambrose, Julia Stephen was the source for Rachel's deceased mother, Theresa Vinrace. As I said earlier, Virginia was always uncertain about her mother's affection, and in the earliest extant version of *The Voyage Out* this fear is apparent in Woolf's fictional depiction of the absent Theresa.

In the earliest extant version Woolf emphasises Rachel's memory of her mother, for it is her mother's presence which hovers over the voyage[8] and seems to be the mysterious force[9] which Rachel will decipher as she journeys out into maturity and simultaneously attempts an inner voyage home. The passage bears quoting in full:

> She was an only child and had spent a curious life, like some restless amphibious creature. Her mother, a great voluptuous woman, the daughter of a parson in the north country, had wished of course to breed sons, whom she figured as bold defenders and besiegers, rough stalwart men, who were to express for her by their excessive vigour and scorn of femininity her own spite against the restrictions of her

sex. But it was not so: here in Cynthia [later Rachel] she reproduced quite literally all that was womanly in herself. Still Mrs. Vinrace was too generous a nature to stint her affections voluntarily; and in time she had as passionate a feeling for her daughter, but it was more jealous, more easily on the defensive, as any that she might have had for her sons. But she died; and left as legacy to her child a number of speculations which as her mother would never answer them, might be considered with the utmost of candour from very different points of view. Her mother, for instance, would put into action her own most hidden impulses; polling a branch weighted with apple blossoms and shaking it so that the petals dropped in a long chain to the ground and the whole burden of autumn fruit vanished in a moment. Such traits in her mother she loved and she feared . . . .[10]

The protagonist of this earliest extant version is left with an overpowering legacy indeed: the memory of a beautiful mother who would have preferred sons, but nevertheless loves her with a jealous and defensive love. This legacy is obviously permeated with a Freudian conception of the Oedipal relationship. In *Moments of Being*, Woolf repeatedly discusses her mother's preference for male children in the family. For the others, she was a more general and distant presence. All her devotion was given to George, who was like his father; and her care was for Gerald, who was very delicate. Yet she 'was hard on Stella because she felt Stella "part of herself" '.[11]

Woolf's attitude towards maternal love is extremely ambiguous in *The Voyage Out*. In fact, reading *The Voyage Out* is like reading *Hamlet* with the bias of Hamlet's sister. Certainly the sexual overtures of the passage in question are persistent. Not only would the desired male children right the mother's powerlessness, but perhaps they would be absolutely desirable barbarian 'besiegers', with excessive vigour; in short, potentially attractive lovers. On the other hand, Woolf conceives of Rachel as an only child who had spent 'a curious life, like some restless amphibious creature'. The word 'amphibious' suggests an indefinite and underdeveloped personality – the very opposite of the stalwart males. Yet anyone who knows

how self-consciously derivative Woolf was in her first novel
would understand that the word is from Sir Thomas Browne's
Religio Medici, a book which we remember Rachel reads with
exhilaration and which Woolf constantly mentions in both her
letters and essays. In *Religio Medici* Browne says,

> We are only that amphibious piece, between a corporeal
> and a spiritual essence; that middle form, that links those
> two together and makes good the method of God and
> nature, that jumps not from extremes, but unites the
> incompatible distances by sane middle and participating
> natures. . . . For, first, we are a rude mass, and in the rank of
> creatures which only are, and have a dull kind of being, not
> yet privileged with life or preferred to sense or reason; next
> we live the life of plants, the life of animals, the life of men,
> and at last the life of spirits: running on, in one mysterious
> nature, those five kinds of exigencies, which comprehend
> the creatures, not only of the world, but of the universe.
> Thus is man that great and true amphibium, whose nature
> is disposed to live, not only like other creatures
> in diverse elements, but in divided and distinguished
> worlds; for though there be but on [world] to sense, there
> are two to reason, the one visible, and the other invisible.[12]

The contradictions inherent in Rachel's experience of a
dualistic world are initially dramatised in her remembered
relationship with her mother and authorially emphasised by
metaphors illuminating that relationship. For in going back to
the original passage we understand that, after Rachel's birth,
her mother feels a passion for her, but it is 'more jealous' and
possessive than her love for her sons would have been. Yet
Cynthia's (Rachel's)[13] very essence is contrary to the bold
sexual qualities which her mother apparently needs. By
nature, she is not possessible.

Let us look again now at the strange legacy Theresa Vinrace
leaves her daughter. 'Her mother, for instance, would put into
action her own most *hidden impulses*; polling a branch weighted
with apple blossoms and shaking it so that the petals dropped
in a long chain to the ground and the whole *burden* of *autumn
fruit vanished in a moment*. Such traits in her mother she loved
and she feared.'[14] At first glance this description appears to be

simply evocative of her mother's sensuous nature. But, as always, Woolf has chosen her words carefully. To poll means to cut off the top of a tree or plant; or 'to lop off a branch'. Earlier meanings were 'to cut off the horns of cattle' and 'to behead'. Both literally and figuratively, this word implies destruction. Petals, of course, connote the most fragile of living organisms: young children, not fully formed. Strangely irrevocable too is the phrase 'and the whole burden of autumn fruit vanished in a moment'. Without any recourse to biographical evidence this sentence ominously expresses the mother's wish to cast aside her late-born children. Added to this is Quentin Bell's information about Julia Duckworth's marriage to Leslie Stephen:

> To this family [the four Duckworth children] they added a fifth in 1879, a girl, whom, since she had a half sister named Stella, they called Vanessa. In the following year a son was born who was named after his great-uncle Thoby. Here they decided to bring their family to a halt.
> But contraception was a very imperfect art in the nineteenth century; less than eighteen months later, another daughter was born. She was named Adeline Virginia.[15]

Is this biographical referent then the raw material behind the seemingly arbitrary pessimism in the novel? Did Woolf's fear of her mother's rejection lie behind the childish romantic posturing towards her mother's inaccessibility? Mitchell Leaska contends that critics who have ignored the predetermined quality of Rachel's death 'have been forced to interpret the book on the airless altitudes of abstraction'.[16] He adds, however, that Woolf herself gives no 'reasonable explanation' for Rachel's death, an omission which reinforces the theme of 'tragic meaninglessness'. While I completely agree with his first assertion, I think that his second contention needs qualification. Though Woolf gives no 'reasonable explanation' for Rachel's death, she does present us with a poetic clue in the earliest extant version. Because of her mother's conflicting legacy, Rachel will be riddled by the dualism of her own nature: part of her is defensive and detached, a spiritual creature trying to transcend the social limitations of her own sex. Another part is sensuous – rejoicing in the pleasures of the earth.

But, if Woolf has implied that the 'natural' Freudian heritage left Rachel by her dead mother is potentially fatal, she may be postulating an ideal relationship between Rachel and her adoptive mother, Helen, as seen through the grid of Jane Harrison's myth of Mother and Maiden. As Jane Marcus has said, 'When Joyce wrote *Ulysses*, he could expect that educated readers (with a little academic assistance) could at once read his book as a modern *Odyssey*, and readers of Eliot's *The Waste Land* hardly needed his footnotes to recognize its sources in *The Golden Bough* and *From Ritual to Romance*.'[17] Yet only recently have critics recognised the influence of Jane Ellen Harrison on Woolf's work.[18]

Many Edwardian readers took seriously indeed Harrison's attempts to resurrect the pre-classical Greek goddesses to their original positive force. We know that Woolf had read Jane Ellen Harrison's *Prolegomena to the Study of Greek Religion* (1908), *Themis: A Study of the Social Origins of Greek Religion* (1912), *Ancient Art and Ritual* (1918) and *Reminiscences of a Student's Life*, published by Virginia and Leonard Woolf at the Hogarth Press (1925).[19] For a number of reasons, not the least of which was Woolf's obsessive relationship with her own mother, she must have been fascinated with a section in Harrison's *Prolegomena* called 'Mother and Maid'. I am not certain whether she knowingly used the myth as a basis for *The Voyage Out*. If she did, it was one of a number of conventions which enriched her early fiction. I do know that Freud, Bergson and Harrison provided an intellectual substructure for many English novelists in the early twentieth century, and Woolf was well read in all three of them. For both objective and subjective reasons, it is at least a good guess that Harrison's ideas were part of the substructure of Woolf's creative process in *The Voyage Out*.

In using myth as an approach to a work of literature, the critic can assume that, when coherent and illuminating parallels are discerned, a work may be interpreted in terms of the myth it resembles. Often what appears as only partly disclosed in the work may be revealed as complete and explicit through the myth. This is admittedly an external reading; it asserts that myth may be brought to the novel after its completion. It is like pressing a coloured transparency over a sheet covered with many hues to reveal the pattern which otherwise resides within them unperceived. But, in Harrison's analysis of the myth of the Mother and Maiden, I have found a transparency which does help bring into perspective the many ambiguous colours and shapes of the novel.

Originally, Harrison claims, there was no specific name for the great mother, nor was she a specific deity.[20] She was simply called the 'Lady of the Wild Things'. The Great Mother was the mother of the dead as well as the living, according to Aeschylus. And the Athenians of old called the dead 'Demeter's people', and during the Nekusia at Athens people sacrificed to the Earth. When the Earth Mother became the Corn Mother, the symbolism of death and renewal was inherent. What is more, Harrison insists that in primitive countries there were two forms of the Earth Mother: they were simply called Mother and Maid, and they were the older and younger form of the same person. Hence they are easily confused. But, as a product of later mythologies, Harrison points out, Mother and Maid appear as Mother and Daughter. Demeter becomes more and more identified with the actual corn. The Mother becomes physical, while the Daughter becomes spiritual; the Mother is of the upper air, the Daughter relegated to the underworld. She goes to a place unknown to the Olympians, for her kingdom is not of this world.

Structurally, Woolf's most revealing treatment of this mythology is the variation she plays on the frame of Mother and Maiden as the woman mature and the woman before maturity. In an effort to imbue Helen with the attributes of the original Great Mother, Woolf initially associates her with vegetation: 'she was working at a great design of a tropical river, running through a tropical forest, where spotted deer would eventually browse upon masses of fruit, bananas, oranges, and giant pomegranates, while a troop of naked natives whirled darts in the air'. During the first dance at the Hotel, Helen's physical movements are likened to the graceful movements of the deer she is embroidering in her primitive design. 'They ought to leap and swing!' she says of the others. Helen's grace is so compelling during the dance that strangers want to touch her and many cannot take their eyes off her. As

Hewet becomes increasingly enchanted by Rachel, St John Hirst is also intrigued by Helen. 'He liked the look of her immensely, not so much her beauty, but her largeness and simplicity which made her stand out from the rest like a great stone woman, and he passed on in a gentler mood.' St John attributes to Helen that same primitive, natural energy which is characteristic of the archetypal Great Mother.

Implicit in this description of Helen was Woolf's idealised relationship with Vanessa. She saw Vanessa as beautiful, noble, all-knowing and all-protective. Yet she wanted to be considered Vanessa's equal. And, unlike Woolf's memory of Julia Stephen, Vanessa need not be bound up by the Oedipal preferences which Woolf associated with the mother in a traditional family.

Yet as the novel progresses, Helen is trapped in the maternal role typical in a traditional family. For Helen, we must remember, has already made the discoveries which Rachel is in the process of making. Appropriately enough, Helen is Rachel's first mentor in the school of sexuality. During the voyage across, Richard Dalloway, an older married man, gives Rachel her first kiss. Helen sees that Rachel is terrified and she tries to put the experience into perspective: 'Men will want to kiss you, just as they'll want to marry you. The pity is to get things out of proportion. It's like noticing the noise people make when they eat or men spitting; or, in short, any small thing that gets on one's nerves' (p. 19).

Yet Rachel magnifies the experience, for she has not acquired that social balance which is characteristic of the mature person. And, as they continue their discussion, Rachel suddenly asks Helen to explain the women who walk the streets in Piccadilly. When she learns they are prostitutes, she says, 'It *is* terrifying – it *is* disgusting.' Rachel, like Persephone, comes to understand the terrors of nature. In the earlier typescript, Rachel's conversation with Helen over Dalloway unequivocally evokes her obsession with the primordial: '"I felt weak, you see," said Rachel. "I felt he could do what he chose with me. I remember looking at his hand. It takes one back to prehistoric times I suppose. It makes one feel queer."'[21]

Unlike the conceptual bulwarks which allow Dalloway to set aside his sexual experience with a young girl as a momentary aberration, one from which he will return to his wife and to his theories about unity, Rachel's 'reaction' carries with it all the force of a primitive encounter with sex, and it cannot be set aside: '"So that's why I can't walk alone!" By this new light she saw her life for the first time a creeping, hedged-in thing, driven cautiously between high walls, here turned aside, there plunged in darkness, made dull and crippled forever' (p.92). This scene is the first of a long series in which Rachel plays Persephone to Helen's Demeter. Rachel is 'plunged into darkness, made dull and crippled forever'.

But if Helen shines her bright rays of realism on Rachel, preaching aggressiveness in social relations, Rachel unwittingly seduces Helen with her sense of wonder. Once, for example, just after they land in Santa Marina, Helen and Rachel are walking after dark and are parted by a crowd of worshippers.

> 'They believe in God,' said Rachel as they regained each other. She meant that the people in the crowd believed in Him; for she remembered the crosses with bleeding plaster figures that stood where foot paths joined and the inexplicable mystery of a service in a Roman Catholic church. We shall never understand!' she sighed.   (p. 114)

Sometimes Rachel's otherworldliness allows Helen to live out the passionate side of her nature which the world rarely sees. Helen really loves the religious festivals, yet when they are with other people she rejects Rachel's beliefs and retreats into cynicism.

Like Rachel's mother, Helen is comforted by the solidity of the male point of view: 'Her friendship with St. John was established for although she fluctuated between irritation and interest in a way that did credit to the candour of her disposition, she liked his company on the whole. He took her outside this little world of love and emotion. He had a grasp of facts.' The attraction she feels towards men is based on their ability to live in the factual world where emotions remain in the background.

Alongside this stratagem for survival stands Helen's pretended inability to fathom people of her own sex. In judging other women, she protects herself from her own emotionalism. Here, then, is her first impression of Rachel: 'Women of her own age usually boring her, she supposed girls would be worse. She glanced at Rachel again. Yes! how clear it was she would be vacillating, emotional, and when you said something to her it would make no more lasting impression than the stroke of a stick upon water' (p. 15).

Woolf's exhumation of this bafflingly contradictory Great Mother means that Rachel must confront the same paradoxical limitation in the most intimate aspects of her life as she does in her social history. Her fascination with the enigmatic quality of Helen's love (which she also experiences as hate) so diminishes her other relationships that she is arrested in her social growth. For Helen is symbolically Jocasta to St John and Terence and Demeter to Rachel. The opposing myths of Oedipus and Mother and Maid are embodied in her, and she externalises those opposing forces between life and death which Rachel encounters in her education. And, though Helen loves the energies associated with a simpler physical world, she has no illusions that this physicality will change the divided nature of the civilised world. Just as Rachel's failure to communicate verbally comes from her fear of social alienation, Helen too has been crippled by social limitations.

Unfortunately, Helen's pessimism is born of experience. Publicly she has borne up under Ridley's childish and tyrannical claims; privately she sees his selfishness as absurd, but has no power to change it. Helen's entire existence has been determined by his idiosyncracies. Thus we see Helen 'on her knees under the table', desperately arranging the study table at its proper height in her husband's sitting room, while he complains, 'Did I come on this voyage in order to catch rheumatism and pneumonia?' (p. 27).

None the less, the narrator continues to analogise Mother and Maiden. Time and again each woman tries to actualise the poetic vision that she has of her lover. Rachel, during her courtship, imagines Terence as a 'young god'. And, as Helen pursues her flirtation with St John Hirst, she romantically frames him in the 'front of the dark pyramid of a magnolia tree' (p. 245). But the anomaly of an imaginary Hirst seen as Gauguin might paint a native is too much for Helen, who has spent her life in the midst of male hypocrisy:

She looked at him against the background of a flowering magnolia. There was something curious in the sight. Perhaps it was that the heavy wax-like flowers were so smooth and inarticulate, and his face – he had thrown his hat away, his hair was rumpled, he held his eyeglasses in his hand, so that a red mark appeared on either side of his nose – was so worried and garrulous. (p. 247)

Thus, though Rachel has seen and released the spirit of her mythical alter-ego, Helen continues to live her life with an all-encompassing melancholy. Gradually, Helen's solicitude for Rachel's well-being becomes a desperate attempt to appropriate her very soul. The more Helen understands that social pretences are absolutely useless, the more she wants to possess the one person who does not require them. Here then is the classic mother–daughter relationship in the divisive patriarchal world. Rachel's memory of her natural mother's jealousy is realised in Helen; Demeter seeks her Persephone to renew the barren field of the upper world.

Understandably, when Rachel's friendship with Hewet deepens, the effect on Helen is disturbing:

Having detected as she thought, a secret, and judging that Rachel meant to keep it from her, Mrs. Ambrose respected it carefully, but from that cause, though unintentionally, a curious atmosphere of reserve grew up between them. . . . Always calm and unemotional in her judgements, Mrs. Ambrose was now inclined to be definitely pessimistic. . . . How did she know that at this very moment both her children were not lying dead, crushed by motor omnibuses? (p. 269)

How complex is Woolf's evocation of Helen: the partial loss of one whom she imagined to be totally kind and solely her own is unthinkably cruel; Mother and Maiden are separated; Rachel has literally been stolen from her sanctified room. Though in past situations Helen's rhetoric has protected her from the involvement she fears, now she openly admits her misgivings. Now, as she sees Rachel walking down the path of illusion, every incident, however minor, has a profound effect on her, and taken together they reinforce her belief that the foundations of social reality are treacherous indeed:

> The little jokes, the chatter, the inanities of the afternoon
> had shrivelled up before her eyes. . . . Her sense of safety
> was shaken, as if beneath twigs and dead leaves she had seen
> the movement of a snake. It seemed to her that a moment's
> respite, a moment's make-believe, and then again the
> profound and reasonless law asserted itself, moulding all to
> its liking, making and destroying. (pp. 321–2)

In *The Voyage Out* Helen's snake embodies that which Woolf
calls fate. Because Helen alone is capable of articulating the
dual existence which civilised people often mask, she is used
constantly to portray society's evils. Thus, travelling to the
native village, she has presentiments that disaster is threatening the lovers:

> How small the little figures looked wandering through the
> trees! She became acutely conscious of the little limbs, the
> thin veins, the delicate flesh of men and women, which
> breaks so easily and lets the life escape compared with these
> great trees and deep waters. . . . Thus thinking, she kept her
> eyes anxiously fixed upon the lovers, as if by doing so she
> could protect them from their fate. (p. 350)

It is not Terence's power over Rachel which Helen fears, but
rather the social assumptions which he unwittingly brings to
their relationship.

However, if we follow the outlines of the myth, keeping in
mind that the original Lady of the Wild Things is both the
bringer of life and the bearer of death, it may be perfectly
plausible also to imagine Helen as the embodiment of Theresa
Vinrace's ghost come back to haunt Rachel. For Helen, as the
vehicle of Rachel's dead mother, embodies the contradictions
of an English patriarchal society to such an extreme degree
that the resolution she triggers has about it the inevitability of
Greek tragedy.

In the last third of the novel, the focus of Woolf's vision
centres on the intensely physical and, at times, dream-like
existence which characterises Rachel's love for Terence and

Helen. In their voyage and symbolic meeting at the mouth of the river, the competing myths of Oedipus and of Demeter and Persephone reach a hallucinatory but definite resolution. Mother, Maiden and lover descend into an unmediated pastoral landscape, and out of their sensual encounter emerges a revelation of their social fate.

With her expedition up the river, Woolf symbolises Rachel's entry into the primeval and signals the reader that she is entering a space which is untouched by social norms. Spatially, this voyage is the innermost place Rachel visits, and, as such, it produces a psychological and pictorial intensity not found in any other section of the novel. Terence, as well as Rachel, enters a hypnotic state in which the boat going up the river 'became identified with himself':

> He was drawn on and on away from all he knew, slipping over barriers and past landmarks into unknown waters as the boat glided over the smooth surface of the river. In profound peace, enveloped in deeper unconsciousness than had been his for many nights, he lay on deck watching the treetops change their position slightly against the sky, and arch them into dreams where he lay beneath the shadow of vast trees, looking up into the sky.   (p. 326)

Here Woolf evokes the richness of the original garden, as 'staring into the profusion of leaves and blossoms and prodigious fruits', Hewet exclaims that the 'Elizabethans got their style from the exuberance of the forest' (p. 328).

Nevertheless, the pastoral experience is incomplete until the individual sees that the innocence he imagines as the essence of nature has always been an illusion. As Eleanor Winsor Leach contends, 'The continual tension between the pastoral impulse and the need to preserve a known identity in the face of the overwhelming power of nature gives rise to conflict and complexity in pastoral.'[22]

Rachel first imagined the river she would visit as 'now blue, now yellow in the tropical sun and crossed by bright birds, now white in the moon, now deep in shade with moving trees and canoes sliding out from the tangled banks' (p. 98). Though the colours were bright and though Woolf suggests sexual over-tones in the image of the canoe, the mood in the early passage is not threatening. As Rachel and Terence actually travel up their river, however, 'the trees and the undergrowth seemed to be strangling each other near the ground in a multitudinous wrestle' (p. 327). Although they are at last alone, 'the noises of the ordinary world were replaced by those creaking and sighing sounds which suggest to the traveller in a forest that he is walking on the bottom of the sea'. And, unlike Rachel's imaginary picture of sensual bliss, nature here is surreal:

> As they passed into the depth of the forest the light grew dimmer. . . . The path narrowed and turned; it was hedged in by dense creepers which knotted tree to tree, and burst here and there into star shaped crimson blossoms. The sighing and creaking up above were broken every now and then by the jarring cry of some startled animal. The atmosphere was close and the air came at them in languid puffs of scent. The vast green light was broken here and there by a round of pure yellow sunlight which fell through some gap in the immense umbrella of green above, and in these yellow spaces crimson and black butterflies were circling and settling. (p. 331)

The image of creepers and knotted trees alternating with the blood-red crimson blossoms evokes a sense of love-play which is unquestionably unpleasant. Motion itself is suggestive of the rhythms of intercourse.

The narrowing of the path and the dense creepers induce a sense of heat and suffocation coupled with what must have been the irritating and inescapable tactile sensations. The 'crimson star shaped blossoms' bursting forth suggest blood, and the 'jarring cry of some startled animal' reflects Rachel's horror at this entrapment.

Ironically, only here at the centre of their pastoral world do Terence and Rachel transcend the inefficacy of words and speak 'in a little language such as lovers use' (*The Waves*):

> 'We love each other', Terence said.
> 'We love each other', she repeated.
> The silence was then broken by their voices which joined in tones of strange unfamiliar sound which formed no

words. Faster and faster they walked; simultaneously they stopped, clasped each other in their arms, then, releasing themselves, dropped to the earth. (p. 332)

Rachel's knowledge, when she ultimately submits to Terence, brings us to that thematic centre of the novel, where the dialectic between nature and society is resolved with a kind of terrible fatality. On the one hand, Rachel has persistently tried to recapture the direct emotions associated with primitive existence. And here she is, finally free of every encumbrance and with another person. On the other hand, her growing intuition that a commitment to Hewet with his advantageous social position, will threaten her already tenuous freedom is enacted physically. For, with the declaration of their love, Rachel lives out the consequences of her wildest hopes, while simultaneously feeling the steel doors of her social prison snap shut.

By degrees she drew close to him, and rested against him. In this position they sat for some time. She said 'Terence' once; he answered 'Rachel'.
'Terrible, terrible', she murmured after another pause, but in saying this she was thinking as much of the persistent churning of the water as of her own feelings. On and on it went in the distance, the senseless and cruel churning of the water. (ibid.)

The objectification of Rachel's entrapment is heard in the wild yet impersonal sound of the water. That she has committed herself to a person who will bring her unhappiness is clear in terms of the pastoral myth exploded. As Terence began the expedition, 'he was completely calm and master of himself' (p. 330). After the love scene he loses his way. Again, the conventions of pastoral are used to point out the psychological and social dilemmas of the characters.

Even more revelatory is the enactment of Helen's passion for Rachel and Terence during this strange expedition up the river. After the lovers' second escape from the rest of the company, they are followed by Helen, and in this scene (which is the most inexplicable in the novel) there is an apparently violent yet erotic interplay amongst the three of them. The conflicting loyalties which, in terms of the novel's realistic mode, arise from Rachel's allegiance to Helen as a mother figure and to Terence as lover are here dramatised in a dream-like setting.

> Voices crying behind them never reached through the waters in which they were now sunk. The repetition of Hewet's name in short, dissevered syllables was to them the crack of a dry branch or the laughter of a bird. The grasses and breezes sounding and murmuring all round them, they never noticed that the swishing of the grasses grew louder and louder, and did not cease with the lapse of the breeze. A hand dropped abrupt as iron on Rachel's shoulder; it might have been a bolt from heaven. She fell beneath it, and the grass whipped across her eyes and filled her mouth and ears. Through the waving stems she saw a figure, large and shapeless against the sky. Helen was upon her. Rolled this way and that, now seeing only forests of green, and now the high blue heaven, she was speechless and almost without sense. At last she lay still, all the grasses shaken round her and before her by her panting. Over her loomed two great heads, the heads of a man and a woman, of Terence and Helen.
>
> Both were flushed, both laughing, and the lips were moving, they came together and kissed in the air above her. Broken fragments of speech came down to her on the ground. She thought she heard them speak of love and then of marriage. Raising herself and sitting up, she too realized Helen's soft body, the strong and hospitable arms, and happiness swelling and breaking in one vast wave. When this fell away, and the grasses once more lay low – and the sky became horizontal, and the earth rolled out flat on each side, and the trees stood upright, she was the first to perceive a little row of human figures standing patiently in the distance. For the moment, she could not remember who they were.   (pp. 346–7)

Here, as before, the condition of their enchantment is suggested in the images of water. However, this time the narrator shifts dramatically from the restraint of the earlier simile to the radical immediacy of metaphor. Oddly enough, water imagery here also signals the ecstatic physical union of

Rachel and Helen, 'their happiness swelling and breaking in one vast wave'.

Omitted from the final version are two sentences in the earliest extant version, which help illuminate the novel. Before their confession of love in Chapter 20, Rachel tells Hewet, 'My mother was the person I cared for . . . and now Helen.' After the confession she cries, 'Oh Terence, the dead. My mother is dead!' Certainly Rachel's regret for her mother complicates her relationship to Terence. In her exaggeration of Helen's size, Woolf embodies Rachel's passion for Helen, a passion which Woolf admitted she felt for Vanessa. As ambiguous as this scene is, two realities emerge which clarify the novel's denouement. First, Rachel feels herself incapable of sexual initiation without the participation of an older woman. This requires the literal sexual love of the 'mother' for 'son' and 'daughter'. Secondly, Helen and Terence's competition for Rachel proves finally to be destructive.

And, if read as Rachel's hallucination, the love object is as much Helen as it is Hewet. Though the images in the final version suggest violence, the passage in the holograph version evokes a mixture of playfulness and violence: 'Helen was upon her. Too breathless to scold she spent her rage in rolling the helpless body hither and thither, holding both wrists in a firm grasp, and stuffing eyes, ears, nose and mouth with the feathery tassels of the grass. Terence heard them panting and gasping more like retriever puppies than grown women.'[23]

In yet another version of the scene (this too was rejected in the definitive text), the competition between Helen and Terence is apparent:

'Are you happy?' she asked.
'Infinitely!' Rachel breathed and was clasped in Helen's arms.
'I had to tell you', she murmured.
'And if you hadn't, I knew', said Helen.
The inevitable jealousy crossed Helen's mind as she saw Rachel pass almost visibly into communion with someone else.
'But you know I love you, Rachel, you're so like Theresa and I loved her.'
'Why did she die?' said Rachel. 'Or do people die?'[24]

The survival of the archetypal Mother and Maid is diminished by the inevitable possessiveness of the Mother in a patriarchal society; and the psychological impasse which has been suggested in the 'realistic' sections is seen here with the visual starkness of a dream.

With the re-emergence of the three into their social world, Rachel's education is complete. Terence and Rachel's return to the hotel signals the anomalies of their coming marriage. For Terence now sees Rachel with the eyes of the Londoner, rather than through the romantic lens of the traveller playing primitive: ' "God, Rachel, you do read trash!" he exclaimed. "And you're behind the times too, my dear. No one dreams of reading this kind of thing now – antiquated problem plays, harrowing descriptions of life in the east end – oh no, we've exploded all that. Read poetry, Rachel, poetry, poetry, poetry!" ' (p. 358). And Helen's behaviour after the engagement is the social counterpart to her possessiveness during the scene on the river. Thus one afternoon at the villa she says, 'You've all been sitting here . . . for almost an hour, and you haven't noticed my figs, or my flowers, or the way the light comes through, or anything. I haven't been listening, because I've been looking at you. You looked very beautiful; I wish you'd go on sitting forever' (p. 379). Rachel's inability to retain her autonomy in the face of their conflicting possessiveness signals her decision to capitulate to oblivion rather than to the slow defeat which would result from a closeness with either of them.

Neither Terence's imaginary life as a writer in London nor Helen's overweaning possessiveness offers Rachel a way to live. Her capitulation to illness, then, is the delirious expression of her chosen suicide:

> All sights were something of an effort, but the sight of Terence was the greatest effort, because he forced her to join mind to body in the desire to remember something. She did not wish to remember: it troubled her when people tried to disturb her loneliness; she wished to be alone. She wished for nothing else in the world. (p. 424)

The realisation that she is tormented by Helen's demands as well as Terence's is especially shocking during her illness. She 'found herself walking through a tunnel under the Thames, where there were little deformed women sitting in archways playing cards, while the bricks of which the wall was made oozed with damp, which collected into drops and slid down the walls. But the little old women became Helen and Nurse McInnis' (pp. 404–5). Rachel's discovery of something inherently other in nature is a way of embodying her realistic social fears.

After Rachel's death the guests take on the formal overtones of mourners in a traditional pastoral poem. They individually express their grief and collectively draw together after a frightening rainstorm: 'As the storm drew away, the people in the hall of the hotel sat down. And with a comfortable sigh of relief, began to tell each other stories about great storms, and produced in many cases their occupations for the evening' (p. 451). Here there is a gentle resurgence in their will to live, and, though the English travellers' victories are small, Woolf infers that Rachel's death magically produces the rain which refurbishes the dry land of their hopelessness. Quietude follows exhaustion, and both the eccentric London society woman and the cynical Cambridge student find rest:

All those voices sounded gratefully in St. John's ears as he lay half asleep, and yet vividly conscious of everything around him. Across his eyes passed a procession of objects, black and indistinct, the figures of people picking up their books, their cards, their balls of wool, their work baskets, and passing him one after another on their way to bed.
(p. 458)

If we assume, as Jane Ellen Harrison did, that what a people does in relation to its gods is one good index to what it thinks, Rachel/Persephone's ritual propitiation to her mother is the inevitable sacrifice to a society still incapable of respecting the spiritual needs of its women.

St Augustine tells a story about the rivalry between Athene and Poseidon in those days before descent was traced through the father. The contest then was decided by the vote of all citizens, men and women alike. Predictably the men voted for Poseidon and the women for Athene, who won by one vote. Because Poseidon was angry, the men decided to appease his wrath by inflicting on the women a triple punishment: their children would no longer to be called by their mother's name, they would lose their vote, and they would no longer be called Athenians after their own goddess. This diminution of the public personality of women through the separation of their sensual energy from their spiritual energy has always been their nemesis. Woolf knew this from observing her mother's life, and through living her own. This knowledge, so painfully acquired, is revealed in the fiction of Helen and Rachel: in their love for each other, in their exclusion from the sources of English power, and in the sad conclusion of their attempts to reclaim their mythological archetypes.

NOTES

1. This essay was conceived as a chapter in my forthcoming book, *The Short Season between Two Silences: The Political and the Mystical in the Works of Virginia Woolf.* In its original form, it is much longer than the present essay. I should like to thank the Faculty Research Committee of the University of California, Santa Cruz, for granting me the time and money necessary for this work. Permission to quote from all manuscript sources has been granted by Quentin Bell.
2. Quentin Bell, *Virginia Woolf: A Biography*, 2 vols (London: Hogarth Press, 1972) vol. I, p. 200. Hereafter cited as *VWB*, followed by volume and page numbers.
3. *The Flight of the Mind: The Letters of Virginia Woolf*, vol. I: *1888–1912*, ed. Nigel Nicolson and Joanne Trautmann (New York: Harcourt, Brace, Jovanovich, 1976) p. 334. Hereafter cited as *L*, I.
4. *L*, I, p. 362.
5. Clive Bell to Virginia Stephen, April 1908 (University of Sussex). Permission to quote from the letter has been granted by Quentin Bell, Nigel Nicolson and Angelica Garnett.
6. Virginia Woolf, *The Voyage Out* (London: Hogarth Press, 1971) p. 17. Page references in the text are to this edition.
7. *VWB*, I, p. 103.
8. Woolf places the initial impetus for the voyage on Theresa Vinrace's influence and then very clearly transfers the mantle to Rachel's shoulders: 'In after years, very probably, the entire village would be represented by this one hour; and the hooting of sirens perhaps the night before. Nothing is stranger than the position of the dead on the living, and the whole scene was the work of one woman who had been in her grave for eight years' (earliest extant version of *The Voyage Out*, p. 15, Berg Collection, New York Public Library).

9. Ibid.
10. In an article in the *Times Literary Supplement* written on 25 Mar 1920, p. 199, called 'Freudian Fiction' (review of *An Imperfect Mother*, by D. Beresford), Woolf contends that it is positively desirable for a novelist to rely on Freudian theories to explain the motives of his characters. Simultaneously she cautions against a slavish application of any theory. And in 1922 Virginia and Leonard Woolf were sufficiently interested in Freud to publish his *The International Psychoanalytical Library*. In addition to that they published *The Ego and the Id* (1927), *The Future of an Illusion* (1928), *Civilization and Its Discontents* (1930) and *Civilization, War and Death* (1939). Virginia Woolf mentions Freud three times in her diary: 2 Dec 1939, 18 Dec 1939 and 9 Feb 1940. Thanks to Quentin Bell, we know that she and Leonard met and talked with Freud at Hampstead in 1939: 'He gave Virginia a narcissus and talked, as everyone then talked, about Hitler. It would take a generation, he said, to work out the poison' (*VWB*, II, p. 209).
11. *Moments of Being, Unpublished Autobiographical Writings of Virginia Woolf*, ed. Jeanne Schulkind (Brighton: Sussex University Press, 1976) p. 96.
12. Sir Thomas Browne, *Religio Medici* (London: Walter Scott, 1886) p. 53. (First authorised edn 1643.)
13. Rachel began her fictional life as Cynthia, and only after four months and several letters to Clive and Vanessa Bell did Woolf decide on the change.
    Cynthia, of course, is one of the variant names of the moon goddess, Artemis, daughter of Zeus and sister to Apollo. Like her brother she is a divinity of light (although hers is the light of the moon rather than the sun), and one part of her legend always associates her with aloofness, with spiritual exhilaration, and with virginity. Artemis was as fine a hunter as her brother, and marriage was repugnant to her.
    On the other hand, Woolf's final choice of a name for her protagonist is not Greek but Hebraic, and, far from recalling the fierce virgin huntress, it signified gentleness, with connotations of sacrifice as well: literally the word meant 'ewe' or 'lamb'. In the very hesitations which accompanied her choice, Woolf reveals the extreme conflicts which confront Rachel throughout the entire work, for it is perfectly apparent that Rachel does indeed embody both the defiant and elusive traits of the Greek Cynthia and the tender and idealistic yearning of the Hebraic Rachel. Out of this conflict in character, Woolf has evoked the drama of opposing worlds.
14. Earliest extant version of *The Voyage Out*, p. 15. Italics are mine.
15. *VWB*, I, p. 18.
16. Mitchell A. Leaska, 'Virginia Woolf's *The Voyage Out*: Character Deduction and the Function of Ambiguity', *Virginia Woolf Quarterly*, Winter 1973, p. 35.
17. Jane Marcus, '*The Years* as Greek Drama, Domestic Novel and Götterdämmerung', *Bulletin of the New York Public Library*, Winter 1977, p. 278.
18. In her 'Pargeting *The Pargiters*: Notes of an Apprentice Plasterer', ibid., Spring 1977, p. 420, Jane Marcus discusses the importance of Harrison's *Themis* to Woolf's composition of *The Years*. She claims that in *The*

Years Woolf takes seriously Harrison's view of the year as ring or *annus*, and its acting out in art of the mother–son ritual of the death and rebirth of the year as the origin of collective life and the collective conscience. Marcus says, 'The line introducing the action of "1891", "For it was October, the birth of the year", may be explained by Woolf's reading of Jane Harrison, who points out that the ancient Greek agricultural year began in the autumn and that the origin of Greek drama lies in the early ceremonies of the "Death and Rebirth of the Year-Spirit" '. Harrison argues that to the Greeks the years 'are not abstractions, divisions of time; they are the substance, the content of time and that this notion that the year is its own content . . . haunted the Greek imagination' – *Themis: A Study of the Social Origins of Greek Religion* (Cambridge, 1912) pp. 185–6. It is worth noting at this point that the sea journey in *The Voyage Out* also began in October (p. 1) and came to an end four weeks later (p. 100); three more months bring the story to March (p. 108); Rachel and Helen eavesdrop outside the hotel in Santa Maria on 15 March (p. 113); the fatal river voyage happens in April (p. 204); and Rachel becomes ill and dies in May (p. 420).

19. Each of these books is cited in the *Catalogue of Books from the Library of Leonard and Virginia Woolf* (Brighton, Sussex: Holleyman and Treacher, 1975) Index, p. 27. A copy of *Ancient Art and Ritual* now in the Washington State University Library is inscribed by Harrison to Woolf, Christmas 1923.
20. The following discussion on Woolf's debt to Harrison is documented in Harrison's *Prolegomena to the Study of Greek Religion* (Cambridge: Cambridge University Press, 1903) pp. 260–76.
21. Unnumbered earlier typescript of *The Voyage Out*, in the Berg Collection of the New York Public Library.
22. Eleanor Winsor Leach, *Vergil's Eclogues: Landscapes of Experience* (Ithaca, NY: Cornell University Press, 1974) p. 35.
23. Unnumbered holograph of *The Voyage Out*.
24. Unnumbered earlier typescript of *The Voyage Out*.

Ed. Note: The manuscripts of *The Voyage Out* have now been sorted out, sequenced and dated by Louise DeSalvo. This process is discussed in a special issue of *Bulletin of Research in the Humanities*, Autumn 1979, in two essays by Louise DeSalvo and also by Elizabeth Heine and Beverly Schlack.

5 *Jacob's Room* as Comedy: Woolf's Parodic *Bildungsroman*

JUDY LITTLE

Early readers of *Jacob's Room* responded to the book's comic elements as well as to its pathos; modern critics, on the other hand, concentrate on the form, and usually comment also on the sad absurdity of Jacob's life, a life cut off prematurely by the First World War. The comedy is of primary importance, however, and it is closely linked to the book's form and to Jacob's 'character', sketchy as his character may seem to be. The novel is in some ways a parody, and many of its peculiarities in form, point of view and characterisation are linked to the parodic impulse. The comedy and the 'form' of *Jacob's Room* derive partly from a strategy of literary attack. The form shows very clearly the marks of its being a playful yet serious rebellion; it is held together by the shadowy structure of the very thing it is against: the *Bildungsroman*.

The parodic mocking of the form generates some mocking of subject as well. The *Bildungsroman*, when it concerns a capable Edwardian male, must deal in part with the hero's experience of British institutions of higher learning, for instance. In *Jacob's Room* the traditional male growth-pattern, full of great expectation, falls like a tattered mantle around the shoulders of the indecisive hero, heir of the ages. The musing and amused narrator mocks the structure of her story; she mocks the conventions of the hero's progress; and, by implication, she mocks the values behind those conventions. In this way, a very mild, even cheerful, feminism often

105

coincides with the narrator's playful wrenching of traditional patterns.

Certainly Virginia Woolf wanted no more than the shadow of a structure in her third novel; she aimed for a 'looseness and lightness', a form with no 'scaffolding': 'Scarcely a brick to be seen; all crepuscular, but the heart, the passion, humour, everything as bright as fire in the mist. Then I'll find room for so much – a gaiety – an inconsequence – a light spirited stepping at my sweet will.'[1] If the form is right, she will find room for everything she wants to put in, including humour, gaiety, inconsequence. Among those who have criticised the result, however, is Virginia Woolf herself. In October 1922, after the publication of *Jacob's Room*, she wrote, 'I expect I could have screwed *Jacob* up tighter, if I had foreseen; but I had to make my path as I went.'[2] The book's peculiarities of characterisation and its patchwork design have often come in for criticism.[3] The greatest artistic liability, according to most critics, is the inconsistency on the part of the narrator; she sometimes disclaims omniscience, especially with regard to Jacob, and at other times readily assumes it, even giving us Jacob's feelings and thoughts on occasion.[4] Awkward and arbitrary as this shifting in and out of omniscience may seem, it contributes considerably to the 'humour' and 'gaiety' which the author hoped to incorporate into the work. Clive Bell was perhaps responding to these qualities when he praised the narrator's 'cool, humorous comment'. Likewise an early reviewer admired the narrator's 'subtle, slyly mocking, and yet poignant vision'. This reviewer wrote also of 'the delicious humour which infects every page'.[5] The 'humorous comment', and especially the 'mocking, and yet poignant vision', often hinge on a radically unconventional switch in perspective, an omniscient narrator suddenly telling us the ironic truth after another narrator – or the same one – has been merely guessing at Jacob's words or thoughts. At other times the movement seems to be in the opposite direction; the narrator pretends to be the omniscient author of a *Bildungsroman*, and then teases the reader – and the form – by asserting that 'it is no use trying to sum people up'.[6]

The *Bildungsroman* was an extremely popular form in the nineteenth and early twentieth centuries,[7] and parody was overdue; actually, there had been a few parodies, or semi-parodies, and Woolf had read them, among many other specimens of this genre. Meredith, for instance, was one of her favourite writers;[8] his *Bildungsromane* tend to be comic, certain elements of the convention often being violated or mocked. His *Evan Harrington* and *Harry Richmond* are comic *Bildungsromane*. In *Richard Feveral*, Richard's father, Sir Austin, keeps a notebook in which he plans the phases of his son's life, labelling them 'The Blooming Season', 'The Magnetic Age', and so on. Sir Austin's notebook reads like the chapter titles of a *Bildungsroman*, as J. H. Buckley points out.[9] Austin Feveral's plans backfire, and his effort to write the script for his son's life – to 'sum him up', as Woolf might say – represents a cruel parody of what could have been a real life; Richard becomes confused and hardened by his father's rigid expectations, and manages a rebellion that wrecks his own life.

In 1918 and 1919 Virginia Woolf reviewed *Bildungsromane* of Compton Mackenzie, H. G. Wells and Dorothy Richardson. Particularly interesting are her remarks about the satirically drawn characters in Wells's novel *Joan and Peter*. Peter's father, an aunt, a schoolmistress, are characters whose motives and actions are too pat and mechanical to be quite believable; they are 'burlesques' rather than characters, and Woolf finds them contributing to the 'crudeness of the satire', which yet by its crudeness convinces the reader of the author's honest anger.[10] Woolf's review is largely devoted to an analysis of these peculiar characters and to the attitude of social criticism which made the author create them.

In a review of *Limbo*, an early collection of Aldous Huxley's short stories, Woolf again gives special attention to the opportunities and to the dangers of satire. She censures Huxley for being too obviously clever, and she feels that his range is limited; if asked to talk about something he believes in, she asserts, he could only stammer. And yet she likes his 'Farcical History of Richard Greenow' well enough to quote it at some length. This story is a raucously parodic *Bildungsroman*, giving us the early life, education and grotesque failure of Richard. His great discovery is that he is a 'hermaphrodite', and his true vocation – writing novels – is carried on by his second self, 'Pearl Bellairs'. He conscientiously objects to the World War, and he dies in an insane asylum. Woolf is especially amused by Huxley's portrait of a 'fellow of Canteloup', Canteloup being a college of Oxford. She quotes a passage in which Huxley juxtaposes the scholar's 'dazzling academic career' with his furrowed face, sloppy eating habits ('his clothes were disgusting with the spilth of many years of dirty feeding') and incessant talking.[11] Huxley's portrait of the Oxford scholar is more sordid than Woolf's satiric sketches of dons in *Jacob's Room*, but the purpose in each case is the same: the educators of the young are seen as ludicrously inadequate. Woolf gives us 'poor old Huxtable', who cannot walk straight, who changes clothes as mechanically as clockwork, who is miserly and priestly. Sopwith, also priestly, is an incessant talker; he is respected, but with growing ambiguity by his one-time undergraduates as they reach a more mature judgement. And Cowan, Virgil's image, or the nearest Cambridge can come to this, is gluttonous and self-indulgent (pp. 37–40).

After quoting Huxley's portrait of a scholar, Woolf continues her discussion:

> There is an equally amusing description of a dinner with the Headmaster of Aesop and Mrs Crawister, a lady of 'swelling port' and unexpected utterance, who talks to the bewildered boys now about eschatology, now about Manx cats ('No tails, no tails, like men. How symbolical everything is!'), now about the unhappy fate of the carrion crow, who mates for life.[12]

Jacob, like Richard Greenow, must sit through a painful meal given by a scholar, Mr Plumer; his wife, like Richard's hostess, is a lady of 'unexpected utterance', her conversation calling a halt to social intercourse rather than facilitating it. Groaning, Jacob leaves the house after this introduction to the suffocating banalities which the world seeks to impose on him (pp. 31–4).

Jacob, however, is 'obstinate'; at least, this is his mother's interpretation of the fact that he does not conform to her notion of obedience (pp. 9, 21). Jacob and the world do not fit each other; he cannot conform to expectations. This basic quality of his mysterious personality is symbolised in the form of the novel – the pat elements of the *Bildungsroman* structure are one by one introduced, and one by one tossed away as irrelevant. Avrom Fleishman has said that *Jacob's Room* extends 'the *Bildungsroman* form into a fitful sequence of unachieved experiences rather than a coherent process', and J. H. Buckley suggests that *Jacob's Room* may be 'potentially a Bildungsroman'.[13] But Woolf's novel is not an effort to extend the *Bildungsroman*; it is, among other things, an attack on this form. It attacks the notion that a conventionalised fictional 'summing up' can fit a real life, or that a young Englishman's storybook socialisation is anything but a burlesque of his real stumblings toward self-discovery. Rather than being a potential *Bildungsroman*, *Jacob's Room* is a lightheartedly decadent one. It seems almost as though Virginia Woolf deliberately chose the traditions of the *Bildungsroman* in order to play havoc with them.

All of the traditional elements are in the novel, but Jacob walks through his story as though he does not see the traditions. He is an orphan, or partly an orphan, because his father has died; but nothing Dickensian is ever made of this, Jacob being neither better nor worse for the fact. He moves, as a young man, from the provinces to London, but the narrator mines no moral riches out of this circumstance. Tom Jones and Pip would have gone badly to seed, and would have emerged with a greater knowledge of humanity and of themselves. But Jacob is not corrupted, and his move to the city is not made into one of the signposts of the novel. Jacob's education is something that barely happens to him, yet all the scenery is there – all the scenery for the awakening of his mind and for his rebelling against stodgy traditions. Finally, Jacob, unlike the typical *Bildungsroman* hero, receives no revelation, no 'epiphany'. Yet opportunity after opportunity is supplied by the author; she deliberately makes Jacob look the other way, or she mocks the offered moment. Virginia Woolf drags in all the *Bildungsroman* scenery; then she lets Jacob walk aimlessly about, as though the stage were bare. The effect is a remarkable tension that gives fictional embodiment to the pathos, and comedy, of Jacob's life – a life which becomes emblematic of all lives to the extent that they do not fit expected patterns, and instead obstinately resist a 'summing up'.

No one takes charge of Jacob's education. There is no Helen Ambrose in this story, as there was in Woolf's first, and more

or less conventional, *Bildungsroman*. There is no Uncle Oswald, as there is in Wells's novel, back from Africa just in time
to salvage from other relatives the education of Joan and
Peter. Certainly no one goes to the lengths that Austin Feveral
goes, keeping a notebook, and giving labels to the stages of his
son's growth. No one cares enough about Jacob's development either to help or to hinder him. There is, however,
Mr Floyd, whose proposal of marriage Mrs Flanders rejects,
and who teaches Latin to her boys. When he leaves the village
he lets the boys choose a gift from him, and Jacob chooses the
works of Byron (p. 19). In any other *Bildungsroman*, and
indeed in any of Woolf's other novels, such a gesture would
cast ripples over the hero's future. And Byron is mentioned
again; Byron, the sea, the lighthouse, the sheep's jaw, are
mentioned by the narrator as belonging to the 'obstinate
irrepressible conviction' which gives youth its sense of identity
(p. 34). Late in the novel Mr Floyd sees Jacob in London, and
at first does not recognise him; Mr Floyd recalls, as though the
recollection proves irrelevant to his present observation of
Jacob, that the young man had once accepted the works of
Byron from him (pp. 173–4). But is Jacob Byronic? Is there
even any irony in his lack of Byronism? He has many love
affairs, he travels in Europe; he tries to write, but his essay is
rejected. He seems to respond to nature, and yet, it is really the
narrator whom a landscape moves to lyrical utterance. Jacob is
generally happier than Byron, and Jacob's passions and his
travels do not issue into imaginative responses to doges and
bridges. When Jacob meets Sandra Wentworth Williams, he
suffers from his desire, but he suffers pitifully and simply; he
writes no impassioned poems.

Jacob's selection of a book from among his early tutor's
volumes proves to be no special signal to his character. Nor
does his university experience assume the importance of a
solemn milestone. Moved on some occasions to a fleeting
appreciation of the atmosphere of Cambridge, Jacob must
also tolerate caricature dons and oppressive luncheons. The
comedy of some of the Cambridge episodes may indeed be, as
Aileen Pippett suggested, Woolf's 'mocking revenge upon the
ancient institutions where she was never able to study'.[14] A few
years later, in *A Room of One's Own*, Woolf does certainly build
some uncomfortable comedy out of the alarmed gentleman in

the fluttering black gown who denies a woman entrance to the library at 'Oxbridge'. Women are 'locked out', denied access not only to the library, but to the entire centuries-old tradition of knowledge and of intellectual training. And yet, Woolf goes on to observe, this circumstance may not be as dangerous as being 'locked in' to the same tradition.[15] The narrator of *Jacob's Room* is similarly outside the male institutions through which she moves the hero. Even the hero, though sometimes stirred by his college experience, is oddly untransformed by it. He too is somewhat on the outside. The narrator refuses to let him be quite 'locked in' – either by the institution or by the fiction pattern to which a well-brought-up male character usually conforms. Jacob's education neither crushes him nor ennobles him; it perhaps has not very much to do with him. Unlike Stephen Dedalus, Jacob apparently develops no potent and complex theory of art or philosophy. Nor does he meet a G. E. Moore.

To Jacob, Cambridge offers Huxtable, Sopwith and Cowan, who are figures of inadequacy – inadequacy rather than destructiveness. These scholars do not display the thin-lipped, rigidly restrained asceticism of the priests in *A Portrait of the Artist as a Young Man*, for instance. We are not made to feel that Jacob must escape from the Huxtables and Sopwiths or risk injury to his soul. Jacob's orientation is not religious, so there is no solemn moment during which someone approaches him about a possible vocation; yet the narrator points to the possibility, perhaps the necessity, of Jacob's making some kind of life choice. Just after the painful luncheon given by Mr Plumer, the narrator speaks of the shock, to a person of about twenty, which the world makes as it begins to oppose 'the obstinate irrepressible conviction which makes youth so intolerably disagreeable – "I am what I am, and intend to be it", for which there will be no form in the world unless Jacob makes one for himself. The Plumers will try to prevent him from making it' (p. 34). There will be no form for his life – no shape for the irrepressible conviction of identity – unless Jacob makes the form. But does Jacob choose at all? In his passivity and lack of initiative he resembles another Jacob, the hero of Beresford's novel *The Early History of Jacob Stahl* (1911). His relatives want Jacob Stahl to choose a profession, and they particularly suggest the taking of Holy Orders. Jacob resists, because 'he had a full share of obstinacy if he lacked determination – his powers of resistance were greater than his capacity for initiative'.[16] Similarly Jacob Flanders, although he too is obstinate, lacks 'determination'. He neither embraces, nor rebels strenuously against, any aspect of his education.

Both the narrator and Jacob have a casual though sensuous attitude towards intellectual endeavour; both seem to take lightly the notion of Jacob's being the heir of the ages. Beresford, on the other hand, fluffs his prose into a brief rhapsody while he contemplates Jacob Stahl as the 'heir of the ages!' He describes the stars cooling and contracting, until at last their energy becomes Jacob.[17] With somewhat more energy H. G. Wells, writing of the war's effect on young people, loads with irony the idea of inheritance. After Peter is badly wounded, his guardian Oswald reflects bitterly on the way the world has treated its 'heir'.[18] Wells's Peter and Woolf's Jacob are brutally deceived heirs, but the narrator in Wells's novel provides voluminous hortatory comment on the failures of British education and on the need for the young heirs to rebuild their world. In *Jacob's Room*, however, neither Jacob nor the narrator reaps any edification out of the notion of inherited responsibilities or opportunities. As Jacob comes to the window of his friend Simeon's room, the narrator observes his face; he looks satisfied,

> indeed masterly; which expression changed slightly as he stood there, the sound of the clock conveying to him (it may be) a sense of old buildings and time; and himself the inheritor; and then to-morrow; and friends; at the thought of whom, in sheer confidence and pleasure, it seemed, he yawned and stretched himself. (p. 43)

The narrator offers only tentative interpretations here, but Jacob's actions are described without ambiguity. He looked satisfied, masterly; he yawned and stretched. The notion of his being 'an inheritor' is very much underplayed; here there is none of the earnestness of Wells or Beresford behind the idea. For this heir the notion does not carry with it any Victorian moral urgency, or even the mildly reformist moral energy of the Edwardian era.[19]

The two undergraduates continue their discussion, and one

of them mentions 'Julian the Apostate'. The narrator is more interested in the lyric atmosphere of midnight and wind than she is in observing which man spoke the phrase. Nevertheless, she definitely asserts that Simeon is the one who says, 'Somehow it seems to matter.' Of the two, he is evidently the more interested in the philosophical ramifications of the emperor's backsliding. Jacob says, 'Well, you seem to have studied the subject.' Then something in both Jacob's consciousness and that of the narrator experiences the pleasure and intimacy which pervade the room following this intellectual discussion:

> He appeared extraordinarily happy, as if his pleasure would brim and spill down the sides if Simeon spoke.
> Simeon said nothing. Jacob remained standing. But intimacy – the room was full of it, still, deep, like a pool. Without need of movement or speech it rose softly and washed over everything, mollifying, kindling, and coating the mind with the lustre of pearl, so that if you talk of a light, of Cambridge burning, it's not languages only. It's Julian the Apostate. (p. 44)

A discussion that might have been the springboard for Jacob's *non serviam*, or for his defining of a 'form' for his life, is instead enjoyed as a sensuous event – by Jacob and by the narrator. Jacob arrives at no great sense of purpose and identity, as Stephen Dedalus does in his lengthy deliberations with Cranly. Jacob *enjoys* his mind and the ideas that he 'inherits' from the past; he does not do anything so practical as tie together his own ego with them.

A later image suggests that the heritage of the ages is to Jacob a neutral pleasure, something to be enjoyed rather than shouldered and carried onward as part of the white man's burden. After leaving Florinda at the Guy Fawkes party, Jacob and Timmy are in high spirits, quoting Greek and feeling generally exuberant: 'They were boastful, triumphant; it seemed to both that they had read every book in the world; known every sin, passion, and joy. Civilizations stood round them like flowers ready for picking. Ages lapped at their feet like waves fit for sailing' (p. 74). For Jacob, intellectual conversation is valuable because it creates intimacy between friends. Ages lap at his feet, beckoning this Cambridge sportsman to a pleasant pastime of sailing. His sense of being an heir is linked, in his own mind, to the fact that Florinda called him by his first name, and sat on his knee. 'Thus did all good women in the days of the Greeks' (p. 75). Jacob here stereotypes both Greece and Florinda. Like the female statues of the Erechtheum, Florinda is pedestalled, a feminine prop for the structure of ancient civilisation as envisioned by Jacob Flanders. This recent Cambridge graduate, unlike the narrator, is only too ready to sum people up – especially women, and especially 'the Greeks'. The comedy of this section is so generously sympathetic that it is hardly even ironic. The hilarity is carried further some time later when Jacob sees Florinda 'turning up Greek Street upon another man's arm' (p. 93).

This does not mean that Jacob never has a serious thought. He and his Cambridge friends do engage in cerebral manoeuvres, but the hint of youthful discovery or youthful rebellion is immediately ploughed under by a context of shared laughter and sensuous enjoyment. The narrator's frequent shifts of distance contribute much to the short duration of any philosophical or rebellious musings. Moving back a little, she suggests that the story may be following a typical *Bildungsroman* pattern; she hints that Bonamy or Jacob may be resenting the fact of Keats's early death – perhaps her characters are about to raise clenched fists against God or the nature of things. But no, she moves in closer, and without any hedging tells us that Jacob, 'who sat astride a chair and ate dates from a long box, burst out laughing' (p. 42).

True, this method of narration, this inconsistency with regard to distance, is perhaps confusing. I am not sure that it is necessarily an ineffective approach, however. Hafley is right when he says that, while one narrator insists on the impossibility of knowing Jacob, another narrator does a good job of disproving this by moving easily into the minds of other characters.[20] There are in a sense two narrators, or one narrator who insists on giving us a twofold vision of Jacob, a vision that shows the conventional pattern which he 'should' follow, and almost simultaneously points out that he is not following the pattern. This method is an extended version of what Woolf does in 'An Unwritten Novel'. There, a 'narrator' within the narrator's head invents an elaborate story about a woman who happens to ride opposite in a train; the narrator calls her 'Minnie Marsh'. But, when the unknown woman leaves the train, the frame narrator must admit that the supposed 'Minnie' really seems happier and more at ease in the world than the storymaking imagination had envisioned. The frame narrator has to admit the mystery which results from the discrepancy between the two portraits – the imaginary one and the one revealed briefly and incompletely by the facts. A similar double narrator prevails in *Jacob's Room*. She is continually sketching the novelistic pattern that growing youths are 'supposed' to follow; then she suddenly provides a close-up of Jacob eating dates or finding in the cheap Florinda the emblem of all things Greek. The effect is comic, and serves often as a parodic gesture in which novels, and other conventional 'plots' in people's minds, are shown to be false.

Even Jacob's mildly rebellious gestures are mocked. He drafts an essay against the prudery of an editor's bowderlised Wycherly, and Bonamy praises it. But, although Jacob goes through all the *Bildungsroman* motions on this occasion, the event becomes a parodic rather than a real instance of rebellion:

> An outrage, Jacob said; a breach of faith; sheer prudery; token of a lewd mind and a disgusting nature. Aristophanes and Shakespeare were cited. Modern life was repudiated. Great play was made with the professional title, and Leeds as a seat of learning was laughed to scorn. And the extraordinary thing was that these young men were pefectly right – extraordinary, because, even as Jacob copied his pages, he knew that no one would ever print them. . . .
>
> (p. 68)

The style here completely demolishes any moral significance which the scene might have had if it had been approached in a more realistic manner, one that used dialogue and allowed us to overhear Jacob's thoughts in this moment of ethical triumph. Instead the passage reads like a list of items which every good novelist should include while narrating the hero's discovery of his own ethic – repudiate 'modern life', make 'great play' with the 'professional title', laugh at the 'seat of learning'. The distance, and the generalities which contribute to the distance, make the scene a parody of a moment of insight and self-assertion.

When the essay is returned from several journals, Jacob throws it in a special box. 'The lid shut upon the truth' (p. 69). In one sense, the closed lid represents Jacob's refusal to face the evidently mediocre statement which he made of his idea; he passively accepts the failure. In another sense the 'truth' is in the essay and in the perception of these young men, as the narrator suggests. Society closes the lid on Jacob's protest, but he did not protest really vigorously. Jacob does not pursue further this minor challenge to things as they are; it does not become an important event on which his development hinges.

Nor does Jacob's development hinge upon love or sex. This conventional item of a *Bildungsroman* makes its appearance in *Jacob's Room*, but the women Jacob meets neither build nor destroy his character. He meets the 'good' girl (Clara), and several versions of the 'bad' girl. He meets a more mature, and experienced woman, Sandra Wentworth Williams, who is already married; perhaps she will do for him what Lawrence's Clara does for Paul Morel in *Sons and Lovers*. Jacob, however, does not arrive at a more complete knowledge of himself as a result of the relationship with Sandra. Instead, he just falls painfully in love, and suffers terribly from this 'hook dragging in his side' (pp. 146, 149).

His affair with Florinda had been one of 'innocence' and simplicity; he accepted in the beginning her assertion of virginity. His relationship with Sandra seems to complement the Florinda relationship, because Jacob now assumes he really knows himself and knows women. As he and Sandra descend the Acro-Corinth, Sandra indulges herself and Jacob in some snippets of her sentimentally melancholy childhood: she was orphaned at four, wandered in the huge library and in the kitchen, and she sat on the butler's knee. Responding, 'Jacob thought that if he had been there he would have saved her; for she had been exposed to great dangers, he felt' (p. 145). Great dangers? Wandering through a library and sitting on a butler's knee? Jacob's imaginings here have no basis in the very slim data he has about Sandra. He is simply playing, safely and momentarily, with the notion of some vague heroism. A few seconds later, he is thinking of 'how little he had known himself before' (p. 146) – before meeting Sandra. But there has been no great change; his seeming growth is ironic, mere imaginary play on his part. Jacob's transformation from 'innocence' to 'knowledge' is parodic, not real. His only 'knowledge' is the uncomfortable sensation of a hook dragging in his side.

It might be argued that the slender sketch of Jacob's growth is an accident or flaw in the construction of the novel, a failure on the part of an author who was trying out a new method. I don't think so. Woolf can give a heavy, substantial representation to a character's consciousness, thoughts, growth and important moments; she did so in *The Voyage Out* and *Night and Day*, and she does so in *Jacob's Room*, but in this third novel she reserves for the narrator a fuller representation of consciousness. Furthermore, other occasions support the sense of Jacob's tenuous, ironic 'growth', and of his parodic, half-hearted travelling through typical *Bildungsroman* territory. Jacob goes to the Acropolis, for instance, and sits down to read:

> And laying the book on the ground he began, as if inspired by what he had read, to write a note upon the importance of history – upon democracy – one of those scribbles upon which the work of a lifetime may be based; or again, it falls out of a book twenty years later, and one can't remember a word of it. It is a little painful. It had better be burnt.
> Jacob wrote; began to draw a straight nose. . . .
> (pp. 149–50)

At this point democracy and the straight nose are interrupted by women on tour. The comedy is doubled and tripled. First Jacob interrupts himself by turning from democracy to a straight nose; then the sightseeing women interrupt the drawing of the nose. To be fair to Jacob, we would have to point out that the narrator may be responsible for the comic thoughts about juvenilia on democracy; she does not say definitely that Jacob himself writes such a 'painful' note. She moves in closer, however, and we do see Jacob drawing a straight nose. His meditations on history are probably not those of a future Gibbon or a Clive Bell. Jacob curses the women for interrupting him, but the comedy of the scene began earlier; he had interrupted himself.

The narrator continues the parodic portrait of a British youth's disillusionment with Athens:

> 'It is those damned women', said Jacob, without any trace of bitterness, but rather with sadness and disappointment that what might have been should never be.
> (This violent disillusionment is generally to be expected in young men in the prime of life, sound of wind and limb, who will soon become fathers of families and directors of banks.) (p. 150)

Jacob's disillusionment here hardly deserves the adjective 'violent' which the narrator ironically applies, looking ahead to the prosaic destiny which – except for the war – ordinarily awaits young men such as Jacob; they become 'fathers of families and directors of banks', not great historians and thinkers. Jacob's 'disappointment that what might have been should never be' approaches cliché in its phrasing; it is parodic, just as his supposed realisation – 'how little he had know himself before' – was parodic.

The narrator puts the cap on this comic scene by letting us see Jacob as he looks at the sculptures of the Erechtheum:

> Jacob strolled over to the Erechtheum and looked rather furtively at the goddess on the left-hand side holding the roof on her head. She reminded him of Sandra Wentworth Williams. He looked at her, then looked away. He looked at her, then looked away. He was extraordinarily moved, and with the battered Greek nose in his head, with Sandra in his head, with all sorts of things in his head, off he started to walk right up to the top of Mount Hymettus, alone, in the heat.   (p. 151)

This is farcical ('He looked at her, then looked away. He looked at her, then looked away'). Jacob's stagey double-take lets all the air out of the potentially epiphanic balloon. And, instead of the idealised 'straight' nose he had been drawing, his head is full of the 'battered Greek nose' which he somehow associates with Sandra. What a descent from Bonamy's prediction that Jacob would fall in love with 'some Greek woman with a straight nose' (p. 139)! For Jacob, no bird-girl stands symbolically on a beach; if she did, he would probably notice her crooked nose instead of rising to the occasion with a lyrical definition of his identity and his vocation.

Jacob's apparently climactic opportunity for love and insight is his night-time visit to the Acropolis with Sandra. Woolf does not describe it. The narrator's own reflections indicate that she has deliberately turned away from this event. As Jacob and Sandra climb, the narrator's perspective widens, giving us Paris, Constantinople, London and Betty Flanders, who sighs 'like one who realizes, but would fain ward off a little longer – oh, a little longer! – the oppression of eternity' (p. 160). Meanwhile Jacob and Sandra have vanished from the narrator's view. 'There was the Acropolis; but had they reached it?' The answer to the narrator's question may be 'Yes', in the sense that Jacob may have literally reached the Acropolis with Sandra. From what we know of Jacob, however, 'No' would be the answer to the more symbolic aspect of the narrator's question. 'As for reaching the Acropolis who shall say that we ever do it, or that when Jacob woke next morning he found anything hard and durable to keep for ever?' (ibid.). It is doubtful that he carried away anything durable from this event – doubtful that he reached the 'Acropolis' of symbolic insight. Later, back in London, he is essentially unchanged, and still suffering from his unmanageable passions. He draws a sketch of the Parthenon in the dust in Hyde Park, and reads a letter from Sandra about her memory 'of something said or attempted, some moment in the dark on the road to the Acropolis which (such was her creed) mattered for ever' (p. 169). Moments belong to Sandra's creed, not to Jacob's. He overlooks them, or distorts them; she, on the other hand, makes moments, contrives them.

Some sort of 'moment' of insight is present even in Woolf's early novels. The newly engaged Katharine Hilbery, for instance, 'held in her hands for one brief moment the globe which we spend our lives in trying to shape, round, whole, and entire from the confusion of chaos'.[21] In *Jacob's Room*, however, the narrator goes out of her way to undercut such occasions. Clara Durrant, writing about Jacob in her diary, wishes that the moment of Jacob's July visit could continue for

ever. 'And moments don't', the narrator offers as a transi-
tional comment, going on to describe Jacob in London
laughing at an obscene joke (p. 70). Sandra's moments – part
of a self-conscious 'creed' – come in for downright ridicule.
The narrator troubles to point out the 'dirty curtains' of the
hotel window in Olympia where Sandra stands, contemplat-
ing the burdened peasants as they return for the evening:

> She seemed to have grasped something. She would write it
> down. And moving to the table where her husband sat
> reading she leant her chin in her hands and thought of the
> peasants, of suffering, of her own beauty, of the inevitable
> compromise, and of how she would write it down.
>   (pp. 140–1)

Her sentimental musings self-consciously place her own
beauty in the middle of the picture. She says, 'Everything
seems to mean so much'; then she notices her own reflection in
a mirror, and she thinks, 'I am very beautiful' (p. 141). After
the big occasion of her visit to the Acropolis with Jacob, she
reflects on their relationship, sucking back again 'the soul of
the moment': ' "What for? What for?" Sandra would say,
putting the book back, and strolling to the looking-glass
and pressing her hair' (pp. 160–1). Neither Clara nor Sandra
looks very deeply into herself; neither makes any real discovery about her life. Sandra, indeed, can look only *at* herself.

Nor is Jacob really the sort of meditative, introspective
character by which an author can make the most of the usual
Bildungsroman format; his obstinately non-reflective personality is, however, fine material for a parody of this traditional
form. The narrator does allow that Jacob's personality may
change with age:

> 'What for? What for?' Jacob never asked himself any such
> questions, to judge by the way he laced his boots; shaved
> himself; to judge by the depth of his sleep that night, with
> the wind fidgeting at the shutters, and half-a-dozen mos-
> quitoes singing in his ears. He was young – a man. And then
> Sandra was right when she judged him to be credulous as
> yet. At forty it might be a different matter.   (p. 161)

Sandra asks 'What for?' in a self-conscious manner that makes a mockery of the question. Jacob never even asks. Probably. The narrator in this passage is once again giving us a tentative view; we must try 'to judge' on the basis of the evidence. Other evidence suggests that Jacob does not ask such questions; except for occasions when he is in love, he enjoys life, and is 'not much given to analysis' (pp. 138–9). Like all young people in a *Bildungsroman*, he is supposed to ask 'What for?' But he maintains his own obstinate mystery, and neither asks for revelation nor receives any.[22]

The narrator, not Jacob or Clara or Sandra, has the imaginative and lyrical responses to Greece and to the English landscape. She gives us the spectacular and melancholy beauty of the Cornish coast as Timmy and Jacob sail close to it (pp. 47–8). She gives us the illuminating meditation on the 'exaltation' of young people such as Fanny Elmer and Nick Bramham whose restless energy, if it were any more intense, would blow them 'like foam into the air'; if we had such continual ecstasy, 'he stars would shine through us' (pp. 119–20). And the narrator, not Jacob, gives us the longest meditation on the immortal beauty of the Parthenon (pp. 146–8). In this book, the narrator has the moments of insight; she is, in her own right, a distinct and important 'character', as recent critics have observed.[23]

Part of her insight emerges in the very 'looseness' and 'gaiety' of the novel's structure, in the sketchy, continually qualified account of Jacob's development. The narrator needs this very flexible perspective, one which allows her to assume omniscience on occasion, and at other times to speak in her own voice, a woman who is older than Jacob and who finds him difficult to know. The flexible perspective allows the *Bildungsroman* elements to be introduced, almost as though they were hypotheses about behaviour; then, with a shift of perspective, the narrator can 'correct' the conventional assumption, and show us how far from the convention the mysterious Jacob is. The parodic approach to his character, his growing up, his love affairs, and his travels, yields both comedy and a solid conviction of his 'obstinate' reality. Jacob is not 'characterised' in a traditional way. Instead, he is teased into a tentative existence, and he walks around, somewhat at a loss, in his own parodic *Bildungsroman*.

The resulting humour is directed not only at a highly conventional literary form, but at the male hero whom the form so often featured. The sympathetic laughter of the narrator is subtly feminist, but she rescues Jacob – by her very refusal to sum him up – from any severe censure. After all, he does not always fit the mocked pattern. His very deviation from the *Bildungsroman* parodies the pattern, and at the same time asserts his own mysterious reality and his specialness as a human being.

NOTES

1. Virginia Woolf, *A Writer's Diary*, ed. Leonard Woolf (London: Hogarth Press, 1975) p. 23.
2. Ibid., p. 54.
3. An early reviewer calls *Jacob's Room* a 'rag-bag of impressions' (*New Age*, 21 Dec 1922, p. 123); see in *Virginia Woolf: The Critical Heritage*, ed. Robin Majumdar and Allen McLaurin (London and Boston, Mass.: Routledge & Kegan Paul, 1975) p. 108. The rapid transitions, according to James Hafley, often contribute to a sense of structural incoherence; see *The Glass Roof: Virginia Woolf as Novelist* (New York: Russell and Russell, 1963) pp. 58–9. J. K. Johnstone criticises the lack of inevitable links among the episodes; see *The Bloomsbury Group* (London: Secker & Warburg, 1954) p. 328.
4. See esp. Hafley, *The Glass Roof*, pp. 52, 53, 55; and Nancy Topping Bazin, *Virginia Woolf and the Androgynous Vision* (New Brunswick, NJ: Rutgers University Press, 1973) p. 98.
5. Clive Bell, 'Virginia Woolf' (*Dial*, Dec 1924, pp. 451–65) in *Virginia Woolf: The Critical Heritage*, p. 147; A. S. McDowall (unsigned review, *Times Literary Supplement*, 26 Oct 1922, p. 683) in *Virginia Woolf: The Critical Heritage*, pp. 96–7. Winifred Holtby also praises the comedy in *Jacob's Room*, especially the portraits of eccentric scholars; see *Virginia Woolf* (1932; repr. Folcroft, Penn.: Folcroft Press, 1969) pp. 123–4.
6. Virginia Woolf, *Jacob's Room* (London: Hogarth Press, 1971) p. 153. Page references in the text are to this edition.
7. For a discussion of the form and its rise in popularity, see J. H. Buckley, *Season of Youth: The Bildungsroman from Dickens to Golding* (Cambridge, Mass.: Harvard University Press, 1974) pp. 1–22; and William C. Frierson, *The English Novel in Transition, 1885–1940* (Norman: University of Oklahoma Press, 1942) pp. 193–210.
8. Quentin Bell sees Meredith as primarily an early influence in *Virginia Woolf: A Biography* (New York: Harcourt, Brace, Jovanovich, 1972) vol. I, p. 138. Woolf discusses Meredith in several essays. In 'Hours in a Library' (1916), she lists the books that a person would have read by the age of twenty; the list includes 'the whole of Meredith'. See *Collected Essays* (London: Hogarth Press, 1972) vol. II, p. 35.

9. Buckley, *Season of Youth*, p. 64.
10. Virginia Woolf, 'The Rights of Youth', a review of H. G. Wells, *Joan and Peter* (*Times Literary Supplement*, 19 Sep 1918), in Woolf, *Contemporary Writers* (London: Hogarth Press, 1965) pp. 90–3. See also her reviews of Mackenzie's books *The Early Life and Adventures of Sylvia Scarlett* (*Times Literary Supplement*, 29 Aug 1918) and *Sylvia and Michael* (*Times Literary Supplement*, 20 Mar 1919) in *Contemporary Writers*, pp. 82–6. She finds Mackenzie's Sylvia too thinly characterised and the action too swift. Woolf stands by Richardson's refusal to use realism, but does not feel that Richardson has mastered her method yet; see Woolf, 'The Tunnel', a review of Dorothy Richardson *The Tunnel* (*Times Literary Supplement*, 13 Feb 1919) in *Contemporary Writers*, pp. 120–2.
11. Virginia Woolf, 'Cleverness and Youth', a review of Aldous Huxley, *Limbo* (*Times Literary Supplement*, 5 Feb 1920) in *Contemporary Writers*, p. 150; and see Huxley, 'Farcical History of Richard Greenow', in *Limbo* (London: Chatto & Windus, 1946) pp. 40–1.
12. Woolf, review of *Limbo*, in *Contemporary Writers*, p. 150. See in *Limbo*, pp. 13–22.
13. Avrom Fleishman, *Virginia Woolf: A Critical Reading* (Baltimore: Johns Hopkins University Press, 1975) p. 46; Buckley, *Season of Youth*, p. 263.
14. Aileen Pippett, *The Moth and the Star: A Biography of Virginia Woolf* (Boston, Mass.: Little, Brown, 1953) pp. 150–1.
15. Virginia Woolf, *A Room of One's Own* (New York: Harcourt, Brace and World, 1957) pp. 7–8, 24.
16. J. D. Beresford, *The Early History of Jacob Stahl* (Boston, Mass.: Little, Brown, 1911) p. 55. In a review of Beresford's later novel *Revolution* (*Times Literary Supplement*, 27 Jan 1921), Woolf mentions his trilogy dealing with Jacob Stahl; she praises Beresford's earlier novels, including *Jacob Stahl*, as 'very memorable'. See Woolf, *Contemporary Writers*, pp. 155–6. The two Jacobs are alike in their passivity, their obstinacy, their reluctance to take a definite course of action, and their painful love relationships. In other respects Woolf's Jacob shows little resemblance to Beresford's. Another namesake is the biblical Jacob, as Manly Johnson argues in *Virginia Woolf* (New York: R. Ungar, 1973) pp. 44–5.
17. Beresford, *Jacob Stahl*, pp. 321–3.
18. H. G. Wells, *Joan and Peter: The Story of an Education* (New York: Macmillan, 1918) pp. 19, 549.
19. Prewar reformers urged society to make minor adjustments but to maintain essentially the same structure; as George Dangerfield phrased it, 'reform' at this time meant 'a passionate desire to preserve, by improvement, the shape of things as they were'; quoted by Frierson in *The English Novel in Transition*, pp. 143–4.
20. Hafley, *The Glass Roof*, p. 52.
21. Virginia Woolf, *Night and Day* (London: Hogarth Press, 1971) p. 533.
22. With regard to Jacob's passivity and his lack of intellectual exertion, it is important to distinguish him from Woolf's brother, Thoby Stephen. It is true that the absurd brevity of Jacob's life suggests parallels with Thoby and with Rupert Brooke. Jane Novak argues for caution,

however, in making such parallels. Thoby had a sense of humour; he had more self-confidence and a greater intellect than Jacob has. See Novak, *The Razor Edge of Balance: A Study of Virginia Woolf* (Coral Gables, Fla: University of Miami Press, 1975) pp. 101–3.
23. See especially Barry S. Morgenstern, 'The Self-conscious Narrator in *Jacob's Room*', *Modern Fiction Studies*, Autumn 1972, pp. 351–61. Others who comment briefly on the narrator as a character are Hafley, *The Glass Roof*, pp. 49–50; and Novak, *The Razor Edge of Balance*, pp. 87–8.

6 *Mrs Dalloway*: the Communion of Saints

SUZETTE A. HENKE

I. INTRODUCTION

All of Virginia Woolf's major novels suggest an intellectual commitment to feminist, pacifist and socialist principles.[1] Throughout her work, Woolf decries the kind of authoritarian power that incites nations to war, makes autocrats of husbands and fathers, and forces individuals into rigid patterns of social conformity. By dislocating traditional form, she subtly incorporates into avant-grade fiction an impassioned, radical ideology.

Mrs Dalloway offers a scathing indictment of the British class system and a strong critique of patriarchy.[2] The work's social satire takes much of its force from ironic patterns of mythic reference that allow the fusion of dramatic models from Greek tragedy and from the Christian liturgy. Woolf envisions an allegorical struggle between good and evil – between Clarissa Dalloway's comic celebration of life and the tragic, death-dealing forces that drive Septimus Smith to suicide: 'Suppose the idea of the book is the contrast between life and death. The two minds of Mrs. D. and Septimus.... All must bear finally upon the party at the end; which expresses life, in every variety ... while Septimus dies.'[3]

It is perhaps more than coincidental that Woolf took notes for *Mrs Dalloway* in a small black copybook that contained earlier reflections on themes of 'propitiation' and 'lamentation' in the *Choephori* of Aeschylus.[4] She mentions in 1922 diary entries that she is working on the novel, reading

125

Aeschylus, and planning her essay 'On Not Knowing Greek'.[5] And several times in her holograph notebook she compares the fictional form to classical drama, asking, 'Why not have an observer in the street at each critical point who acts the part of chorus?'[6]

Narrative action in *Mrs Dalloway* is set in a larger symbolic context of ritual sacrifice and eucharistic communion. Just as medieval drama detailed the life and death of Christ through the Catholic liturgy, so Woolf's novel presents death and transfiguration within the frame of a pagan Mass. Septimus Smith serves as the traditional scapegoat, the Christological figure whose martyrdom is precipitated by the 'sins of the fathers' guilty of tyranny, greed and political power-mongering. Woolf satirises contemporary rites of tragic sacrifice – rituals of war and coercion that victimise the young, the helpless, the visionary and the deviant.[7]

The theme of the scapegoat resides at the heart of Greek tragedy and, in transmuted form, comprises one of the central tenets of the Catholic liturgy. Woolf incorporates into her fiction both Greek and Christian models, despite the fact that she grew up in an aggressively godless household.[8] The offering of the Mass apparently constitutes a primary metaphor in Woolf's novel – with Septimus Smith serving as Christ the victim and Clarissa Dalloway functioning as 'high priest'. As celebrant of a pagan Mass, Clarissa reminds us of the sacred words of transubstantiation: 'Take thou and eat: for this is my body.' She offers to her dinner guests not only physical sustenance but the spiritual nourishment of a communion sanctified by the death of Septimus. She is high priestess and empathic victim – a worshipper of life whose spring 'fertility rite' is blessed by the scapegoat who 'revitalises the community that destroys him'.[9]

Septimus dies that Clarissa may live. His death is an escape from authoritarian forces that would rape his consciousness, trammel his soul, and imprison him in a madhouse down in Surrey. By 'throwing it all away', Septimus makes of his life an unspoiled, gratuitous offering. He has preserved the chastity of spirit that Clarissa jealously guards in the privacy of her attic room. His visionary idealism remains intact, untouched by the 'world's slow stain' of compromise and defilement.[10]

Described as a virgin mother and a nun, Clarissa makes her

own life an 'offering' to the forces of spiritual fertility. Lolloping like a mermaid in her silver-green dress, she embodies female beauty, naturalness and a consciousness of sensuous joy. Her dinner party constitutes a sacramental paean to life and regeneration.[11]

Clarissa's devotion is directed not to the patriarchal Jehovah of the Judaeo-Christian tradition, but to a composite ancestral figure whose primary aspect is maternal. 'And it was an offering; to combine, to create; but to whom?'[12] Most readers have assumed that Clarissa's query is rhetorical, since she herself never directly answers the question. Yet her life is an offering to her parents, especially to her mother:

> For she was a child, throwing bread to the ducks, between her parents, and at the same time a grown woman coming to her parents who stood by the lake, holding her life in her arms which, as she neared them, grew larger and larger in her arms, until it became a whole life, a complete life, which she put down by them and said, 'This is what I have made of it! This!' And what had she made of it? What, indeed?   (pp. 63–4)

In this momentary fantasy, Clarissa imagines herself in the dual aspect of child and woman, running down to her parents by the lake at Bourton and bearing in her arms the gift of her own completed life. She longs to bring both parents back from the dead. With feelings of wonder, pride and amazement, she yearns to give them the consummate present of her mature adult self.

Clarissa's unique allusion to her dead mother heightens the symbolic import of the memory. The vision is part dream, part recollection. It suggests that Clarissa unconsciously offers the final gift of self-actualisation to the phantasmal image of the mother she remembers. To the young Clarissa Parry, Bourton must have seemed an Edenic paradise sanctified by maternal benevolence. After the loss of her mother, Clarissa felt it incumbent on her to re-create the beatific communion shattered by Mrs Parry's death. Her gatherings serve as a perpetual tribute to the absent mother, creative acts of social artistry based on the primary model of family affiliation.

Clarissa's parties are works of art that challenge mortality and strive to reinstate the prelapsarian delights of infant joy.

II. CLARISSA AND THE PRIME MINISTER: ART VERSUS WAR

Like all Virginia Woolf's major novels, *Mrs Dalloway* is imbued with political resonances. The work tacitly questions tyrannical authority in all its forms, from nationalistic power-mongering to conjugal appropriation. The unnamed antagonists of the book are life and death, Eros and Thanatos – a comic impulse toward love, communion and creative survival pitted against tragic instincts toward war and destruction.

The dialectical movement of the novel centres around the two great forces described in *Three Guineas* – art and war. If only we knew the truth about both, Woolf insists, 'the enjoyment and practice of art would become so desirable that by comparison the pursuit of war would be a tedious game for elderly dilettantes'.[13] In *Mrs Dalloway* Woolf pays tribute to the delicate and ephemeral art forms that grow out of the daily lives of women. Like Mrs Ramsay in *To the Lighthouse*, Clarissa Dalloway is a 'good liver' – a social artist who brings people together in new, imaginative configurations. With painstaking care, she weaves an evanescent web of friendship that creates new possibilities for love, affiliation and collective joy.

In 'The Prime Minister', Woolf's short story draft of *Mrs Dalloway*, Clarissa and the head of state are clearly juxtaposed in symbolic antagonism. They are enemies in the eternal struggle between civilisation and culture. The Prime Minister is a 'generalised' figure of 'authority' who represents male dictatorial power. Clarissa, in contrast, emerges as a 'particular character' who embodies the feminine capacity to create, preserve and sanctify life.[14]

'What, then, is this "patriotism" that leads you to go to war?' Woolf asks in *Three Guineas*. In *Mrs Dalloway* she provides an objective correlative that suggests an answer. The gray, funereal presence of an anonymous state car casts an aura of solemnity over the London crowd. It elicits a surge of inchoate emotion, so deep as to remain inarticulate, yet strong enough to urge the citizens to man cannons and defend the honour of the British Empire in a pub brawl. 'But now mystery had brushed them with her wing; they had heard the voice of authority; the spirit of religion was abroad with her eyes bandaged tight and her lips gaping wide' (p. 20). Nationalism is portrayed allegorically as a blind and gaping figure, a spirit of groupthink that engulfs the will. The grotesque caricature is both ludicrous and threatening: behind it lurks Woolf's perpetual fear of authoritarian forces that lead to cultural devastation. Woolf recognises a genuine danger in social pressures that force men and women to relinquish autonomy in deference to a higher power, be it political, religious or familial. As a faceless member of the crowd, the individual becomes a puppet of demagogic manipulation.

Woolf declares in *Three Guineas*: 'Inevitably we look upon societies as conspiracies that sink the private brother, whom many of us have reason to respect, and inflate in his stead a monstrous male, loud of voice, hard of fist, childishly intent upon scoring the floor of the earth with chalk marks' (*TG*, p. 105). Seen in the context of Clarissa's party, the Prime Minister is a fairly innocuous authority figure: 'One couldn't laugh at him. He looked so ordinary. You might have stood him behind a counter and bought biscuits' (p. 261). The Prime Minister is fatuous and absurd. Yet his ludicrous costume attests to that dangerous tendency 'for educated men to emphasize their superiority over other people, either in birth or intellect, by dressing differently, or by adding titles before, or letters after their names' (*TG*, p. 21). The Prime Minister embodies the social conspiracy of patriotism. He 'goes through mystic rites and enjoys the dubious pleasures of power and dominion' (*TG*, p. 105). He belongs to a political fraternity of lawgivers who can at any moment sink the private brother in monstrous demands of territorial expansion or wrench the soul into socially acceptable, well-proportioned modes of behaviour.

In both *Mrs Dalloway* and *Three Guineas*, Woolf perpetually decries not only war, patriotism and nationalistic ardour, but also the auxiliary vices of force and possessiveness that bolster the dictatorial spirit. 'Proportion' and 'Conversion' both support a hierarchical structure of authority that places kings and lawmakers in positions of leadership, generals in control of military battalions, and tyrannical husbands at the head of

Edwardian households. Woolf asks in *Three Guineas*, 'And are not force and possessiveness very closely connected with war?' (*G* p. 30). Her query associates the military forces that engulf Septimus in wartime with the brutal tactics of Sir William Bradshaw. Law and medicine collude with government to convert the deviant into passive ciphers of British convention.

III. CLARISSA AS NUN: PRIVACY VERSUS PASSION

Ironically, Clarissa Dalloway sentimentalises the effects of the Great War on the British populace: 'This late age of the world's experience had bred in them all, all men and women, a well of tears' (p. 13). Her attitude is romantic and maudlin. She admires the nobility of character and stoic temperament evoked by the recent war, but remains oblivious to the cracked stoicism endured by men like Septimus Smith.

In another life, a future incarnation perhaps, Clarissa would wear a different body and be 'interested in politics like a man' (p. 14). But in this world she feels it necessary to avoid the masculine terrain of law and government. Though ignorant of international politics, she is nevertheless a shrewd judge of character, and she proves highly sensitive to the political dimensions of human interaction. She shares with Septimus Smith an instinctive disdain for Sir William Bradshaw and for all the emissaries of Conversion that threaten the privacy of the soul.

The title of Woolf's novel is partially ironic since, in actuality, there *is* no 'Mrs Dalloway'. The name designates a fictitous persona, a social mask that disguises the former Clarissa Parry. Along with her 'narrow pea-stick figure' and her 'face, beaked like a bird's' (ibid.), Clarissa's married name serves as an outer skin covering the invisible, ineffable core of private identity. 'She had the oddest sense of being herself invisible; unseen; unknown; . . . not even Clarissa any more; this being Mrs. Richard Dalloway' (ibid.).

Peter Walsh reflects that, 'with twice his wits, she had to see things through his eyes – one of the tragedies of married life. With a mind of her own, she must always be quoting Richard'

(p. 116). Richard Dalloway is politically conservative and somewhat obtuse; he manifests 'a great deal of the public-spirited, British Empire, tariff-reform, governing-class spirit' (p. 116). Yet Clarissa, in choosing to marry him instead of Peter, made an instinctive and judicious choice in the interests of self-preservation. Peter's dynamic personality would have excited and enthralled her. Had she married him, she would have enjoyed 'this gaiety all day'. But Peter's obsessive ideal of romantic fusion would have engulfed Clarissa and forced her soul. 'For in marriage a little licence, a little independence there must be between people living together day in day out in the same house; which Richard gave her, and she him.... But with Peter everything had to be shared; everything gone into' (p. 10). As Woolf counsels in *Three Guineas*, 'it should not be difficult to transmute the old ideal of bodily chastity into the new ideal of mental chastity' (*TG*, p. 82). Hence the nun-like isolation of Clarissa's attic room, emblematic of virginal solitude. Clarissa is both virgin and mother: like the Christian figure of Mary, she remains spiritually aloof and emotionally inviolate.

Peter Walsh is not only possessive but infantile in his passionate demands. Woolf admits in her notes that 'there is something helpless, ridiculous about him as well as terrifying'.[15] Like Mr Ramsay, Peter fuses an aggressive male ego with a pathetic masculine helplessness. Though Peter deposits his garland before Clarissa as goddess, he can worship her only in the abstract guise of *magna mater*. He suspects that she has 'grown hard' and a 'trifle sentimental' (p. 73). He thinks her cold, conventional, unresponsive and lacking in female sympathy. Yet Peter himself manifests a frightening conventionality when he takes 'pride in England; in butlers; chow dogs; girls in their security' (p. 82). His idea of womanhood is stereotyped and chivalric.

Although women are attracted to Peter because he is 'not quite manly', his epicene qualities are less androgynous than infantile. He constantly demands feminine nurturance to soothe his battered ego. Peter dreams of the ideal woman as a great nurse who comforts and soothes, who offers sensuous gifts flowing from a warm, fertile body. His vision of the solitary traveller evokes a fantasy of Clarissa as he would like her to be: a beneficent mother dispensing 'charity, comprehension, absolution' (p. 86).

Peter's ideal mother–wife is a bottomless source of sensate and emotional warmth, a perpetual fountain of sympathy. Yet Peter can never elude an unconscious, stereotyped imprint of the female as a dangerous seductress. He secretly fears that, beneath the surface aspect of maternal solicitude, woman tempts man to a life of unbridled naturalness. Under the implacable gaze of the Earth Mother he envisions, civilisation becomes meaningless and absurd. An archetypal Ceres proffers 'great cornucopias full of fruit to the solitary traveller' (ibid.). But in a more alluring guise, the female merges with a band of sirens 'lolloping away on the green sea waves' (ibid.), beckoning fishermen to a watery grave. Peter's fantasy suggests that woman entices her mate to obliterate his ego in the general flux of universal life and 'blow to nothingness with the rest' (p. 87).

In waking life, Peter is a notorious womaniser. He knows that marriage to Clarissa would have been disastrous for them both, and he reflects that the 'other thing' was easier – the facile lovemaking that characterises his romantic affair with Daisy. With a touch of condescension, he tells himself that 'women . . . don't know what passion is. They don't know the meaning of it to men' (p. 121). Certainly, his romantic temperament cannot fathom the mystery of Clarissa's spiritual virginity. He thinks her 'cold as an icicle'. 'That was the devilish part of her – this coldness, this woodenness, something very profound in her, . . . an impenetrability. Yet heaven knows he loved her' (p. 91). Even now Peter tries to project onto Clarissa the ill-fitting role of *magna mater*; he cannot accept her fiercely defended emotional privacy.

Peter's jealousy and possessiveness evoke in him a secret disdain for physical maternity. Wanting to be coddled and 'babied', he resents women's giving birth. In an earlier draft of the novel, he laments 'the inevitable result upon almost every woman without exception having children; [for it was the very devil; that] it made them dull; [Cowlike] made them give up caring for things'.[16] A perpetual child himself, Peter is 'on the defensive against people who think him old. That was why he ran away from Elizabeth.'[17] And that is why he chooses a child-bride less than half his age. At the heart of Peter's attraction to

Daisy is a compulsive need to assert his youth, vitality and potency. Daisy will desert her own children, 'sacrifice all' and offer him the flattering idolatry of girlish infatuation. In deciding to marry Richard Dalloway instead of Peter Walsh, Clarissa chose privacy over passion. She forfeited romantic intensity for companionate love. Marriage to Peter would have entailed a schizoid modality of existence, a constant tension between amorous fusion and personal creativity. Peter's chivalric ideal sanctioned a grasping, appropriative love, a 'togetherness' that would have crushed Clarissa's individuality. In the domestic sphere, Peter is an innocuous version of the male dictator 'who believes that he has the right, whether given by God, Nature, sex or race is immaterial, to dictate to other human beings how they shall live, what they shall do' (TG, p. 53). In the end, a redemptive selfishness rescued Clarissa. Had she married Peter, she might, like Septimus, have gone mad.

Clarissa Dalloway lacks the kind of generosity and effusiveness that someone like Mrs Ramsay displays in To the Lighthouse – nobly, heroically, altruistically, but at the expense of her own soul. Clarissa apparently failed Richard at some crucial juncture in their marriage, first at Clieveden, 'then at Constantinople, and again and again' (p. 46). Through some cold contraction of the spirit, she could not provide him with 'feminine' warmth. Yet Clarissa's coldness may also be a survival strategy, a salutary egotism calculated to preserve her own carefully guarded psychological space. We are never told the precise nature of her conjugal failure. Perhaps she simply abjured the traditional female duty of ego-enhancement and refused to mirror her husband's image at twice its natural size.

The 'nun-like' Clarissa is passionately in love with sensuous existence. Hearing Big Ben strike the hour, she cuts her life into blocks and tastes the delicious days, months and years left her. The sense of an ending enriches her present. A victim of influenza and heart disease, she feels like Lazarus risen from the grave. Like Septimus Smith, she has witnessed the senseless death of a loved one – her sister Sylvia, accidentally killed by a falling tree. The incident forced Clarissa to come to terms with mortality. Knowing the fragility of human existence, 'she enjoyed life immensely. . . . She enjoyed practically everything' (p. 118).

Clarissa slices like a knife through cant and illusion. A thoroughgoing sceptic, she adopts an existential vision of absurdity. Thus Peter imagines her thinking: 'As we are a doomed race, chained to a sinking ship, . . . as the whole thing is a bad joke, let us, at any rate, do our part; mitigate the sufferings of our fellow-prisoners (Huxley again); decorate the dungeon with flowers and air-cushions; be as decent as we possibly can. Those ruffians, the Gods, shan't have it all their own way' (p. 117). Clarissa's existential vision is the Janus-image of Septimus Smith's 'mystical madness'. Whereas Septimus is convinced that everything has a transcendent meaning that eludes mankind, Clarissa believes that we must constantly create meaning in the face of absurdity. Hence her benevolent philosophy of 'doing good for the sake of goodness' (p. 118).

IV. ANDROGYNY, HOMOSEXUALITY, AND THE SORORITY OF WOMEN

Both Clarissa Dalloway and Septimus Smith are repressed homosexual characters who refuse to conform to the stereotypical patterns ascribed to their sex. Septimus fled to the trenches to learn stoic 'manliness'. Clarissa chooses an attic room as a refuge from the traditional female role of angel in the house: 'Like a nun withdrawing, or a child exploring a tower, she went upstairs. . . . There was an emptiness about the heart of life. . . . The sheets were clean, tight stretched in a broad white band from side to side. Narrower and narrower would her bed be. The candle was half burnt down and she had read deep in Baron Marbot's *Memoirs*' (pp. 45–6).

A spiritual 'virginity preserved through childbirth' clings to Clarissa 'like a sheet' (p. 46). In the manner of a shroud, a white band of linen winds round her bed – a bed that will grow narrower until it shrinks to the size of a coffin. The attic room and the deserted tower are symbols of Clarissa's intrinsic solitude, her psychological conviction of isolation and dread: 'She had a perpetual sense . . . of being out, out, far out to sea and alone; she always had the feeling that it was very, very dangerous to live even one day' (p. 11).

Like Septimus Smith, Clarissa fears ego-engulfment and a disintegration of the self. She cannot respond to male demands for sympathy and refuses to condone emotional symbiosis in marriage. She feels that she has disappointed Richard by her inability to offer him the kind of romantic passion usually expected in heterosexual relationships: 'She could see what she lacked. It was not beauty; it was not mind. It was something central which permeated; something warm which broke up surfaces and rippled the cold contact of man and woman' (p. 46).

Yet in moments of candour and intimacy she responds passionately to the sensuous beauty of other women. She 'could not resist sometimes yielding to the charm of a woman' (ibid.). Clarissa 'did undoubtedly then feel what men felt. Only for a moment; but it was enough' (p. 47). Female contact has the force of revelation in Clarissa's past, lyrically described in images of erotic ecstasy. She recalls a moment of wonder when Sally Seton kissed her on the lips and offered a flower from the garden at Bourton. Enthralled with the sacred presence of Sally clad in 'pink gauze', Clarissa swoons in romantic delight. She is convinced, like Othello, that 'if it were now to die 'twere now to be most happy' (p. 51). The sentiment is melodramatic in its suggestion of bliss immortalised by death. But Clarissa's love for Sally is possibly the most intense emotion she will ever experience. It gives her a transcendent moment of happiness, the glorious revelation of 'a match burning in a crocus; an inner meaning almost expressed' (p. 47).

Clarissa's lesbian attraction to Sally is celebratory and openly expressed. 'But nothing is so strange when one is in love', she reflects, and thinks parenthetically, 'and what was this except being in love?' (p. 51). Her virginal passion for Sally is graced by an adolescent purity, unclouded by the sexual masks and societal roles that often muddle adult heterosexual relations. 'The strange thing, on looking back, was the purity, the integrity, of her feeling for Sally. It was not like one's feeling for a man. It was completely disinterested, and besides, it had a quality which could only exist between women, between women just grown up' (p. 50). As Woolf reminds us in A Room of One's Own, women are rarely allowed to *like* each other in modern fiction. And few artists have attempted to depict the genuine affection that gives rise to love between women – a love unspoiled by a desire for social appropriation or marital fusion. The lesbian dimension of Sally's attraction is more overt in the manuscript version of the novel. Peter muses that 'in the old days, you couldn't deny, Sally had cared for her all right'. When he and Sally meet at the party, they discuss their former rivalry for Clarissa's affections. Sally apparently shares Peter's romantic conviction that true love comes but once in a lifetime. And like him she cherishes an enduring image of Clarissa as her own first, inimitable love: 'One is never in love more than once, he said. And what could she say? That life was a tragedy. That it was better to have loved [than not]. . . . All of what [she said] was true; all very true; [and she loved her, as one lover, they said, old had – wild]'.[18]

Woolf eventually deleted the bracketed passages, thus expunging from the final version of the text Sally's proclamation of love for Clarissa. Yet Peter's colloquy with Sally is more comprehensible if one realises that both characters experience the same excitement and exhilaration in Clarissa's presence. They have gathered to pay homage to a figure whom they jointly venerate in memories of an earlier passion.

Recalling her own precious moments of love for Sally, Clarissa refuses to interfere with her daughter Elizabeth's 'falling in love' with Miss Kilman: 'It proves she has a heart' (p. 204). But she cannot help feeling apprehensive about Elizabeth's choice of a lover who is predatory and insensitive, obscene in her spiritual asceticism, and vampiric in her greed for power. The unfortunate Miss Kilman is one of Mrs Dalloway's alter egos. Had the dice of the gods been cast differently, Clarissa might have loved Doris and befriended her. And, with still another roll of the dice, Miss Kilman might have been Mrs Dalloway. Clarissa could have become an idealistic university woman, a socialist and a follower of William Morris. Miss Kilman envies Clarissa her leisure, her money, her daughter and her man. Richard is one of the few males who take an interest in the isolated spinster. Unable to threaten Clarissa's social status or her conjugal felicity, Doris Kilman preys on Elizabeth. She strikes where she senses her enemy most vulnerable.

Woolf despises the 'conversion aspects' of 'love and re-

ligion'. Yet she refuses to indict Miss Kilman entirely. In some
sense, the tutor has correctly assessed her own plight: she has
been cheated by fate and lacks 'reserves' of happiness. 'All her
soul rusted with that grievance sticking in it' (p. 16). Kilman
passionately hates in the name of love. Her antagonism
towards Clarissa takes the form of obsessive fantasy: 'And
there rose in her an overmastering desire to overcome her; to
unmask her . . . ruin her; humiliate her; bring her to her
knees crying, You are right!' (p. 189).

Frustrated in her courtship of Elizabeth, Kilman stuffs
herself with chocolate eclairs and makes food a surrogate for
love. Greed and gluttony define a life of spiritual penury. But
Woolf has a certain amount of sympathy for this 'unlovable'
woman frustrated to the point of indignant rage. Kilman
suffers from the spiritual constrictions that grow out of
poverty. Despite her quick mind and her knowledge of
history, she is unable to invade the male-dominated teaching
profession. An erstwhile German sympathiser, she defines
herself as a political refugee from British imperialism. Without professional credentials, Kilman tutors the daughters of
educated men and directs her anger against women who have
ingratiated themselves with males in power.

In spite of her fear of 'Elizabeth's seducer', this 'woman who
had crept in to steal and defile', Clarissa eventually concludes,
'She hated her: she loved her. It was enemies one wanted'
(p. 266) – enemies to sharpen the soul and stir the passions. At
some level, Clarissa feels a sororal attachment to women as
different from herself as Doris Kilman and Lady Bruton. She
recognises 'some feminine comradeship which went beneath
masculine lunch parties and united Lady Bruton and Mrs.
Dalloway, who seldom met, and appeared when they did meet
indifferent and even hostile, in a singular bond' (pp. 160–1).

Even Elizabeth Dalloway, 'inclined to be passive', feels the
stirrings of female affiliation. Better educated than her
mother, she entertains professional aspirations: she plans to
'become a doctor, a farmer, possibly go into Parliament'
(p. 207). She feels herself 'a pioneer, a stray', venturing into
the unknown teritory of the Strand. It is significant that she
sees this undiscovered world predominantly in terms of
female attachment: 'She liked the geniality, sisterhood,
motherhood, brotherhood of this uproar. It seemed to her

good' (p. 209). The social hierarchy has sufficiently changed to alter the exclusively male fraternity of the Strand. In *Three Guineas* Woolf expressed hope for a generation of independent women united in professional solidarity. By allowing Elizabeth Dalloway a glimpse of that same vision, Woolf suggests that the adolescent girl may yet blossom into a 'new woman' who unites the cleverness and ambitions of Miss Kilman with the humane sympathies of someone such as Clarissa.

The relationship between Clarissa and her daughter is fragile and thinly sketched. Yet Elizabeth, who admires the intelligence and social insight of Miss Kilman, ultimately turns back to her mother when she attends the evening party despite her tutor's remonstrations. Poised on the brink of womanhood, Elizabeth will develop under Clarissa's delicate, unobtrusive and respectful cultivation. Unlike Miss Kilman, Clarissa will not 'force' her daughter's soul. She leaves room for the psychological space and spiritual freedom necessary to adolescent maturation. Though Elizabeth is 'Daddy's girl', she has been influenced by her mother more than she realises. And it is she who will carry on the tradition of sorority and compassion handed down from mother to daughter.

V. SEPTIMUS SMITH: ALTER-EGO AND SCAPEGOAT

In her holograph notes, Woolf speculates that Septimus Smith might be 'founded on R. His face. Eyes far apart – not degenerate. Not wholly an intellectual. Had been in the war. Or founded on me?' His portrait is to 'be left vague – as a mad person is – not so much character as an idea'. 'Why not have something of B. in him? The young man who has gone into business after the war: takes life to heart: seeks truth – revelations – some reason.'[19] Woolf's composition of what she called the 'mad scenes' in the novel largely reflects her own 'schizophrenic' experiences. But the more realistic aspects of Septimus's life as a young, self-educated clerk may have been based on her contact with a student she had taught at Morley College in London. The initial 'R.' furthermore, could refer to Roger Fry, whose Quaker intensity, brooding isolation and immitigable honesty Woolf describes in her diary. She portrays Roger as 'lean, brown, and truculent', an 'obstinate young man . . . who will *not* say what he does not believe to be true'.[20]

Both Septimus Smith and Clarissa Dalloway are visionary seers who experience moments of heightened perception, transcendental states of psychic illumination or 'inner light'. Septimus perceives the exquisite beauty of trees in Regent's Park, and Clarissa celebrates the intense wonder of a June day in Westminister. Both characters are highly sensitive, imaginative and wilful. If Clarissa is a social artist of human relations, Septimus is her *Doppelgänger* – the uncontrolled, demonic side of the creative imagination.[21]

Clarissa and Septimus are obsessed in different ways with a compulsive need for personal autonomy. They share a mutual horror of psychological engulfment, metaphorically rendered in fantasies of conflagration. In an act of self-preservation, Clarissa retreats to her attic room; Septimus leaps to his death and to salvation. Through his suicide, Septimus communicates with Clarissa, who understands his gesture of defiance against an authoritarian society that would force his soul.

Gulled by the feverish rhetoric of nationalism, Septimus consented to sacrifice individual liberty to collective aggression. As a soldier in battle, he became a cog in the machinery of death and tacitly condoned the insanity of war. He returned from the inferno, like Lazarus, only to create his own private hell.

Before the war, Septimus was too androgynous to conform to society's masculine stereotype. Shy and stammering, he read Shakespeare's plays, wrote romantic poetry, and fell hopelessly in love with Miss Isabel Pole. Under her tutelage, his soul blossomed. But in the trenches Septimus was educated in the stoic ways of manhood. He suppressed feeling, won promotion, and coolly dismissed the loss of his friend Evans. In an effort to diminish pain, he was forced to exorcise the ability to feel. Consummate indifference in the midst of chaos proved a wartime survival strategy. Septimus learned his lesson too well. Adopting a 'manly' posture of detached rationality, he embraced the widespread, socially acceptable madness of modern society. Like the mechanically marching soldiers admired by Peter Walsh, he was 'drugged into a stiff yet staring corpse' (p. 77).

In his messianic mission, Septimus now preaches universal love and environmental protection. His world is aflame with the presence of God. He hallucinates a literal engulfment by vegetative life, gaping abysses and tongues of fire. The trees and leaves take root in his body, shredding the skin and leaving sensitive nerve-endings exposed on a rock. The visionary madman is endowed with a mystical sense of the divine animation of nature. He communicates with the birds and trees, but feels powerless to transmit his 'dehumanized' message to his fellow men and women. Like Christ or Apollo, he suffers the ostracism of a divine prophet, 'the scapegoat, the eternal sufferer' (p. 37).

Tracked down by human nature, that 'repulsive brute' with 'blood-red nostrils' (p. 139), Septimus feels like a trapped animal who has no choice but to sacrifice his body to save the privacy of his soul. The pack will devour him, just as the Bacchae consumed Pentheus. Septimus preserves his autonomy in a final, wilful act of self-destruction. He is the Christ-figure sacrificed for the sins of mankind – for cruelty, egotism and authoritarian brutality. A victim of the Great War, he is doomed to expiate the sins of the grey-haired men in Whitehall who sentenced him to battle.

Septimus is sane in his insanity, lucid in his vision. Despite the growing pressure of hallucination, he has a clear recognition of the enemies that seek to curtail his freedom and lock him up as a prisoner down in Surrey. He refuses to submit to the demonic authority represented by Holmes and Bradshaw. Despising the emissaries of patriarchal institutions, he abjures the responsibility of fatherhood and will not collude in the perpetuation of a corrupt and brutal society. He abdicates his 'manly' role as husband and father by a sexual rejection of his wife.[22] Rezia treasures the Mediterranean ideal of home and family and desperately wants 'a son like Septimus' (p. 134). 'She could not grow old and have no children!' (p. 136). But Septimus is convinced that 'love between man and woman was repulsive to Shakespeare. The business of copulation was filth to him before the end' (p. 134). He turns a deaf ear on Holmes's platitudes about marriage and 'duty to one's wife' (p. 139).

Rezia feels shunned and rejected by Septimus, whose madness she interprets as petulant behaviour. In her diary, Woolf acknowledges Lydia Lopokova as 'a type for Rezia' and on one occasion addresses Lydia as 'Rezia' by mistake.[23] As the foreign-born wife of John Maynard Keynes, Lydia Lopokova felt somewhat confused by her husband's homosexual preferences. In making Lydia the prototype for Rezia, 'simple, instinctive, childless',[24] Woolf subtly suggests a homosexual attraction between Septimus and Evans – an affection sublimated in the ingenuous metaphor of two romping dogs. Evans's death released Septimus from the threat of homosexual consummation. But the spectre of Evans returning from Thessaly may elicit in Septimus profound guilt over a suppressed desire for Greek love.

It is significant that Septimus experiences one of his last moments of joy when he helps Rezia design Mrs Peters's hat. Taking up his wife's craft, he revels in the feminine art of sewing an aesthetically pleasing and useful design. As he helps Rezia fashion the hat, he freely admits the 'female' side of his nature and assumes the androgynous aspect that might have made him lovable to Evans.

Before her husband's death, even Rezia Smith comes to realise that Holmes and Bradshaw have no right to say 'must' to Septimus. She determines to defy the magic medicine-men and to go with her husband to Bradshaw's sanitarium. Her decision comes too late; human nature has already appropriated its victim. But Septimus recognises and celebrates his wife's conversion. He sees her in the guise of a flowering tree, part of the vegetative world with which he can communicate: 'a miracle, a triumph, the last and greatest' (p. 224).

VI. THE PARTY: SACRIFICE AND REVELATION

Woolf declared in her notes for *Mrs Dalloway*, 'All must bear finally upon the party at the end; which expresses life, in every variety . . . while Septimus dies.'[25] Clarissa's party is analogous to the Catholic offering of the Mass, a ritual culminating in sacramental communion. Just as the Catholic Eucharist dramatically re-enacts the last supper shared by Christ with the Apostles, so Clarissa performs the Christological function of offering both physical and spiritual nourishment to those at her dinner-party. Like Christ, she feels that the guests literally feed on the vitality of their host. As she stands at the head of the stairs, flames of tension consume her body. She is planted like a rigid stake, immobilised on the cross of social mortification: 'Why seek pinnacles and stand drenched in fire? Might it consume her anyhow! Burn her to cinders! Better anything, better brandish one's torch and hurl it to earth than taper and dwindle away' (p. 255).

> The best rationale for Clarissa's parties resides in her own transcendental theory which, with her horror of death, allowed her to believe, or say that she believed (for all her scepticism), that since our apparitions, the part of us which appears, are so momentary compared with the other, the unseen part of us, which spreads wide, the unseen might survive, be recovered somehow attached to this person or that. (pp. 231–2).

If human beings survive through the people and places they have known, then parties constitute artistic acts that defy mortality. By bringing individuals together, Clarissa makes them 'immortal' for one another. She creates a scene that wrenches her guests from the dullness of habitual activity and serves as a stage for moments of heightened consciousness. Social pleasantries and trivial conversations belie the communal form that Clarissa imposes on the shape of reality. Her parties are delicate and evanescent in appearance, but beneath the surface, clamped together with bolts of steel. The interaction of personalities in ritual gesture establishes a lasting, collective relationship crystallised in bonds of joyful affiliation.

If Clarissa is a nun who preserves the monastic sanctity of the soul, her parties are a paean to life, a hymn to continuing existence. Her own moment of illumination is precipitated by the news of the death of Septimus, a young man who has hurled his torch to extinction. Though the two have never met, Clarissa feels that she understands his suffering and rebellion. She re-creates the moment of his fall and empathically identifies with the martyred scapegoat: 'Always her body went through it first, when she was told, suddenly, of an accident; her dress flamed, her body burnt. He had thrown himself from a window. Up had flashed the ground; through him, blundering, bruising, went the rusty spikes' (p. 280).

In the act of suicide, Septimus has preserved his autonomy, his idealism, and his spiritual freedom. Clarissa's own life has been battered and soiled by daily living, by the contamination of the 'world's slow stain'. Her ideals have been tempered, her beliefs eroded in the gradual process of adaptation and compromise. Yet the impulse to celebrate existence still runs through her and illuminates her presence: '[She had kept going.] She was alive.'[26]

Woolf declared in her holograph notes that Septimus 'feels that other people are engaged in living but that he is not. He must somehow see through human nature – see its hypocrisy, and insincerity, its power to recover from every wound, incapable of taking any final impression. His sense that this is not worth having. That only the best is worth while.'[27] Later Woolf writes, 'There must be a reality which is not in human beings at all. What about death for instance? But what is death? Strange if that were the reality.'[28] Similarly, Clarissa Dalloway speculates, 'A thing there was that mattered. . . . This he had preserved. Death was defiance. Death was an attempt to communicate' (p. 280). Clarissa, too, feels like a martyr, sacrificing herself for the momentary revelation made possible by her art. Consumed in flames, crucified by public criticism, she nevertheless returns to life like the Phoenix reborn out of the ashes of immolation.

Woolf adapts from Christianity the symbol of the virgin mother, the *mater dolorosa*, who laments the death of the murdered god but who, simultaneously, recognizes his martyrdom as a triumph and a transfiguration. In the guise of blessed mother and high priestess, Clarissa celebrates Septimus's offering. And, as pagan fertility goddess, she accepts the sacrifice, thereby displacing the father God of the Judaeo-Christian tradition.[29]

Septimus has chosen one way to preserve his soul untrammelled. Clarissa learns another from the old woman she sees going to bed next door. The woman seems ageless, an eternal figure of the female spirit sheltered by houses, rooms, distances and solitude. She is emblematic of the feminine life-force that endures and creates. Her image recalls the phantom of Clarissa's mother, a benevolent spirit present throughout the novel in the mode of absence. Like a mother mourning the loss of a son in battle, Clarissa returns to the party after absorbing, interpreting and assimilating the meaning of Septimus's death. Understanding the precious and unique gift of life, she is ready to offer her guests the illumination that will transfigure the gathering into a beatified communion of saints.[30] She serves as an agent of art and social affiliation, creative modes of survival in the midst of tragic absurdity. *Mrs Dalloway* ends with an epiphany – a revelation, not of God, but of the divinity present in every human being, summed up in the moment by the radiant presence of Clarissa: 'For there she was' (p. 296).[31]

NOTES

1. As Jane Marcus points out, contemporary 'readers have been led to believe that Virginia Woolf's acute sex and class consciousness derived from a Victorian virginal and "ladylike" misunderstanding of politics (Leavis, Forster, Bell) or, more recently, were part of her "madness". But Woolf's socialism and feminism were very much a response to nineteenth- and twentieth-century experience' – ' "No More Horses": Virginia Woolf on Art and Propaganda', *Women's Studies*, IV, nos 2–3 (1977) 269–70. Marcus explains that 'Woolf's socialism was part of a serious intellectual stance which incorporated pacifism as well as feminism. Woolf writes in the tradition of Wollstonecraft, Olive Schreiner and Sylvia Pankhurst' – 'Middlebrow Marxism: *Mrs Dalloway* and the Masses', *Virginia Woolf Miscellany*, Spring–Summer 1976, p. 4. I am greatly indebted to Jane Marcus for her generous advice and editorial assistance in the composition of this essay.
2. See Alex Zwerdling, 'Mrs. Dalloway and the Social System', *PMLA*, XCII (1977) 69, for a discussion of politics and social class in the novel.
3. Virginia Woolf, *Mrs Dalloway* holograph notes, 9 Nov 1922, in the Berg Collection of the New York Public Library.
4. Ibid., 9 Nov 1922 – 2 Aug 1923, and *Choephori* notes, Jan 1907, in the Berg Collection of the New York Public Library.
5. See, for instance, Woolf's diary entry for 14 Oct 1922: 'I must get on with my reading for the Greek chapter. I shall finish the Prime Minister in another week. . . . I must now concentrate on Essays: with some Aeschylus' – *The Diary of Virginia Woolf*, vol. II: *1920–24*, ed. Anne Olivier Bell (New York: Harcourt, Brace, Jovanovich, 1978) p. 208.

6. Virginia Woolf, *Mrs Dalloway* holograph notes, 19 Nov 1922. Jane Marcus has suggested that Woolf's elevation of 'the role of the chorus in the modern novel to its position in Greek drama . . . was the aesthetic equivalent of a revolutionary political act, a socialist's demonstration of faith in the people' – '*The Years* as Greek Drama, Domestic Novel, and Götterdämmerung', *Bulletin of the New York Public Library*, Winter 1977, p. 279.
7. As Avrom Fleishman explains in *Virginia Woolf: A Critical Reading* (Baltimore: Johns Hopkins University Press, 1975) p. 77, 'Woolf deepens her portrait of the outsider by relating him to the archetype of the scapegoat, which has traditionally accompanied the communal ideal. By the exclusion, sacrifice, or crucifixion of one of its members the group establishes or reaffirms its own organic ties.'
8. Raised in an atheistic environment, Virginia Stephen entertained fairly vague notions of Christianity. She once believed that Christmas was the celebration of the Crucifixion, and her misconception so amused the rest of the family that it earned her the nickname of 'Goat'. Nevertheless, Woolf's overt use of Christian symbolism in her novels may have constituted a tacit rebellion against an atheistic scepticism she associated with patriarchal intolerance. She witnessed considerable hostility between her father, Sir Leslie Stephen, and his sister Caroline Emilia. In her letters, Woolf refers to Aunt Caroline as the 'Nun' and the 'quacking Quaker'. But she also reports intense conversations with her aunt on the subject of mystical experience: 'We talked for some nine hours; and she poured forth all her spiritual experiences. . . . All her life she has been listening to inner voices, and talking with spirits: and she is like a person who sees ghosts, or rather disembodied souls, instead of bodies' – *The Flight of the Mind: The Letters of Virginia Woolf*, vol. I: *1888–1912*, ed. Nigel Nicolson and Joanne Trautmann (New York: Harcourt, Brace, Jovanovich, 1975) p. 229. It seems possible that Caroline Stephen, author of *The Light Arising: Thoughts on the Central Radiance*, may have inspired Woolf's life-long interest in the religious and 'mystical' dimensions of reality.
9. See Emily Jensen's 'Clarissa Dalloway's Respectable Suicide' in *New Feminist Essays on Virginia Woolf*, vol. II; and Avrom Fleishman's *Virginia Woolf: A Critical Reading*.
10. Mrs Dalloway thinks about 'the contagion of the world's slow stain', a phrase from Shelley's *Adonais*, in 'Mrs. Dalloway in Bond Street' – Virginia Woolf, *Mrs Dalloway's Party* (1923; rpt. New York: Harcourt, Brace, Jovanovich, 1973) p. 22. See also Jean M. Wyatt, '*Mrs Dalloway*: Literary Allusion as Structural Metaphor', *PMLA*, LXXXVIII (1973) 450–1.
11. Jane Marcus calls our attention to the fact that Woolf was strongly influenced by the writings of the classical scholar Jane Ellen Harrison, whose 'work was an attempt to lay bare the matriarchal origins of pre-classical Greek thought'. Harrison indicted Zeus as an 'archpatriarchal *bourgeois*' – '*The Years* as Greek Drama', in *Bulletin of the New York Public Library*, Winter 1977, p. 277n.
12. Virginia Woolf, *Mrs Dalloway* (New York: Harcourt, Brace and World,

1925) p. 185. Page references in the text are to this edition.

13. Virginia Woolf, *Three Guineas* (New York: Harcourt, Brace and World, 1938) p. 97. Further references are to this edition, cited as *TG*.

14. Virginia Woolf, *Jacob's Room* holograph notebook, in the Berg Collection of the New York Public Library, p. 132.

15. Woolf, *Mrs Dalloway* holograph notes, 22 July 1923.

16. Woolf, *Mrs Dalloway* fragments, 7 Jan 1924, in the Berg Collection of the New York Public Library, p. 153. Brackets indicate passages deleted in the final manuscript.

17. Woolf, *Mrs Dalloway* holograph notes, 18 June 1923.

18. Woolf, *Mrs Dalloway* fragments, 7 Jan 1924, pp. 153, 159.

19. Woolf, *Mrs Dalloway* holograph notes, 19 Nov 1922.

20. Woolf, *Diary*, vol. II, pp. 311, 325.

21. For further discussion, see Phyllis Rose, *Woman of Letters: A Life of Virginia Woolf* (New York: Oxford University Press, 1978) ch. 7.

22. In 'Middlebrow Marxism' (*Virginia Woolf Miscellany*, Spring–Summer 1976) Jane Marcus suggests that Septimus Smith's principal 'social sin' against the British Empire is his refusal to father a child. 'Septimus is indeed alienated, from a patriarchal as well as imperialist and capitalist state. . . . Because he cannot conform to that state's concept of masculinity, money and power, he, like many scapegoats, punishes himself. He is not a homosexual but a repressed homosexual. It is the repression of his love for Evans which causes his guilt at his failure to feel' (p. 5).

23. Woolf, *Diary*, vol. II, pp. 265, 272.

24. Woolf, *Mrs Dalloway* holograph notes, 9 Nov 1922.

25. Ibid.

26. Woolf, *Mrs Dalloway* fragments, 7 Jan 1924, p. 153.

27. Woolf, *Mrs Dalloway* holograph notes, 22 July 1923.

28. Ibid., 2 Aug 1923.

29. We might again recall the influence of Woolf's mentor, Jane Ellen Harrison: 'Pre-classical Greece, in Jane Harrison's recreation of it, shows woman as a splendid spiritual source of society's rituals of breaking apart and coming together, of "natural" time and the death and rebirth of the Year-Spirit' – Marcus, '*The Years* as Greek Drama', in *Bulletin of the New York Public Library*, Winter 1977, p. 279.

30. In an article entitled 'Virginia Woolf's All Souls' Day', J. Hillis Miller identifies the mysterious song of the female beggar in *Mrs Dalloway* as Richard Strauss's 'Aller Seelen', a lament in which a bereaved woman imagines meeting her dead lover on All Souls' Day, the 'day of a collective resurrection of spirits. . . . Like Strauss's song, *Mrs. Dalloway* has the form of an All Souls' Day in which Peter Walsh, Sally Seton, and the rest rise from the dead to come to Clarissa's party' – *The Shaken Realist*, ed. Melvin J. Friedman and John B. Vickery (Baton Rouge: Louisiana State University Press, 1970) p. 115. The Catholic liturgy for All Souls' Day is devoted to the salvation of those who suffer the cathartic fires of purgatory. We might extend the analogy further, however. If Clarissa's party is indeed eucharistic, then her guests from the purgatorial past are symbolically sanctified by the gathering. Cognisant of a divine, epiphanic presence, they witness a 'beatific vision'

and become members of the heavenly communion of saints.
31. For a Heideggerian analysis of this final epiphany, see Lucio P. Rutolo, *Six Existential Heroes* (Cambridge, Mass.: Harvard University Press, 1973) ch. 1: 'Clarissa Dalloway'.

7 Where the Spear Plants Grew: the Ramsays' Marriage in *To the Lighthouse*

JANE LILIENFELD

> They had reached the gap between two clumps of red-hot pokers. . . . No, they could not share that; they could not say that. . . . They turned away from the view, and began to walk up the path where the silver-green spear like plants grew, arm in arm. His arm was almost like a young man's arm, Mrs. Ramsay thought, thin and hard, and she thought with delight how strong he still was, though he was over sixty, and how untamed and optimistic . . . .[1]

Virginia Woolf projects the Ramsays' relation onto the landscape throughout *To the Lighthouse*. Here we see that the Ramsays' marriage, based on love, has imperfections like the hedge.[2] To associate them in this way with the rootedness of Mrs Ramsay's garden might confuse us as to the soil of their union. Is their relation, so embedded in the flux of the waters, the hills of the land, a perception of certain eternally true modes of male–female union?

The beautiful Mrs Ramsay, appearing to be magnanimity robed in charm and grace, has captivated scores of readers. One group, well-represented by Bernard Blackstone,[3] David Daiches,[4] Lord David Cecil[5] and Roger Poole[6] sees her as the motherly, all-giving Angel in the House. To these critics, she has no flaws and is thus unable to ward off harrassment by her desiccated husband, to whom she lovingly sacrifices herself.

Opposition to this idealised view was first ventured by Glenn Pedersen[7] and Mitchell Leaska.[8] They find that Mrs Ramsay – feather-brained self-satisfied manipulator – is actually the reason for her husband's unhappiness and her son's failure to reach the lighthouse.

These diametrically opposed views depend on a common perception: all assume the Ramsays' marriage is the eternal union of the masculine and feminine principle. The masculine principle, seen by James Ramsay as 'the arid scimitar of the male', 'bitter and barren', must, in this view, of necessity draw sustenance from the female principle, the 'leafy voluptuousness', of the wife–mother's self-sacrificing love. It is indeed surprising that Virginia Woolf, outspoken as a feminist, known to object to traditional views of sex roles, should be seen to have created a novel celebrating their unquestioned existence.

She did not, of course. Woolf's vision of the Ramsays' marriage is a mature, sharp critical examination not only of the relations between her own parents,[9] but also of the destruction wreaked by the Victorian social arrangement on human capacities for freedom and growth. Woolf offers alternatives, for the very women Mrs Ramsay urged to 'marry, marry, marry' explode the prison represented by the Ramsays' relation and turn her prescriptions into their critical opposites, thus making Part III of the novel a re-evaluation by the 1920s of their Victorian predecessors. Using the tools of feminist criticism, this essay will examine in detail Woolf's vision of the Ramsays' marriage, proving that as she celebrates and criticises it she makes clear the urgency for creating new modes of human love and partnership. I shall show that the Ramsays' marriage is time-bound, founded on middle-class Victorian roles and values. Arguments that the family as structured by the patriarchy is the bulwark of morality, the state and stable human character have not changed much since the 1850s.[10] It is this ideological persuasion about patriarchal marriage that underlies most criticism of the marriage in *To the Lighthouse* and obscures Woolf's point that the Ramsays' marriage is debilitating to both parties.

In order to examine the framework of the Ramsays' marriage, it is necessary to make explicit Woolf's hints about the novel's time scheme. Part III takes place in 1919 as the Great War has ended; in it Mr Ramsay tells Macalister that he is seventy-one. Since Mr Ramsay was over sixty in Part I, we know that Part II covers ten years, making Part I occur in 1909. Since Prue is eighteen in Part I, the Ramsays must have been married at least nineteen years, having married about 1889 or earlier. Thus we can argue that the Ramsays had been raised in the England of the 1860s, a time of momentous intellectual turmoil.

Burns's historical analysis of mid-Victorian England[11] reveals that underneath the staid and increasing prosperity of the Victorian middle classes were festering issues. One of these, women's inequity before the law, was fiercely protested. The 1860s saw Emily Davies and her sisters organise the assault on the male colleges of Cambridge that finally, in 1948, enabled women to have full rights there. Barbara Leigh Smith Bodichon's committee kept the issue of women's legal rights before the public for decades, and was victorious in the passing of the Married Woman's Property Act of 1882, the year of Woolf's birth. A strong buttress of this protest was John Stuart Mill's urging of women's suffrage in his 1866 Parliamentary Bill, and in his publication in 1869 of *The Subjection of Women*.[12]

Growing out of this mid-Victorian revolt were the arguments of the 1880s advocating marriage reform, the widening of women's roles, political action for women, and an end to sex-role imprisonment for men as well as women.[13] This feminist activity had its theoretical underpinnings in social theories of character and family structure. The Victorians invented the idea that culture itself was relative,[14] and out of this fertile soil grew protests such as Morgan's, Engel's and Westermarck's that 'human sexual arrangements'[15] were not eternal, natural law, nor ordained by God. Engels saw that men had enslaved women socially, legally and politically, and on their bent backs had invented patriarchal rule.[16] He urged revolutionary change in patterns of ownership, the family and the state.

Attacks even less extreme than Engels's horrified and frightened traditional upholders of the *status quo*. Leslie Stephen, the original of Mr Ramsay, was typical of speakers for the tradition. To him, the family was both the crystalline form of all cultural bonding and the specific mode of order imposed on civilisation.

Stephen's statements in 'Forgotten Benefactors' and *The Science of Ethics*[17] reveal fears that the reforms saluted by Engels and others were aimed at the underpinning of his own house. To Stephen it was natural law that a wife should have no legal rights, no right to her own property or money, no training for any job, nor any hope of obtaining one. Though he bound Julia Stephen tightly, she resisted covertly.[18] This resistance he met with the emotional blackmail to which he admitted in *The Mausoleum Book*.[19] But the daughters of Leslie and Julia Stephen were keen observers, and their mother's maintaining of her selfhood and the revolutionary theories of women's new chances filtering down in the culture were not lost on them. They smashed the patriarchal superstructure of marriage as Leslie Stephen enforced it, and reworked the emotional mode of the marriage bond. In it they encompassed friendship, artistic alliance and sisterhood.[20] Part of the history of this struggle lies in the argument of *To the Lighthouse*.

In order to buttress male control of the actual world, Victorians developed an ideology of women's limited potential; this in turn justified the very narrow opportunities for mental vigour allowed the Victorian middle-class woman. Mrs Sarah Stickeney Ellis's idealised marriage and conduct books insist on the strictly circumscribed family role allowed such women, and are a running commentary on Mrs Ramsay's behaviour.[21]

In her marriage manual *The Wives of England: Their Relative Duties, Domestic Influence, and Social Obligations*, Mrs Ellis insists that wives are by nature inferior to husbands:

[You should remember] the superiority of your husband simply as a man. It is quite possible that you may have talent, with higher attainments, and you may also have been generally more admired, but this has nothing whatever to do with your position as a woman, which is, and must be, inferior to his as a man.[22]

It is quite clear that Mr Ramsay's behaviour is based on this assumption, but not so clear that Mrs Ramsay agrees with it.

Mrs Ellis's admonitions about women's constitutional and behavioural inferiority were the superstructure of women's whole training. In the family girls were a poor second to their brothers, who went off to public school and then university while the girls stayed at home to be tutored by 'a little woman with a red nose who is not well educated herself but has an invalid mother to support'.[23] Virginia and Vanessa Stephen remained home while Thoby and Adrian Stephen went to school, and their inferior education, much like Mrs Ramsay's, paid for 'Arthur's Education Fund'.[24]

Wittily agreeing with Mrs Ellis, John Ruskin in his famous lecture of 1865, 'Of Queens's Gardens', admonished, 'It is not the object of education to turn woman into a dictionary.'[25] Ruskin joins Mrs Ellis in insisting that woman must accept God's law as laid down by man: she may be polished, but she is not to be critical; she may be beautiful, but should not be argumentative. So educated, it is no wonder that Mrs Ramsay has no systematic grasp of facts or the practice to shape them into logical structures. Mill uneasily admitted that middle-class women were badly crippled by their narrow education and even narrower prospects: women saw no overarching theoretical principles, no truth, but only the particulars of the moment.[26] So circumscribed, their minds were in the state of 'an educated Elizabethan woman's'.[27]

Mrs Ramsay's training has the desired effect. While she is not as stupid as her husband needs to think her in order to buttress his own self-worth, Mrs Ramsay is frightened of her own potential for intellectual achievement. 'Books, she thought, grew of themselves. She never had time to read them' (I, v, p. 43). Watching her read a sonnet, her husband 'wondered what she was reading, and exaggerated her ignorance, her simplicity, for he liked to think she was not clever, not book-learned at all. He wondered if she understood what she reading. Probably not, he thought. She was astonishingly beautiful' (I, xix, p. 182). Mrs Ramsay's indirect interior monologue illuminates Mill's and Woolf's realisation that the stupider the wife appears to the husband, the more desirable she becomes.[28] To make the wife so childlike intellectually that she must remain emotionally dependent was the object of her education and upbringing.

What did it all mean? To this day she had no notion. A square root? What was that? Her sons knew. She leant on them; on cubes and square roots; that was what they were talking about now; . . . she let it uphold and sustain her, this admirable fabric of the masculine intelligence, which ran up and down, crossed this way, and that, like iron girders spanning the swaying fabric, upholding the world so that she could trust herself to it utterly, even shut her eyes or flicker them, for a moment, as a child. . . .

(I, xvii, p. 159)

The swaying fabric which sustained also entrapped. Mr Ramsay's rational constructs depend on the ideology of Mrs Ramsay's limited sphere.[29] Cam uncritically recognises that her father 'liked men to work like that [as fishermen in danger of drowning] and women to keep house, and sit beside sleeping children indoors' (III, iv, p. 245). Because she has partially given her assent to Mr Ramsay's division of the world into the masculine and feminine sphere, Mrs Ramsay is thus a prisoner of the drawing room.

According to Mrs Ellis, one prisoner of the drawing room should help another: 'In every mistress of a family, the poor in every neighbourhood should feel they have a friend.'[30] To them the wife should give not merely money, but also 'a few useful hints on the best methods of employing scanty means'.[31] Perhaps without the condescension of Mrs Ellis, Julia Stephen had entered the lives of the poor in St Ives, Cornwall. Her efforts resulted in the regular employment of a nurse in the town, and many were made more comfortable by her in the poor homes of the fishing village.[32] Fully aware of the limitations of this ideology which squandered women's energy on sustaining a *status quo* dangerous both for the visiting women and for the poor trapped in the structures of a *laissez-faire* economy, Virginia Woolf reminds us that Mrs Ramsay

visited this widow or that struggling wife in person with a bag on her arm, and a notebook and a pencil with which she wrote down in columns carefully ruled for that purpose wages and spending, employment and unemployment, in the hopes that she would one day cease to be a private woman whose charity was half a sop to her own indignation, half a relief to her curiosity, and become what with her untrained mind she greatly admired, an investigator, elucidating the social problem. (I, i, pp. 17–18)

Mrs Ramsay is here on her way to the vision her adopted daughters live out: one must take action to improve the lives of women shackled to the domestic sphere. In this passage lies an implicit sisterhood which impels Mrs Ramsay towards struggling wives, towards the best in Minta Doyle and Lily Briscoe.

Mrs Ramsay's service to others begins with her self-sacrifice to her husband and children.[33] Explaining this entrapment and its seeming acceptance by so many women, Mill points out 'Women are brought up from earliest years ... to live for others, to make complete a negation of themselves, and to have no life but in their affections.'[34] These affections must be severely restrained by the marriage bond.[35] 'Only in the married state can the boundless capabilities of woman's love ever be fully known or appreciated.'[36] Engels saw clearly that, unless women's passions were simultaneously denied and curtailed, patriarchal descent might be endangered.[37]

Giving oneself fully to one's husband, Mrs Ellis argues, is the wife's first duty. The 'master of the house should be considered as entitled to the choice of every personal indulgence'.[38] 'It is unquestionably the right of all men (no matter their character or position) to be treated with deference and made much of in their own homes.'[39] 'The great business of [a married woman's] life is to soothe and to cheer, not to depress, to weary, or to annoy.'[40] According to Mrs Ellis, this angel did not require anything beyond the good done by her self-abnegation.[41] For, 'if the wife can thus supply to the extent of [her husband's] utmost wishes, the sympathy, the advice, the confidence, and the repose, of which he is in need, she will have little cause to think herself unfulfilled'.[42] To many critics, the Ramsays' marriage could not conform more nearly to the ideal praised by Ruskin, Mrs Ellis and Leslie Stephen.

Virginia Woolf makes it clear that Mrs Ramsay does not agree. The sequestered wife's unconscious anger at her position shapes her behaviour, as for example in I, vi and vii, the argument about going to the lighthouse. Mr Ramsay is infuriated by Mrs Ramsay's comforting James and saying the winds might change. He stamps his foot and says, 'Damn you' (I, vi, p. 50), enraged at 'the extraordinary irrationality. ... The folly of women's minds'. It is, of course, this very irrationality in sustenance of which women are denied any intellectual training.

After Mr Ramsay's chastened apology, Mrs Ramsay ruminates on her submission to her family and her self-abnegation

> They came to her *naturally since she was a woman*, all day long with this and that; one wanting this, another that; the children were growing up; she often felt she was nothing but a sponge sopped full of human emotions. Then he said, Damn you. He said, It must rain. He said, It won't rain; and instantly a Heaven of security opened before her. There was nobody she reverenced as she reverenced him. She was not good enough to tie his shoe strings, she felt.
>
> (I, vi, p. 51; italics mine)

A woman striving for honesty, Mrs Ramsay nevertheless denies her fury. She finds the children's demands reasonable if exhausting, but cannot quite subdue herself over Mr Ramsay's argument, so strongly must she keep down anger. Mrs Ramsay's anger explodes into an excessive paean of devotion. Typical Victorian hypocrisy, idealisation and a refusal to admit and work through anger are the bases of much of the Ramsays' interaction, for Mr Ramsay, like his wife, is forced to lie, conceal, submit.

Seeing his wife silent in her garden, Mr Ramsay resents her separateness from him, then thinks, 'he would have been a beast and a cur to wish a single thing altered' (I, xii, p. 106). No, he would have been a normal human being. Could he have admitted some of his less mature feelings to his wife, he might not have needed to exact from her so much support. He seeks to answer his wife's 'half teasing, half complaining' remark that their marriage interfered with his work: 'He was not complaining, he said. She knew that he did not complain. She knew that he had nothing to complain of' (I, xii, pp. 106–7). Seizing and kissing his wife's hand, Mr Ramsay's beautiful gesture brings tears to her eyes. But to deflect attention to their passionate attachment or to the Victorian myth of women's holiness does not blot out the fact that he does sometimes regret his marriage and feel as trapped by it as she does.

Because she has felt so angry, Mrs Ramsay gives even more of herself when Mr Ramsay comes again to her in I, vii. Still vulnerable from his fantasies of intellectual struggle, Mr Ramsay appears, and Mrs Ramsay, in James's view, seems 'to pour erect into the air a rain of energy, a column of spray', while she is simultaneously alight, 'burning and illuminating'; into 'this delicious fecundity, this fountain and spray of life, the fatal sterility of the male plunged itself, like a beak of brass, barren and bare' (I, vii, p. 58). The imagery makes clear that this is James' point of view.[43] To James his father is 'lean as a knife, narrow as the blade of one' (I, i, p. 10), a good image of James's fear and hatred of his father's power over his mother. James watches his father displace him as he stands erect between his mother's legs.

Like James, Mr Ramsay wants nothing less than to be 'assured that he too lived within the heart of life; was needed; not only here, but all over the world' (I, vii, p. 59). Mrs Ramsay, upright in her gray skirt, gives off the light of the lighthouse to her husband (ibid).[44] There is sexual invitation in her dancing fire. Their home is her body, and she bids Mr Ramsay roam it with the rhythms of intercourse (I, vii, p. 59–60).

James, enraged, experiences himself as the trunk of the tree his mother offers to his father, and so feels attacked when his father plunges into his mother's body.[45] But James's image of rapacious plundering is very different from the joyous entering of rooms his mother offers his father, for her waving boughs of fruit deliberately entice the bird. As her husband finishes drinking sustenance from her, Mrs Ramsay experiences a relief as after orgasm, so that 'in exquisite abandonment to exhaustion' she feels throb through her 'the rapture of successful creation' (I, vii, p. 61).

The imagery makes clear that Mr Ramsay is simultaneously suckling at the breast and entering his wife. A good Victorian wife, Mrs Ramsay dares not discuss her husband's intellectual problems. Thus, rather than encouraging him to tell her in detail what he is so afraid of not having accomplished, she offers sustenance to her husband as 'a nurse' does to 'a fractious child' (I, vii, p. 60). Through her mode of sustaining him, she encourages his immaturity. But, honest and intelligent, Mrs Ramsay admits to herself the flaws in 'the rapture of successful creation'.

Mr Ramsay's self-questioning is so strong, and his inability to face it so large, that he accepts, even as does his wife, the limits of the marriage relation. The hedge is not just a signpost of his many past efforts, its leaves being written on with discarded words; it signals the barrier to the efforts he has made for the family situation: 'Years ago, before he had married . . . he had worked ten hours at a stretch. One could worry things out alone' (I, xii, p. 105). But now 'the father of eight children has no choice'. To look at 'the figure of his wife reading to his little boy, he turned from the sight of human ignorance . . . and the sea eating the ground we stand on, which had he been able to contemplate it fixedly might have led to something' (I, viii, p. 69). He lets family life obscure his view of truth, and so 'he had not done the thing he might have done' (I, viii, p. 70). Had he examined philosophically the very ground he stands on, he would, like the honest man he is, have been bound to admit its shortcomings.

But his wife on whom he stands examines the texture of their interchange. She admits her 'physical fatigue' is 'tinged'. So thorough was her training that the man is not to be questioned that 'she did not let herself put into words her dissatisfaction' (I, vi, p. 61). Yet she 'heared dully, ominously, a wave fall'. Mr Ramsay's demands have wrenched askew the 'iron girders' keeping her safe from the ocean's threat. The wave falls through her reading to her son the tale of 'The Fisherman and his Wife', which aptly suggests the price of concealing the flaws in the Ramsays' marriage. In the fairy tale, the fisherman's wife 'wills not as I'd have her will', he says to the flounder. Disgusted with his limited wishes, his wife says, 'if you won't be King, I will' (I, x, p. 87). Even so, Mrs Ramsay recognises her enjoyment of her kingly rights.

Mrs Ramsay, who 'did not like, even for a second, to feel finer than her husband', recognises how she ought to feel: 'Of the two he was infinitely more important, and what she gave the world, in comparison with what he gave, negligible' (I, vii, p. 62). Here she cannot admit that her unacknowledged power over Mr Ramsay gratifies her (ibid.). She must subdue herself, lie to her husband, keep her discontent from her children, and get along somehow with the worry that her husband's intellectual abilities are lessening as he ages (ibid.). It is an unfair bargain to each participant, this marriage relation.

John Stuart Mill understood such relations as the Ramsays':

> Women are schooled into suppressing [their aggressions] in their most natural and healthy direction, but the internal principle remains, in a different outward form. An active and energetic mind, if denied liberty, will seek for power; refused the command of itself, it will assert its personality by attempting to control others.... Where liberty cannot be hoped for and power can, power becomes the grand object of human desires.[46]

Mrs Ramsay manipulates Mr Ramsay by withholding herself from him as in I, xii and xix, but others she manipulates through ambition, aggression, and a desire for mastery.[47]

For example, she cannot look too closely at her matchmaking between Paul Rayley and Minta Doyle. 'And here she was, she reflected, feeling life rather sinister again, making Minta marry Paul . . .; she was driven on, too quickly she knew, almost as if it were an escape for her too, to say that people must marry; people must have children' (I, x, p. 203). Neither Minta nor Paul can resist her. Paul seems to feel it is to Mrs Ramsay he has proposed, 'because he felt somehow that she was the person who had made him do it' (I, xiv, pp. 118–19). Minta is more mysterious, though Mrs Ramsay does recall to mind a woman's accusations once of ' "robbing her of her daughter's affections".... Wishing to dominate, wishing to interfere, making people do what she wished – that was the charge against her, and she thought it most unjust' (I, x, p. 88).

A circumscribed Victorian woman, Mrs Ramsay has no direct power outside the domestic sphere. She can leave no mark upon the world other than her image in the lives of others. And it is a form of immortality she had wanted in matching Minta and Paul, for, as she climbs the stairs to the nursery, she thinks 'how, wound about in their hearts, however long they lived she would be woven' (I, xviii, p. 170).

Only over her children does she exert a mastery as over Paul and Minta, so it is just that Mrs Ramsay should doubly experience her claims to immortality as she climbs toward her last little ones in the nursery. 'She would have liked always to have a baby. She was happiest carrying one in her arms. Then people might say she was tyrannical, domineering, masterful, if they chose; she did not mind' (I, x, p. 90). 'The ideology of motherhood' is designed to keep women powerless, for the only power they are allowed in patriarchal society is their ambiguous hold on small children.[48] Though she may drain others of autonomy, Mrs Ramsay has no real power. And, though she may extend in imagination her own parents' furniture to Minta and Paul, it does not become the seat of the Rayleys' marriage.

The model of marriage which Mrs Ramsay wishes passed on to the young people is composed of many silences, many withholdings. Mrs Ramsay does not, for example, like her husband to see her thinking. In I, xii, during the walk in the garden, she asks what he had been thinking. 'He did not like to see her look so sad, he said. Only wool gathering, she protested, flushing a little. . . . No, they could not share that; they could not say that' (I, xii, p. 104). Mr Ramsay's reaction to this self-withholding is to remember his times of solitude before marriage. Mrs Ramsay does not want to be unguarded, as much for protection as from the self-restraint Mrs Ellis insisted on in wives, for 'the position of looking up to another is extremely unpropitious to complete sincerity and openness with him . . . there is an unconscious tendency to show . . . the side which is the one he likes most to see', as John Stuart Mill so perceptively named it.[49]

But Mrs Ramsay's silences always retain their ambiguous character. As much as she feels they could not share her philosophical sadnesses, she knows that in silence they speak. Her silence serves to insulate her against her husband, while it equally grants a medium in which to give herself to him in a manner both can accept.

Their sexual relation remains a hint swathed in silence.[50] Immediately after Mrs Ramsay refuses to share her thoughts about the lighthouse with her husband comes the passage with which this essay began. The couple turn from the gap in the hedge – their relations – and walk off arm in arm. Mrs Ramsay feels a sexual thrill of pride run through her as she admires the shape and firmness of her husband's arm (I, xii,

p. 107). Their physical closeness is indicated by such a trifle as 'she thought, intimating by a little pressure on his arm that he walked up hill too fast for her, and she must stop a moment' (I, xii, p. 108). They know through years of knowledge communicated through intimacy what their unspoken signals mean. That pressure speaks of a closeness which survives resentment, a physical respect for one another's pace which partly balances the reasons for the silence in which it unfolds.

A physical and emotional need draws the Ramsays together at the end of the day in Mr Ramsay's study. 'She had come to get something she wanted' (I, xix, p. 176), and 'He liked to think that everyone had taken themselves off and that he and she were alone' (I, xix, p. 181). Soon 'the shadow, the thing folding them in was beginning, she felt, to close round her. . . . Through the crepuscular walls of their intimacy, for they were drawing closer together, involuntarily coming side by side, quite close, she could feel his mind like a raised hand shadowing her mind' (I, xix, p. 184). This image intermingles 'the iron girders' of 'the swaying fabric' Mr Ramsay has built for his wife's insulation with something more threatening than comforting, implying as it does a force gathering to descend and swamp.

Mr Ramsay's pressure on his wife in the study is at once comforting and aggressive. She meets it with an equal aggression, a sensible reaction considering her circumscribed position. He asks with his eyes, she thinks, for her to tell him 'that she loves him'. Rather than do so, making excuses to herself about her inability to use language, Mrs Ramsay 'stood at the window with her reddish brown stocking in her hands, partly to turn away from him, partly because she remembered how beautiful it often is – the sea at night. . . . She knew he was thinking, You are more beautiful than ever. And she felt herself very beautiful' (I, xix, pp. 185–6). Women have through the centuries realised their concerns through exactly such indirect action, as Mrs Ramsay does by not telling her husband she loves him.

Her silence becomes physical rejection; instead of speaking, she turns her back on her husband and goes to the window to look at the sea. Now in touch with that element of herself which is the sea and the lighthouse, Mrs Ramsay is certain her husband knows she loves him. But what proof does she have of this? Not one word of this indirect interior monologue issues from him. The wife reassures herself that her behaviour means the same to both, but, in reality, from what does her happiness come? It surges through her very manipulations. Subtly, she gives him verbally an assurance of agreement, for she says the weather will prevent tomorrow's trip to the lighthouse. Mrs Ramsay's repetitions to herself of the words, 'he knew', similar to Mr Ramsay's earlier insistence that 'he was not complaining',[51] renders ambiguous what they assert. What he knows is that she has triumphed.

Is she aware of the ambiguity of her 'triumph' – that favourite word of hers? Mrs Ramsay has done what was expected of her; yet the way she has done so has altered the meaning of her behaviour. She has given in to her expected role, and appears to have subdued her will to that of her husband. But she has not poured out love in a romantic transcendence of barriers.[52] In fact, the romantic transcendence possible in this instance would mean that Mrs Ramsay is dominated by a husband to whom she gives every last part of herself, as Mrs Ellis suggested Victorian wives should do.[53] In resisting, Mrs Ramsay salvages that secret part of herself in touch with the lighthouse from which she draws the energy to continue in her demanding role. Yet she knows herself profoundly and powerfully tempting to her husband as she deliberately arrays herself, like the lighthouse, in her beauty against the night sky.

But, and this is the measure of Mrs Ramsay's sophistication, neither has lost completely. The Ramsays love one another, in spite of their private lies and manoeuvrings; they communicate very well in silence. Further, does Mr Ramsay want his wife to say she loves him? Perhaps his not saying so outright is equally indicative with her silence that both want certain barriers maintained.

In the economy of the novel, Mrs Ramsay's ascension into unattainability as 'The Window' closes, anticipates the loss which comes suddenly as Mrs Ramsay is snatched by death (II, iii, p. 194). A rejecting goddess even as she is just a Victorian housewife, reticent, glad to get a little power over her husband in what is a very unequal allotment, Mrs Ramsay in I, xix, pp. 185–6 merges again into the body of the black night and the

lighthouse tower, as she had earlier done in I, xi, pp. 95–7. In
I, xix, pp. 185–6, she is 'to the Lighthouse'. She faces her
husband; she is the lighthouse itself, and he is further
frustrated in his quest for R. Now unattainable, his wife is part
of that for which he has always striven.

Virginia Woolf's subtle vision of this marriage makes clear
that it contains unresolvable ambiguities. The Ramsays do
love one another; yet their marriage compromise restricts
growth, keeps each frustrated, and does not allow mature
intellectual interchange. If Mr Ramsay had been able to admit
his wife's great intelligence, he need not have faced his
intellectual fears alone. If he could have confided to her in
clear discourse the very problems he fantasises about, their
union would have enabled him to face his tasks and perhaps
have brought him closer to R. On the other hand, had Mrs
Ramsay had some direct say in the things closest to her
husband's heart, if she had had some access, too, to self-
fulfilment outside the limited domestic sphere, she would not
have insisted on her husband's dependence on her, nor
dominated Minta, Paul and Lily. For at the dinner party, when
she hears the conversation turn to the subject of artists'
immortality, she knows her husband's worst fears will be
activated. In a moment of openness she thinks, 'But she
wished it was not necessary [that she assign Minta to assuage
his fears]. Perhaps it was her fault that it was necessary' (I, xvii,
p. 162). It is partly her fault that he is dependent on her false
praise rather than capable of facing and dealing with his
hesitancies about his work. It is no wonder Mr Ramsay is
obsessed by his boots – he cannot walk further than the
garden in which his trapped wife encloses him. His needs
coalesce with her role restraints, and thus each is a lesser being
than together and separately they might have become. It is an
unfair bargain, finally, this marriage bond, and it needs to be
reformed.

The fact that the complexities of the Ramsay's marriage are
clear is a tribute to Woolf's power to deal in herself with very
deep and painful feelings. At the time of writing *To the
Lighthouse*, she admitted to being obsessed with her parents.
The most deeply felt and less verbally available rages and
losses Woolf formed into archetypal images and scenes, thus
conveying symbolically what psychoanalysts call 'primary

process feelings', those feelings we experience before we attain language, from the most primitive layers of the self and psyche.[54] On a more rational plane, Woolf showed a flawed marriage in so truthful a way that those who do not accept feminist views of the world have always found the Ramsays to be male and female traits personified, and their marriage the best way for role mates to live together.[55] The language of ambiguity in which the marriage is clothed, however, and the motivations which force each partner to compromise reveal that Woolf was criticising as well as remembering and creating. This criticism shapes the third section of the novel, where Lily Briscoe and Minta Doyle break free of Mrs Ramsay's impositions of her own role restraints on their lives.

Minta Rayley is present only in Lily's memory in part III, but Lily has thought through the dissolution of the Rayleys' marriage. It has become a partnership wherein each member lives a separate life. Minta accepts the fact that Paul has a mistress with whom he shares his political concerns. It is implied that Minta leads a full social and sexual life without Paul (III, v, pp. 257-8). That 'they were excellent friends, obviously' (III, v, p. 258) does not change the fact that this marriage flouts Mrs Ramsay's expectations for the couple she united. Mrs Ramsay had expected what Paul had fantasised about:

> The lights coming out suddenly one by one seemed like things that were going to happen to him – his marriage, his children, his house; and again he thought, as they came out on the high road, which was shaded with high bushes, how they would retreat into solitude together, and walk on and on, he always leading her, and she pressing close to his side (as she did now). (I, xiv, p. 118)

Paul here visualises a perfect Patriarchal marriage. The 'high bushes' refer back to the Ramsay's gaping hedge. The possessive pronouns which ring with such insistence remind one that Woolf had no illusions about what marriages like Paul's give the unaware male. In fact, Paul is much worse in this fantasy than Mr Ramsay ever is in reality, for Mr Ramsay loves his wife and regards her and his children as theirs, not as some possession solely under his domain. In a buried mark of sisterhood, even as Mrs Ramsay did not always follow where her husband directed, neither does Minta.

Minta's suggested promiscuity is a political action, for it is one way to transcend Victorian restraints on women as males' property. The imagery of garish red and gold in which Minta is always celebrated (III,v, pp. 257–8; I, xvii, p. 149) is highly sexual and in part III Minta is free to luxuriate in a power the Ramsays only discreetly expressed. Interestingly, Minta and Paul's companionship, and their acceptance of one another's intellectual and sexual freedom, could be based on Vanessa and Clive Bell's opening their marriage to include others by 1912.[56]

Mrs Ramsay has manipulated Minta but not vanquished her. Lily Briscoe, however, was in much more danger from Mrs Ramsay's expectations and manipulations than Minta. In some ways Lily Briscoe is the least powerful person in 'The Window', and thus is well chosen to represent the Ramsay girls, who are also powerless under their mother's dominion (I, i, p. 14). Unlike flaming Minta, Lily has no sexual resources to ease her relations with men. Nor are her dealings with Mrs Ramsay free of Lily's anxiety. So great is Lily's love for Mrs Ramsay that it sometimes makes her self-destructive. Under pressure of Mrs Ramsay's expectations in 'The Window', Lily is many times untrue to her feelings of right and wrong. For instance, she is forced to salve Mr Tansley's wounded feelings at the dinner party (I, xvii, pp. 137–8), and her relation with Mr Bankes, whom Lily likes and admires very much, is sometimes strained by her guilt over not wanting to follow Mrs Ramsay's wishes that she marry him.

But Lily Briscoe's complex resolution of her love for and dependence on Mrs Ramsay in part III is a psychological paradigm for women who seek autonomy. In Lily's moving beyond Mrs Ramsay's mode of behaviour we see a major transition in women's use of the power of selfhood, as the centre of power shifts away from the narrow scope of the home to the outer world of work and self-actualisation. Lily comes to cherish in herself powers different from those that motivate Mrs Ramsay. Sorting through her memories and feelings for the older woman in part III, criticising her and the men they had known in common, Lily disentangles herself from Mrs Ramsay's expectations for her in relation to these men, for Lily 'had never married, not even Mr. Bankes' (III, V, p. 260). Mourning Mrs Ramsay, Lily arrives at new ways of loving herself and others.[57]

Readers have long known what is now certain, that Lily Briscoe is an artistic surrogate for the author, and that Lily's formal task is analogous to Woolf's.[58] But as a woman Lily has generally been dismissed as a narrow, scared alternative to Mrs Ramsay; a poor dried-up spinster whose lack of social and sexual panache seriously harms her completeness as an adult, for this is the very way both Ramsay parents judge her (I, iii, p. 29; III, ii, p. 225). But at this moment in our culture we are questioning whether a Mrs Ramsay is the apogee of female development. It is clear now that Lily's refusal to marry, and her avoidance of heterosexuality as Mrs Ramsay had envisioned it, are not a failure to be womanly, for being womanly no longer means being defined by one's relations to men or to one's reproductive system.

Lily's interior union with Augustus Carmichael, (III, V, *passim*) and her friendship with Mr Bankes , (III, xii, p. 263) prepare her to deal with Mr Ramsay, to whom she turns at last (III, xiii, pp. 308–9). Accepting both the Ramsays as flawed but monumental human beings, no longer trapped into seeing them as all-encompassing archetypes, Lily Briscoe realises that her imaginings about their lives have ceased to imprison hers. She realises that she has rejected Mrs Ramsay's strictures about what is proper behaviour for 'real women', strictures that had crippled Lily's talent and prevented her from finishing her painting. Lily, as she puts the final stroke to her picture, can now accept her validity as a single woman, an artist whose power comes not from manipulating others' lives for fulfilment, but one whose mature vision encapsulates and transcends reality. Mrs Ramsay's mode is thus blasted apart, and the single woman and the married woman are each enabled to reach beyond the domestic sphere and the life and work of the husband or lover to act in the world of maturity and decision. Once Lily has become autonomous she can imagine walking beyond the spear plants in Mrs Ramsay's garden, 'not alone anymore but arm in arm with somebody', either man or woman.

NOTES

1. Virginia Woolf, *To the Lighthouse* (New York: Harcourt, Brace, 1927) I, xii, pp. 104–7. References in the text (by part, chapter and page) are to this edition.
2. Mitchell Leaska, *Virginia Woolf's Lighthouse: A Study in Critical Method* (New York: Columbia University Press, 1970) pp. 117–20; and his *The Novels of Virginia Woolf from Beginning to Ending* (New York: John Jay Press, 1977) pp. 151–2.
3. Bernard Blackstone, *Virginia Woolf: A Commentary* (New York: Harcourt, Brace, Jovanovich, 1969) p. 100.
4. David Daiches, *Virginia Woolf* (New York: New Directions, 1963) p. 86, for example.
5. Lord David Cecil, 'Virginia Woolf', *Poets and Story Tellers: A Book of Critical Essays* (London: Constable, 1949).
6. Roger Poole, in *The Unknown Virginia Woolf* (London: Cambridge University Press, 1978), not only finds that the Ramsays' and the Stephens' marriage were a blend of what we now recognise as the sex-role stereotypes of masculine and feminine, but also argues that this division into male and female modes of thought and spheres characterised the marriage of Leonard and Virginia Woolf. For his discussion of Mrs Ramsay as 'the female mind', see pp. 260–1.
7. Glenn Pedersenn, 'Vision in *To the Lighthouse*', *PMLA*, LXXIII (1958) 585–600.
8. Leaska, *Virginia Woolf's Lighthouse*, p. 120.
9. Virginia Woolf, 'A Sketch of the Past', *Moments of Being, Unpublished Autobiographical Writings*, ed. Jeanne Schulkind (Brighton, Sussex: University of Sussex Press, 1976) pp. 64–137. See also Sir Leslie Stephen's *Mausoleum Book*, ed. Alan Bell (Oxford: Clarendon Press, 1977).
10. Compare Lee Holcombe, 'Victorian Wives and Property: Reform of the Married Woman's Property Law, 1857–1882', in *A Widening Sphere: Changing Roles of Victorian Women*, ed. Martha Vicinus (Bloomington: Indiana University Press, 1977) p. 15, to Christopher Lasch, *Haven in a Heartless World: The Family Besieged* (New York: Basic Books, 1977) *passim*.
11. William L. Burns, *The Age of Equipoise* (New York: W. W. Norton, 1964).
12. On the agitation for the reform of women's education, see Rita McWilliams-Tulberg, 'Women and Degrees at Cambridge University, 1862–1897', in *A Widening Sphere*, pp. 117–45. For a discussion of women's legal situation, see Holcombe, ibid., pp. 3–28. See also John Stuart Mill, *The Subjection of Women* (1869), ed. Alice Rossi, in *Mill and Taylor, Essays on Sex Equality* (Chicago: University of Chicago Press, 1970).
13. Cf. Mona Caird, *Is Marriage a Failure?* and *The Morality of Marriage and Other Essays* (1897), to Mrs Sarah Stickney Ellis, *The Wives of England: Their Relative Duties, Domestic Influences, and Social Obligation* (New York: Appleton, 1843).

h

14. Walter Houghton, *The Victorian Frame of Mind* (New Haven, Conn.: Yale University Press, 1957) p. 179.
15. Frederick Engels, *The Origin of the Family, Private Property and the State*, ed. E. B. Leacock (New York: International Publishers, 1973), is based on the findings of the anthropologist Morgan.
16. Engels, *Family*, pp. 120–3. Socialist family theory, investigated by Engels in his insistence on the radical effect industrial capitalism had on family structure, is the basis of most feminist theory of the family: for example, of Annie Oakley, *Woman's Work: The Housewife, Past and Present* (New York: Vintage, 1976); and Nancy Chodorow, *The Reproduction of Mothering: Psychoanalysis and the Sociology of Gender* (Los Angeles and Berkeley, Calif.: University of California Press, 1978). This view is under intense debate among all schools of family theorists. Peter Lazlett, going beyond his earlier *The World We Have Lost* (New York: Charles Scribner's Sons, 1965), argues in his edition of *Household and Family in Past Time* (Cambridge: Cambridge University Press, 1972), that the family has always been nuclear – a very radical theory and a radical change from his earlier views (see *Household*, pp. 2–86, esp. p. 29). Disagreeing with Lazlett, Lawrence Stone, *The Family, Sex, and Marriage in England 1500–1800* (New York: Harper & Row, 1977) sets himself diametrically opposite Engels as well (see esp. pp. 661–2). These scholars have not emphasised or even remarked on a point their findings nevertheless make explicit: women have been second-class citizens to men in all traditional family arrangements across recorded time. For feminist criticism of patriarchal family theory see the superb article by R. Rapp, E. Ross and R. Bridenthal, 'Examining Family History', *Feminist Studies*, Spring 1979, pp. 174–200.
17. Leslie Stephen, *The Science of Ethics* (London: Smith and Elder, 1907) p. 128.
18. 'Jean Love finds Julia Stephen's nursing career a deliberate attempt on her part to get out of the house and away from her husband's and children's demands – demands she covertly encouraged and expected.' Personal communication, Harvena Richter.
19. Stephen, *Mausoleum*, pp. 57–65, esp. p. 60.
20. See, for example, Ellen Hawkes's essay in this volume, as well as Jane Marcus, 'Some Sources for *Between the Acts*', *Virginia Woolf Miscellany*, Spring 1977, pp. 1–3.
21. Ellis, *Wives*. See also William B. Mackenzie, *Married Life: Its Duties, Trials, Joys* (1852); John Maynard, *Matrimony, or, What Marriage Is, and How to Make the Best of It (1866);* and Mrs Beeton's *Book of Household Management*. Sarah Ellis writes so well, and is clearly so intelligent, one wishes she had been on the other side. It is illuminating to compare these books to such as *The Total Woman*, available today.
22. Ellis, *Wives*, 24–5.
23. Virginia Woolf, *Three Guineas* (New York: Harcourt, Brace and World, 1938) pp. 4–5.
24. Ibid.
25. John Ruskin, 'Of Queen's Gardens', in *Sesame and Lilies* (New York: Putnam's, n.d.) pp. 170–1.

26. Mill, *Women*, p. 190.
27. Virginia Woolf, *The Voyage Out* (London: Hogarth Press, 1965) p. 31.
28. Mill, *Women*, p. 142.
29. To socialists, such ideology keeps intact women's unpaid support of the family under industrialised capitalism. To feminists, such ideology prevents women from taking control of their own lives and from living separately from men if they so desire.
30. Ellis, *Wives*, p. 215.
31. Ibid., p. 213.
32. It was in upholding this fabric with its narrow lines and visiting the poor and sick that many of the most militant Victorian feminists understood from their work that Victorian economic horrors were indubitably interwined with women's oppression. As Ray Strachey puts it in a work Woolf knew (see *Three Guineas*, p. 148, n. 12), 'as they realized the evils of society, [they] grew dissatisfied with the powerlessness of their own sex, so that quite a short probation in this school [of "social work"] was enough to produce feminists by the score – *The Cause* (repr. Bath: Cedric Chivers, 1974) p. 88. Quentin Bell, in *Virginia Woolf: A Biography* (New York: Harcourt, Brace, Jovanovich, 1972) vol. I, p. 38, discusses Julia Stephen's nurturance as a force in all the lives she touched.
33. See Adrienne Rich, *Of Woman Born: Motherhood as Experience and Institution* (New York: W. W. Norton, 1976) for a full explanation of this. See also L. Blum, M. Homiak, J. Housman and N. Scheman, 'Altruism and Women's Oppression', eds C. Gould and M. Wartofsky, *Women and Philosophy: Toward a Theory of Liberation* (New York: Putnam's, 1976) pp. 222–47.
34. Mill, *Women*, p. 141.
35. Jill Conway, 'Stereotypes of Femininity in a Theory of Evolution', in *Suffer and Be Still*, ed. M. Vicinus (Bloomington: Indiana University Press, 1972) pp. 140–5.
36. Ellis, *Wives*, p. 111.
37. Engels, *Family*, pp. 120–3, and *passim*.
38. Ellis, *Wives*, p. 76.
39. Ibid., p. 67.
40. Ibid., p. 123.
41. Virginia Woolf later parodied the being whom Coventry Patmore – a close friend of Woolf's grandmother – and Mrs Ellis had enshrined as the Angel in the House.
42. Ellis, *Wives*, p. 117.
43. Leaska, *The Novels of Virginia Woolf*, p. 133.
44. See my '"The Deceptiveness of Beauty": Mother Love and Mother Hate in *To the Lighthouse*', *Twentieth Century Literature*, 23 Oct 1977, pp. 345–76, for a mythic interpretation of Mrs Ramsay.
45. According to Freud, children do imagine intercourse between parents as assaultive behaviour.
46. Mill, *Women*, p. 238.
47. Any reading of novels by Dickens, Trollope and Gaskell, or any opera by Gilbert and Sullivan, will show that married middle-class Victorian

women were expected to be matchmakers.
48. Blum *et al.*, in *Women and Philosophy*, p. 237. Chodorow, *The Reproduction of Mothering*, is a brilliant investigation of motherhood in patriarchy, as in Rich, *Of Woman Born*. See also Jane Flax, 'The Conflict Between Nurturance and Autonomy in Mother–Daughter Relations and within Feminism', *Feminist Studies*, 4, June 1978, pp. 171–89.
49. Mill, *Women*, p. 512.
50. Lytton Strachey found that *To the Lighthouse* had no sex in it. This disgusted him; see Michael Holroyd's biography (New York: Holt, Rinehart & Winston, 1968) vol. II, p. 531, n. 1.
51. See above, p. 155.
52. The romantic transcendence of barriers between selves Woolf found a novelist's convention, and rejected it in her first novel, *The Voyage Out*. This convention, to her, lied about love's complexity.
53. In *The Novels of Virginia Woolf*, pp. 122–5, and *Virginia Woolf's Lighthouse*, pp. 65–76, Leaska asks of Mrs Ramsay what Mrs Ellis asks of Victorian wives.
54. See my '"The Deceptiveness of Beauty"', in *Twentieth Century Literature*, Oct 1977, pp. 350–5; and also Helen Storm Corsa, 'Death, Mourning, and Transfiguration in *To the Lighthouse*', *Literature and Psychology*, XXI 3 Nov 1971, pp. 115–31, for a superb, albeit Freudian, reading of the movements of the unconscious in *To the Lighthouse*.
55. See Cecil, in *Poets and Story Tellers*; Blackstone, *Woolf: A Commentary*; and Daiches, *Virginia Woolf*.
56. Bell, *Woolf*, vol. II, p. 169.
57. See, for instance, Lily's maturity in helping Mr Ramsay stand on his own two feet, and use his boots, III, ii, pp. 229–30.
58. Thomas Vogler, *Twentieth Century Interpretations of 'To the Lighthouse'* (Englewood Cliffs, NJ: Prentice-Hall, 1970) pp. 10–13. On the last page of the holograph of *To the Lighthouse* in the Berg collection of the New York Public Library, Woolf has divided the page into thirds, even as Lily's painting is divided. Down these patches she has drawn a central line, as Lily does, to finish her painting. Psychic unity lies in that strong stroke.

8 Why is *Orlando* Difficult?

J. J. WILSON

Virginia Woolf asked this question, in real or feigned amazement, of Lady Cecil in a letter dated 28 October 1928.[1] Fifty
years after its first publication, people are still finding *Orlando*
difficult. So we know now that Lord Lascelles served as model
for the Archduchess Harriet, that 'Mar' was a term of
endearment used in the Sackville-West/Nicolson ménage, that
Volumnia Fox appears as a character in Marjorie Strachey's
Bloomsbury novel – this in-formation, at first leaked and now
flooding to us, fascinating as it all is, allows us to peek in the
keyholes without actually opening the doors to the author's
full intent and meaning.[2] It would seem, then, that *Orlando* is
not merely or mainly a *roman à clef*.

What is its genre? We get little help from the critics, who
generally avoid the issue by emphasising *Orlando*'s enigmatic
or idiosyncratic nature, as Jean Guiguet warns in his *Virginia
Woolf and Her Works*. They refuse to see it as 'an authentic
repository of the author's thought'. 'Brilliant but incongruous', says Mitchell Leaska, thus explaining its omission from
his *The Novels of Virginia Woolf: From Beginning to End*. Another
ambitiously titled book, *Feminism and Art*, seems almost to
overlook *Orlando*, a work one would think central to the topic.
James Naremore treats it out of sequence, with *Between the
Acts*, and thus misses the significance of its timing in Woolf's
development. A. D. Moody mutters, 'It would be difficult to
say at all simply what it is about', devoting to the task only half
a paragraph.[3]

Professors like to include *Orlando* on reading lists as a
kind of literary aphrodisiac for their unaroused students,
but, again, it is read for the wrong reasons, superficially, and
out of its context, and thus the book fizzles out, falls flat, and

is too easily dismissed as a *jeu d'esprit*, ice/escapade.

Literary context – yes, my key to Orlando is not the key to Vita's heart (though I thrill to that motive and motif in the book) nor even the key to Knole's 365 rooms (though I visited there recently and the guide called me 'the *Orlando* lady' because I kept recognising items from Woolf's inflated inventories[4]), but rather the well-worn, even old-fashioned, key of genre identification – not gender, mind you, but more simply literary labelling, description of the source, form and function of this kind of book as distinct from other books.

At this point, if I were having that conversation promised to Lady Cecil in the letter previously cited ('But I enjoyed writing it, and I should enjoy still more answering any questions about it, if put in person'), Virginia Woolf would, with a hoot of laughter, be telling me in her non-didactic, rapid, mellow voice that professors of literature were donkeys and Americans the most asinine of all. But that is the great advantage of genre analysis: one does not need to listen to the author's protestations, because genre designation, like that of gender, is *ex post facto*; the author cannot tell at the moment of conception what has been created.

Virginia Woolf admits to the unconscious nature of her work on the Ur-*Orlando*: '*Orlando* was the outcome of a perfectly definite, indeed overmastering impulse.'[5] 'I want to kick up my heels and be off.'[6] This permissive holiday mood led her to join a jolly band of literary vandals, or Robin Hoods at least, who roam the respectable world of letters in escape from the Mr Bennetts and in pursuit of the Mrs Browns. Let us eavesdrop on the animated conversation of these prophet–pariahs as they stride through the streets, full of carnival energy ('Trick or Treat') and literary theories:

A. I always considered novels as pretty frivolous productions; I finally found out that they were good for the vapours. . . . I wish we could find another name for the works of Richardson, which raise the spirit, touch the soul, spread everywhere the love of the good, and which we call also 'novels'.

B. Well, anyhow, I'm glad to be quit this time of writing 'a novel' and hope never to be accused of it again. . . . I have an idea that I will invent a new name for my books to supplant 'novel'. A new ——

A. One word, one gesture, have sometimes taught me more than the gossip of a whole town.

C. A dead donkey can be more instructive than a living philosopher. It is all a question of one's point of view.

B. Yes, one line of insight would have done more than all those lines of description; but let those pass as the necessary drudgery of the novelist. . . . But: is life like this? Must novels be like this?

C. Shall we for ever make new books, as apothecaries make new mixtures, by pouring out of one vessel into another? Are we for ever to be twisting and untwisting the same rope?

A. I want to renovate numerous areas . . . .

B. And I could revolutionise biography in a night! It's useless to repeat my old experiments; they must be new to be experiments.

D. I am like those creatures that cannot grow without successive metamorphoses.

C. I hate set dissertations!

B. For us those conventions are ruin; those tools are death.[7]

This exchange is made up of direct quotes from writers who, though separated by centuries, nationality, and so forth, clearly have a lot in common. I am not here trying to establish influence (though one could), but parallels, and, though I have picked my cast (the endnotes will sort them out for you) from the eighteenth and twentieth centuries, the membership can be traced back to the *epylliae* (mock epics), Chaucer's *Tale of Sir Thopas, Don Quixote*, much of Shakespeare and Rabelais, Austen's *Northanger Abbey*, Carlyle's *Sartor Resartus*, Mark Twain's *Connecticut Yankee in King Arthur's Court*, and many others which will occur to you as the criteria become clearer, which should happen whenever I can bring myself to stop writing dialogue and get down to the facts.

Even from the partial listing above, it can be seen that these works often have more in common with one another than they do with other books by their own authors. Indeed they belong to the same genre, cross-fertilising, identifiable, interdependent, and determining in form and content to a greater extent than one would think possible with such original, individualistic minds. This genre, or sub-genre, is called, for want of a better name, the 'anti-novel'.[8] A writer in order to join this mystic and, alas, mythic clan must have, aside from a natural tendency to anti-Petrarchanism, a proven mastery of the conventional novel form. An anti-novel is not usually the product of the first flush of youthful rebelliousness, but, as Woolf herself said, required 'a strong dose of the assurance of middle age'.[9] And of its regrets perhaps; they are all, being by nature rebels and outsiders, considerably bored and depressed by their own success. Here is a reconstruction of Diderot, writing to Sophie Volland of his mood at the crucial time:

Well now that last volume of the *Encyclopaedia* has finally been published, and I feel free to travel, to start all over again really. I've written two or three rather gay little works on my holiday, which I think you'll enjoy. . . . These pieces are so fantastical that I've felt perfectly safe in including lots of people we know, and part of the fun will be in your recognising them. Don't expect any straight narrative, however, or any straight answers. *Mes pensées sont mes catins*, and, as things in themselves are nothing, they have no real sweetness or bitterness, and our mind is what makes them what they are, I don't feel bound by any absolutes.

One might almost think him to be describing *Orlando*! Meanwhile (in the suspension of linear time or mere chronology) Virginia Woolf, who liked as we know to be a hare far ahead of those hounds the critics, is writing in her journal,

Yes, *To the Lighthouse* is almost too much of a success. And what to do now that that's done? I feel dull, stale, dutiful, can't think what to write next – indeed feel nearer suicide, seriously, than since 1913. . . . For the truth is I feel the need of an escapade after these serious poetic experimental books whose form is always so closely considered. Perhaps

Lytton is right and I should try a framework that will admit
of anything.... I want to embody all those innumerable
little ideas and tiny stories which flash into my mind at all
seasons. I think this will be great fun to write; and it will rest
my head before starting the very serious, mystical poetical
work which I want to come next. But what will it be?[10]

Not surprisingly, given this pronounced contempt for the
label and the limitations of the novel genre, both writers try to
eschew it in their next productions: *Orlando: A Biography*; 'Ceci
n'est pas un conte', protests Diderot – too much. Such is their
odi et amo relationship to fiction that they cannot leave it alone,
and so must write an anti-novel to free themselves of this
possession.

Abrams's *Glossary of Literary Terms* defines the anti-novel as a
work 'deliberately constructed in a negative fashion, relying
for its effects on omitting or annihilating traditional elements
of the novel, and on playing against the expectations established in the reader by the novelistic methods and conventions
of the past'.[11] Of course, anti-novels vary in many areas, but
nowhere so much as in degree. Some are nihilistic, some
revolutionary, some mere irresponsible vandalism, but the
anti-novel most true to the type we are here adumbrating is
mainly a declaration of independence. 'L'avant-garde c'est la
liberté', says Ionesco, and Elizabeth Bowen, in her afterword
to the Signet edition of *Orlando*, sees it as a necessary step for
Virginia Woolf in working free, a fantasy serving to shatter
some rigid, deadening mould of so-called 'actuality'. Or, as
put less temperately by Woolf in an article written the very
month of Orlando's conception, to come out against 'pose,
humbug, and solemnity'.[12]

The basic nature of the anti-novel is utopian and the satire
of literary conventions is closely related to a criticism of all
conventions. In a pluralistic society, forms provide a means of
evaluating reality; they can reveal and even renovate our ways
of seeing, challenge our temporary philosophical and
psychological equilibriums. Anti-novelists are anti-librium.
They are against not form, but formula, lashing out at all
empty observances of convention, uninspired recordings,
euphemism, 'False compare', affectation, discrepancies between appearance and reality, and so on. No wonder they so

often have recourse to the comic muse, that traditionally effective enemy of cant. And as comedy can lead to clarification through release, even to that beneficial catastasis, or reordering of concerns, the anti-novel can be an important experience in the novelists' development and, they hope, in their readers' too.[13]

Yes, the *hypocrite lecteur* is invariably taken to task by the anti-novelist on a rampage, and in *Tristram Shandy* the author is quite stern with one lady, making her go back and reread an entire chapter: 'Tis to rebuke a vicious taste which has crept into thousands besides herself, – of reading straight forwards, more in quest of the adventures, than of the deep erudition and knowledge which a book of this cast, if read over as it should be, would infallibly impart with them'.[14] Diderot too, in his anti-novel *Jacques le fataliste*, will try to raise his readers' standards by frustrating their expectations, along with those of Jacques's master, of hearing about love affairs – the usual subject-matter of novels, after all.

Now I realise that I cannot count on all Woolf common readers or even scholars to have read this novel of Diderot's, which perhaps because of its very austerity is less well known than his salacious and successful *La Religieuse*. Please bear with me, however, while I recapitulate those parts of it which will, I swear, serve ultimately to illuminate *Orlando*.

There is in the book a servant, Jacques, and his master, nameless but reasonable, accessible, clubbable, a man who pays the bills and plays by the rules (he knows, we are assured, Aristotle, Horace, de Vida and Le Bossue). Most novel readers tend, quite naturally, to identify with him. It is not until we see his inability to cope with any unusual situation and observe his prurient and slavish interest in 'les amours de Jacques' that we begin to suspect we have picked the wrong master. Diderot soon dispels any doubts we might have: 'le maître de Jacques? ... Il était homme. – Homme passionné comme vous, lecteur; homme importun comme vous, lecteur; homme curieux comme vous, lecteur; homme questionneur comme vous, lecteur ....'[15] By forcing the reader to reject this humiliating and limiting analogy, Diderot hopes to liberate us all from our ignoble reading habits and expectations. And, if he loses a few, so what – as Gide will say much later, 'Tant pis pour le lecteur paresseux; j'en veux d'autres.'[16] And Woolf takes up the charge, describing the other, non-lazy, ideal kind of reader, those who do their part

> in making up from bare hints dropped here and there the whole boundary and circumference of a living person; can hear in what we only whisper a living voice; can see, often when we say nothing about it, exactly what he looked like, and know without a word to guide them precisely what he thought and felt and it is for readers such as these alone that we write . . . .[17]

Woolf has also provided us with a false father-figure, the kindly, inadequate biographer who lets the reader in on all of his little problems. Watch out! this wonderful Gulliver of the biographical world, this scapegoat – or, rather, Woolf in sheep's clothing – is, of course, a booby trap well within the anti-novel's anti-tradition. Not recognising *Orlando* as an exemplum of the anti-novel genre, even the perceptive and careful critic John Graham is taken in by this ingenuous dodge, finding in the honest biographer a 'genuine desire to learn the truth'. He says that *Orlando* 'was the first of Virginia Woolf's novels in which the narrator frankly reveals himself' – which, if we remember *Jacob's Room*, is just not so; but, even if it were, the revelations by this particular narrator are only apparently frank! Graham goes on to wonder if the biographer is not a 'rudimentary model' for the supra-personal lyrical voice in *The Waves*.[18] The biographer, far from being, as Graham suggests, a 'tentative sketch' of the desired new vehicle, is the slow coach which is no longer adequate to the travellers in the world of fiction; emphasis is on obsolescence – it will not be enough to streamline him, as he is the old sterile order that must give way to the new creative chaos in any comic ritual or in any revolution.

It is wise to remain alert to the subversive motives of *Orlando*, for the unwary fall victim to the stuffy comments of our friendly biographer, the pseudo-scholarly index, and other such disarming devices in the arsenal of the anti-novelist's guerrilla warfare. In the so-called 'Writer's Preface', for example, the mask drops, the hoax is obvious; the arbitrariness and acerbity of sentiment and tone are unmistakable to anyone accustomed to the habits of the rabid anti-novelist. And, yet, in spite of such preposterous sentences as, 'I have had the advantage – how great I alone can estimate – of Mr. Arthur Waley's knowledge of Chinese', in spite of deliberate juxtapositions in the list of credits of such strange bedfellows as Lord Macaulay and Emily Brontë, the author's small nephew and Madame Lopokova, and, in spite of the quite nasty slap at 'a gentleman in America who has generously and gratuitously corrected the punctuation, the botany, the entomology, the geography, and the chronology of previous works of mine and will, I hope, not spare his services on the present occasion', this spite-full preface has been accepted literally by a surprising number of readers. I read passages such as that quoted below from David Daiches's book on Woolf with the kind of horrified fascination one feels watching someone slip on a banana skin:

> The author's preface is illuminating. 'Many friends have helped me in writing this book', she begins. 'Some are dead and so illustrious that I scarcely dare name them, yet no one can read or write without being perpetually in the debit of Defoe, Sir Thomas Browne, Sterne, Sir Walter Scott, Lord Macaulay, Emily Brontë, De Quincey, and Walter Pater, – to name the first that come to mind'. This is the literary past in virtue of which contemporary writing [Mr Daiches continues unswervingly] is what it is (again we see the interest in the revelation of the present moment to the flux of experience in general) and it is interesting to see what writers Virginia Woolf singles out as 'the first that come to mind' as factors on which modern fiction depends. The preface continues with expressions of gratitude for help rendered by friends, scholars, historians, critics, which help us to realize the seriousness with which Virginia Woolf took her job of historical reconstruction.[19]

Banana skins come thick and fast once we are in the book itself, and critics are considered fair game by all anti-novelists, who show them no mercy, having been shown none. Remember the exchange of invective in Beckett's *Waiting for Godot*, where Vladimir receives the final insult: 'Moron! Vermin! Abortion! Merpion! Sewer-rat! Curate! Cretin! ESTRAGON (*with finality*): Crritic! VLADIMIR: Oh! (*he wilts, vanquished, and turns away*).' And, as Sterne put it, 'Grant me patience, just heaven! – Of all the cants which are canted in this canting world, – though the cant of hypocrites may be the worst, – the cant of criticism is the most tormenting!', Elsewhere he says heavily, 'Mark only; – I write not for them.'[20] In *Orlando* there are overt statements against critics (for example, 'that time hangs heavy on people's hands is the only explanation of the monstrous growth', in chapter 4), but most devastating is the personification in the 'in'glaw'rious' figure of Nick Greene, the villain too in *A Room of One's Own*, of course. To the archetype of Old Nick, Woolf has added the least charming characteristics of Robert Greene, who in 1592 had the temerity to criticise the only god left standing in *Orlando*, the one true father, Shakespeare; and there are elements of Sir Edmund Gosse, who in the very month that *Orlando* was invented had the temerity to criticise Virginia Woolf herself for lack of respect for her father.[21]

From the gentle teasing of readers to this savaging of critics is but a step in the volatile, hyperbolic, revenge-fantasy world of the anti-novelist, but Woolf escalates her rejection of the so-called authorities into a general debunking of the great-men theory of history. Remember Orlando's boredom during the tea parties with Pope, Addison and company: 'How women in ages to come will envy me! And yet – .'[22] In finding great men dull, Woolf asserts again her belief in the private present moment rather than in the public ceremonial monument. More than a criticism of biographies and history books, this attitude leads to Woolf's rejection of Victorianism ('generals and generalisations'), paternalism – indeed, male-dominated society. Her stylisation of the ambassador's role and the mock magnificence of the coronation scene in *Orlando* help us to maintain that detachment which she will say in *Three Guineas* is the only proper attitude for 'daughters of educated men' to 'military displays, tournaments, tattoos, prize givings, and all such ceremonies'.[23] This rollicking ridicule of the patriarchy is Woolf's special contribution to the anti-novelist's stance outside the establishment, but none of its proponents are overweighted to the male version of reality. I wish I had read more women's literature of the past, because there must be other anti-novels lurking there. The *Women's Bible* would be one, for starters. In contemporary literature and the other arts, everything done with a feminist perspective seems to

partake of the anti-novelist spirit of revenge and reconstruction; I am thinking of some science fiction and also of Marge
Piercy's *Woman of the Edge of Time* (1976).
    In this context the change in gender, and of costume,
becomes more than just a tourist trap. After all, Carolyn
Heilbrun sees part of our hope for future salvation in
androgyny, 'a movement away from sexual polarization and
the prison of gender toward a world in which individual roles
and the modes of personal behavior can be freely chosen'.[24]
Thus the significance of Orlando (in the manuscript version,
by the way, Woolf experimented with giving her name the
feminine ending after the trance-formation) 'spending her
morning in a China robe of ambiguous gender', changing into
knee britches for clipping the nut trees, and wearing flowered
taffeta for courting.[25] Those aware that they were reading an
anti-novel would have been wary from that opening sentence:
'He – for there could be no doubt of his sex, though the
fashion of the time did something to disguise it...'! Like
Chaucer professing to us his admiration for the Shipman and
the Monk, Woolf uses the device of saying just what she does
not want us to think. Oh, it is a highly manipulative genre, the
anti-novel, forcing us to think for ourselves and indeed to
rethink all our so-called givens, be they taboos, institutions, or
other forms of limitations, such as gender, time, space, even
death.
    For it is a book about death, after all, as was *Jacob's Room* and
as will be *The Waves*. (It is interesting how many great
twentieth-century novelists use reincarnation at least as
metaphor – for example, Yukio Mishima's final tetralogy,
Gabriel Marquez's *Hundred Years of Solitude*.) On the second
page of the holograph copy of *Orlando* Woolf wrote,

A Biography
This is to tell a person's life from the
year 1500 to 1928.
Changing its sex,
taking different aspects of the character in
different centuries. The theory being that
character goes on underground before we
are born; and leaves something afterwards
also.

The castle at the end of Diderot's *Jacques le fataliste* bears this notice: 'You were here before coming and you will still be here when you have left.' Whether in memories, works of art, family histories, old houses, reincarnation, or metamorphoses, Orlando will not be unhorsed by that great opponent, death – their ship does not sink, as Rachel's does in *The Voyage Out* – and *Orlando* stays true to its comic lineage.

It is true that anti-novels, being anti-Aristotelian, never know quite how to end. Diderot teases us by refusing to give an account of Jacques's *amours*, and John Fowles gives the readers a choice in his *French Lieutenant's Woman*. The original impulse or repulse is usually balanced out by the play therapy of the writing itself. They have done what they set out to do, as Cervantes put it: 'to destroy the Authority and Acceptance the Books of Chivalry have had in the World and Among the Vulgar'. Anything more is likely to be either anti-climax (as in 'An Unwritten Novel') or apocalypse (as in 'The Shooting Party'). Woolf originally planned 'to end with three dots ... so' and in the manuscript version wrote:

> Shel cried Orlando!
> ... the wild goose —
> the secret of life is ...

THE END   March 17th, 1928

Is she telling us that the quest is just a wild-goose chase?[26] That the present moment is all we can be sure of? But maybe she is also telling us that endings on a dominant tonic, like perorations, are men's kettle-drum rolls, while with women 'this culmination and peroration should be dashed from us on a laugh casually'.[27] To learn how not to have to end his plays with a pistol shot was Chekov's great ambition; may it also be the ambition of our new androgynous and fully human history. But this begins to sound like a peroration – am I really ready to stop talking about the difficulties of *Orlando*?

I did not get to point out the many marvellous puns. (For example, the ghastly play on the gardener's name, or, more charmingly, 'And sometimes there's an inch of silver – six words – in the bottom of the net.' Notice the six words in the last part of the sentence. And there are others.) I did not get to

tell how, in an expunged passage of the manuscript, she
equated motherhood and having a litter of puppies; I did not
get to compliment her panache in parodying her own lyrical
method or her foresight in describing *Lady Chatterley's Lover*
before it had been published.[28] Never mind, you have all read
the book yourselves – the best method, as Woolf reminds us in
'How Should One Read a Book?' Please read it again and see if
these few tips on the useful tool of genre will help with the
book's difficulty; it cannot but open it up to analysis better
than the view of it as *sui generis*. Of the many genres into which
Orlando could fit (*Bildungsroman*, picaresque, quest novel,
satire, fantasy, fairy story, *conte philosophique*, feminist pamphlet, literary history, or even that which it purports to be, a
biography), the anti-novel seems the least Procrustean and
describes best its origins and functions.

Nothing could have better prepared Virginia Woolf for
writing *The Waves*, that book of which she says in curiously
stilted language in one of the manuscript versions: 'the author
would be glad if the following pages were read not as a novel'.
And what genre would better, by its lively history and flexible
form, answer Woolf's original questions: Is life like this? Must
novels be like this?[29] We have seen how closely linked these
questions are in her mind. The answers? Ah well, the secret of
life is . . . but experiencing *Orlando* as an anti-novel has raised
my standards for novels, for criticism, for biographies, for
heroes, for life itself – and death? What's that?

NOTES

1. *A Change in Perspective: The Letters of Virginia Woolf*, ed. Nigel Nicolson
   and Joanne Trautmann, vol. III (London: Hogarth Press, 1977) p. 553.
   Further references are to this edition, cited as *L*, III.
2. *L*, III, p. 433, n. 2; *Harold Nicolson: Diaries and Letters*, ed. Nigel Nicolson
   (London, 1966) vol. I, p. 48; III, p. 381, n. 2; I give my sources here,
   though my point is that the trivia retrieved does not automatically make
   us better readers of *Orlando*. For its own sake, if you want it, however,
   Nigel Nicolson's *Portrait of a Marriage* (New York: Atheneum, 1973)
   and Vita Sackville-West's *Knole and the Sackvilles* (London: Lindsay
   Drummond, 1949) are the two best sources. Her *Pepita* is fun. There is a
   biography on Violet Trefusis by Philippe Julian and John Phillips
   (Boston, Mass.: Houghton Mifflin, 1976); her autobiography is not
   much use.

3. Jean Guiguet, *Virginia Woolf and Her World*, trs. Jean Stewart (New York: Harcourt, Brace and World, 1965) pp. 270ff., 297; Mitchell A. Leaska, *The Novels of Virginia Woolf: from Beginning to End* (New York: John Jay Press, 1977); Herbert Marder, *Feminism and Art: A Study of Virginia Woolf* (Chicago and London: University of Chicago Press, 1968); A. D. Moody, *Virginia Woolf* (New York: Grove Press, 1963); James Naremore, *The World Without a Self: Virginia Woolf and the Novel* (New Haven, Conn., and London: Yale University Press, 1973).

On the other hand, Paul Moody's recent essay (*Southern Review*, July 1977, pp. 438–55), gives the book full credit for containing philosophical ideas essential to our understanding of the modern temperament.

4. Cf. Frank Baldanza, 'Orlando and the Sackvilles', *PMLA*, LXX (1955) 274–9; and Charles G. Hoffmann, 'Fact and Fantasy in *Orlando*: Virginia Woolf's Manuscript Revisions', *Texas Studies in Literature and Language*, Fall 1968, pp. 435–44.

5. Virginia Woolf, *A Writer's Diary*, ed. Leonard Woolf (London: Hogarth Press, 1959) p. 136 (7 Nov 1928).

6. Ibid., p. 105 (14 Mar 1927). Also: 'How extraordinarily unwilled by me but potent in its own rights, by the way, *Orlando* was! as if it shoved everything aside to come into existence' – ibid., p. 120 (20 Dec 1927).

7. A is Diderot; B, Virginia Woolf; C, Laurence Sterne; D, André Gide. People have pointed out the connection between *Orlando* and *Tristram Shandy*, of course – the blank page in chapter 5 especially – and we know that Sterne directly influenced Diderot, but I am not seeking here to show influence, rather commonality of mood and of purpose, of ideal and of grievance. Ionesco could have joined the gripe session; he says he writes plays (called predictably *anti-pièces*) because he hates plays, manifesting the same hostility to conventional forms. As Frank Kermode has pointed out, 'only the most trivial work [conforms] to pre-existent types' – *The Sense of an Ending* (London: Oxford University Press, 1966) p. 24.

I should like to recommend to readers interested in influence A. G. Fredman's *Diderot and Sterne* (New York, 1955). Woolf wrote on Sterne, of course, and several novels by Diderot (though not *Jacques*) are listed as having been in the Woolfs' library.

8. I do not intend here the *nouveau roman*, though there is some overlap. Robbe-Grillet, for example, called for 'new forms for the novel, forms capable of expressing (or of creating) new relationships between man and the world' – 'The Use of Theory', *For a New Novel*, trs. Richard Howard (New York: Grove Press, 1965) p. 9.

9. Virginia Woolf, 'The "Sentimental Journey" ', *Second Common Reader* (New York: Harcourt, Brace, 1932) p. 68.

10. Again I have used the pastiche method, taking direct quotes from Diderot's letters to Sophie Volland and from *A Writer's Diary* during 1927. I have not had to make anything up. I should add here that Diderot had written a number of skilful if rather slimy novels by this time, and Virginia Woolf's *To the Lighthouse* was being found 'satisfactory' even in *Scrutiny*, x, no. 3 (1942) 297.

11. M. H. Abrams, *A Glossary of Literary Terms*, 3rd edn (1970), s. v. 'genre'.

12. Elizabeth Bowen, in Virginia Woolf, *Orlando*, Signet edn (New York: New American Library, 1960) p. 221. Hereafter cited as *O*, followed by chapter and page nos. 'The Biography', *New York Herald Tribune*, 20 Oct 1927 (review of Harold Nicolson's *Some People*) repr in *Granite and Rainbow* (London: Hogarth Press, 1958). Remember Virginia Stephen's participation in that forerunner of Yippie agit-prop, the Dreadnought Hoax.
13. I am much indebted to C. L. Barber's *Shakespeare's Festive Comedy* (Princeton, NJ: Princeton University Press, 1959) for these views on the function of comedy.
14. Laurence Sterne, *The Life and Opinions of Tristram Shandy, Gentleman* (New York: Rinehart, 1959) vol. v, ch. 1. (First published 1762.)
15. *Jacques le fataliste*, p. 649 – all page references are to the Garnier edition of the *Oeuvres Romanesques*, ed. H. Bénac (Paris, 1961); the novel has been translated into English by J. Robert Loy. (The parallels with Beaumarchais's *Marriage of Figaro* are interesting, by the way.)
16. André Gide, *Journal des Faux-Monnayeurs* (Paris: Gallimard, 1926) p. 117.
17. *O*, ii, p. 47.
18. John W. Graham. '"The Caricature Value" of Parody and Fantasy in *Orlando*', *University of Toronto Quarterly*, July 1961, pp. 345–66, esp. pp. 363–5. This essay has been reprinted in Claire Sprague's collection of critical essays on Woolf (Englewood Cliffs, NJ: Prentice-Hall, 1971) and is very thoughtful and worthwhile. Unfortunately, by missing the genre, Professor Graham is thrown off about the biographer and also expends a good deal of time explaining why *Orlando* is 'a freak', and does not follow the law of 'its literary nature, which is fantasy', p. 357. *Orlando* fulfils its anti-novel nature neatly.
19. David Daiches, *Virginia Woolf* (Norfolk, Conn.: New Directions, 1942) pp. 98–9. Woolf's published correspondence shows her embroilments because of this preface, and much later, in a letter now in the Sussex collection, Leonard is still gently explaining its ironic nature to Clemence Dane. After all, Borges saw fit to translate *Ordando*, which should be fair warning; Charles Mauron did the French version.
20. Sterne, *Tristram Shandy*, vol. iii, chs 12, 20.
21. Maud Bodkin speaks of the encounter with the true father in terms quite relevant to the role of Shakespeare in *Orlando* in her *Archetypal Patterns in Poetry* (London: Oxford University Press, 1934) pp. 303–4; the curious reference to Gosse's dismay at her lack of proper family feeling (in reaction to *To the Lighthouse*) is included in a letter to Vita Sackville-West, dated 6 March 1927 (*L*, iii, p. 344). Gosse, given his own autobiography, would have been further shocked by Woolf's side-swipe at her father's life work, the *Dictionary of National Biography*, in *O*, vi, p. 200.
22. *O*, iv, p. 39; and of course many other references to her anti-Carlyle position, notably in *A Room of One's Own*, section vi – the parallels between these two *soeur jumelles* leap to the eye, of course, but, as people like being lectured to more than they like being puzzled, *A Room of One's Own*, with its sugar-coated message, is swallowed more easily. But this is an old fight of Woolf's; she has Ralph Denham in *Night and Day* saying,

'I hate great men. The worship of greatness in the nineteenth century seems to me to explain the worthlessness of that generation' – *Night and Day* (London: Duckworth, 1919) p. 20.

23. From *Three Guineas*, Harbinger edn (New York: Harcourt, Brace and World, 1938) ch. 3, p. 108.

24. Carolyn G. Heilbrun, *Toward a Recognition of Androgyny* (New York: Harper & Row, 1973) pp. ix–x.

25. *O*, iv, p. 144.

26. Her idea for the ending of *Orlando* is in *Writer's Diary*, p. 105 (14 Mar 1927). Again, Gide's remarks on his *Faux-Monnayeurs* are oddly parallel: 'Could be continued. . . . It is with these words that I should like to terminate my F. M.' – *Journal*, part III.

27. *O*, vi, p. 204. Chaucer's own tale is actually broken off by that literary critic/talk-show host who judges that it 'is nat worth a toord' – perhaps the Host too misunderstood the anti-novel nature of that bourgeois imagery. Virginia Woolf later tended to dismiss *Orlando* as 'a bad joke'. Easier than explaining.

28. *O*, vi, pp. 205, 209. Why are there so many deformed hands of men in women's fiction? Think of it: aside from Stubbs. and Colonel Abel Pargiter, there is Rochester in *Jane Eyre*, the father in Lisa Alther's *Kinflicks*. . . . Freud would have loved it.

29. Virginia Woolf, 'Modern Fiction'. *The Common Reader* (New York: Harcourt, Brace, 1925) pp. 153–4.

Ed. Note: The manuscript of *Orlando* has been edited by Madeline Moore and the relevant correspondence between Vita Sackville-West and Harold Nicolson published in *Twentieth Century Literature*, vol. 25, no. 3/4, Autumn/Winter 1979, pp. 303–55.

9 Private Brother, Public World

SARA RUDDICK

Inevitably, we look upon societies as conspiracies that sink
the private brother, whom many of us have reason to
respect, and inflate in his stead a monstrous male, loud of
voice, hard of fist.... (*Three Guineas*)

I was fighting with Thoby on the lawn. We were pommelling each other with our fists. Just as I raised my fist to hit
him, I felt: why hurt another person? I dropped my hand
instantly, and stood there and let him beat me. I remember the feeling. It was a feeling of hopeless sadness.
It was as if I became aware of something terrible; and of
my own powerlessness. (*Moments of Being*)

'Wait until these omnibuses have gone by. Do not cross so
dangerously. These men are your brothers.' In persuading her I was also persuading my own soul.
(Bernard, spoken to Rhoda, *The Waves*)

We have recently become sensitive to daughter–mother and
sister relationships. We have always welcomed attention to the
powerful effect fathers have on their daughters' lives. But a
girl's relation to her brothers is relatively uncharted. For
Virginia Woolf that relation was profoundly important. When
in *A Room of One's Own* she asks us to imagine the life of
Shakespeare's *sister*, she asks us to reflect upon a sexual,
domestic and political opposition which the very term sister–
brother connotes. When, in *Three Guineas*, she identifies
herself as the daughter of an educated man, she is speaking to

185

one of the sons of that privileged class, to a brother and man of power whom a sister has reason both to suspect and to admire. In *Night and Day, To the Lighthouse, Flush, The Years* and *Between the Acts* actual and surrogate brother–sister relationships are explored. Woolf herself acknowledged the importance of her brother Thoby for *Jacob's Room* and *The Waves*, the two novels inspired by and often taken to be a tribute to him.

Though real brothers are various and complicated, the brother-figure, the older brother of a younger sister, has certain conventional social characteristics. The brother is a male who is *not* a father, *not* a lover. Even if superior by dint of age and gender, he, like his sister, is subject to parental power. Even if sexually active and sexually attractive, he preserves rather than violates his sister's physical, sexual autonomy. Because he is male, a brother is a sister's guide to the male world, the 'real' adult world. Having learned to control his superior physical strength and multiple aggressions in the context of familial love and hate, he may protect his sister in a world where he is strong and routinely 'aggressive', she vulnerable and innocent. Just because he is a tamed animal, neither lover nor father, he may be his sister's guide and 'comrade–twin',[1] free from the corruption of sex and power.

Virginia Woolf had two brothers: Thoby, seventeen months her senior, and Adrian, seventeen months her junior. Although Adrian was a childhood rival, he does not seem to have profoundly affected Woolf's adult life or fiction. By contrast, Woolf fairly worshipped Thoby, mourned him after his death at twenty-six, then attempted to understand and recreate him in her fiction. Woolf also had two half-brothers, sons of her mother, fourteen and twelve years old when she was born. George and Gerald Duckworth invert the archetypal brother–sister relation. Their fraternalism was joined with unexpected paternalistic power; they violated their sister's sexual autonomy. Though exercising their brotherly right to introduce her to the 'real' world, they were blind to her values and needs. It is partly by contrast with these 'bad' brothers that Thoby so clearly embodies the brotherly virtues of guidance and protection. Hence Virginia Woolf's relation to him resonates with typical sisterly hopes and illusions.

He is inevitably the brother to Woolf's sister, both because of his literary and emotional importance to Virginia and because of his more generalised embodiment of mythic brotherhood.²

Near the end of her life, Virginia Woolf remembered the days after her mother's death. 'We lived through them in a hush, in artificial light. Rooms were shut. People were creeping in and out' (*MB*, p. 92). Of that mournful time, she has one memory of great beauty. Stella Duckworth, overcoming George Duckworth's objections, allowed Virginia to accompany her to Paddington Station to greet Thoby, returning for the funeral services.

> It was sunset, and the great glass dome at the end of the station was blazing with light . . . I walked along the platform gazing with rapture at this magnificent blaze of color, and the train slowly steamed into the station. It impressed and exalted me. It was so vast and fiery red. The contrast of that blaze of magnificent light with the shrouded and curtained rooms at Hyde Park Gate was so intense. (*MB*, p. 93)

The days of mourning were tragic for Woolf, not because of the actual, painful loss of her mother, but because of the hypocrisy and sentimentality involved in the mourning. Julia Stephen became 'unreal', her family 'solemn', 'self-conscious'. Once, before returning to school, Thoby sided with reality against morbid fantasy. 'It is silly going on like this' Woolf remembers him pronouncing. But then, of course, he left, as through the years he always did, while his sister stayed on in the house dominated by two tyrannical men, her father and step-brothers.

Thoby seems to have had two aspects: an indoor and an outdoor persona. The outdoor boy speaks with brisk authoritative common-sense. He tells his sisters that they should accept their place in the world, the patriarchal circus. 'If George wanted us to go to parties, why not? If father wanted us to walk with him, why not?' This boy had been his father's special pride and, in consequence, had earlier than most 'felt the burden, the glory of being a man' (*MB*, p. 117). He resolutely resisted discipline when small, 'managed' his elderly father during his last illness. He hiked, sailed, led the children on butterfly expeditions, hunted on holidays with his brother Adrian. 'A Greek god but rather too massive for the drawing room' (*L*, I, p. 75), this robust, sensible young Englishman would have become a judge and, 'had he been put on, he would have played his part most royally' (*MB*, p. 120). Even as a boy 'he had taken stock of his own power; dominated his friends in his own way; and was sure he would come into possession of his gifts all in good time' (*MB*, p. 108).

This beautiful, capable, outdoor boy had also his indoor settings: the staircase of Hyde Park Gate, where he and Virginia, walking back and forth, up and down, first discussed the Greeks; the lovely wealthy school halls peopled with friends and great ghosts of the past. Shyly and awkwardly at first, Thoby offered his gifted sister this indoor world: his many friends, first in stories, then in person; the Greeks; the Elizabethans; above all Shakespeare. Woolf seems to have felt that Shakespeare was to Thoby what Thoby himself was to her: 'his other world; the place where he got the measure of his daily world; where he took his bearings' (*MB*, p. 119). This indoor boy, Woolf tells us, would never have been a 'typical Englishman'. 'He was melancholy; original; not able to take ordinary ambitions seriously' (*MB*, p. 120).

When they were older adolescents, Thoby and Virginia's relation was constrained. Thoby shared no confidences, made no compliments, exchanged no kisses, avoided 'emotional scenes', most certainly refused to see or hear his sisters' justified anger at the restrictions imposed by their domestic world. In her letters to him, Virginia is often skittish and coy, deprecating her 'feminine weakness in the upper region', addressing him as 'milord' (*L*, I, pp. 39 and *passim*). Only for a brief while, when Thoby relocated his world in Bloomsbury, shortly before his death, did Virginia have a chance to live among the friends and ideas she had previously known only through Thoby's report and her fantasy.

Thoby 'relished his inheritance and his part in life' (*MB*, p. 119). His world held out possibilities of beauty and adventure which Woolf wholeheartedly wished to share. But, from a remarkably early age, she was impressed by the sheer force of this civilisation, by its violence, both institutional and gratuitous. If Thoby primarily represented the beauty of this civilisation, he at least once represented its brutal power:

Week after week passed at St. Ives and nothing made any
dint upon me. Then, for no reason that I know about, there
was a sudden violent shock; something happened so violently that I have remembered it all my life. I will give a few
instances. The first: I was fighting with Thoby on the lawn.
We were pommelling each other with our fists. Just as I
raised my fist to hit him, I felt: why hurt another person? I
dropped my hands instantly, and stood there, and let him
beat me. I remember the feeling. It was a feeling of hopeless
sadness. It was as if I became aware of something terrible;
and my own powerlessness. (*MB*, p. 71)[3]

It is important, in interpreting this powerful memory, to recall
that brother and sister were close in age, though Thoby was
bigger and more robust. In the remembered scene, both
children are equally 'aggressive' and physical. Woolf neither
charges Thoby with bullying nor appropriates to herself
preternatural pacifist inclinations or any other spiritual
superiority. It is in the midst of *mutual* combat that Virginia
stops. The thought that runs through her mind is a 'moral'
one: 'why hurt another person?' But another thought lurks
behind the emotions she immediately suffered: I am not
powerful enough to hurt this person', a true thought which
refers to gender – to social as well as physical reality. Sisters
typically are, or become, smaller and more vulnerable than
their brothers, while the world the brothers have created
conspires to keep them so. Therefore, whatever initial differences there may be in the impulse to fight, sisters may well lose
interest in doing so. Woolf's sadness and hopelessness have
another source. Whatever she does, whatever her moral
perceptions, fighting will continue. The good Thoby 'beats'
his unresisting sister, as brothers have the sheer power to do.
Though many brothers individually will use that power
rarely, subtly or not at all, society will protect and often
encourage their 'terrible' capacity for hurtful battle: 'Inevitably we look upon societies as conspiracies that sink the
private brother, whom many of us have reason to respect, and
inflate in his stead a monstrous male, loud of voice, hard of
fist . . .' (*TG*, p. 105). While the Duckworth stepbrothers were
'socialised' at the outset, it would take much to transform the
private brother, Thoby, into a 'monstrous male'. But society

sanctioned, for him as for the stepbrothers, the boyhood dream and temptation of unanswerable, unaccountable strength. Thoby died at twenty-six of typhoid fever. Virginia nursed him in his illness, then faced the world without him. He became for her the prototype of a beautiful, privileged young male whose character can never be assessed. The mystery of separate sensibility and separated existences was made permanent. Woolf could not lay mystery to rest by testing and developing a living relation, even though her adult experiences modified her past memories. To test out childhood fantasy in adult living is difficult enough. To explore fantasy with only the resources of memory and imagination is a formidable task.

In the third part of *To the Lighthouse*, Cam and James meet again after their mother's death. James is reminiscent of Thoby (*MB*, p. 117 and *passim*) as he steers a sailing boat under his father's watchful and eventually proud eye. At first the children are joined in uneasy alliance against their father's tyranny, then in uneasy sympathy for him. Despite the watchful tension with which each perceives the other's tentative intimacy with a dangerous father, the sibling pair remain united. Yet James is the stronger. While he rightly fears that his sister will lapse into sympathy, a lapse which, for him, is sheer weakness, Cam looks upon him as the 'lawgiver, with the tablets of eternal wisdom laid open on his knee'. 'Of all the human qualities she reverenced justice most. Her brother was most god-like' (*TTL*, p. 251). And, in the end, when James earns Mr Ramsay's praise, he pretends to be 'perfectly indifferent', not deigning to look at his sister.

The brother–lawgiver is both foreboding and attractive as a fine outdoor boy. In a short story, 'The Introduction', Woolf uses a vocabulary reminiscent of her memoir of Thoby to paint a more bitter portrait of the lawgiver as a young man.[4] The protagonist, Lily Everett, is introduced to Bob Brinsley, just down from Oxford. Brinsley is 'in direct line from Shakespeare . . . and parliaments and churches . . . and the telephone wires too'. Lily has nothing to offer him but a mind which has been judged first-rate by a professor. When her accomplishment dwindles in the presence of 'massive masculine achievement', she is willing to play the part of a woman, to be a 'butterfly', a 'frail and beautiful', 'limited and circumscribed' creature 'with difficulties and sensibilities and sadnesses innumerable'. But, face-to-face with Brinsley, she is stopped in her play-acting by some terrifying suspicion. As Brinsley talks arrogantly about himself and, laughingly, about 'some girl', Lily imagines him pulling the wings off a fly. She feels herself attacked. In Plato's great metaphor, the wings on one's back are the wings of the soul. The beauty of a rightly beloved person warms the roots of the wings that 'for long had been so hardened and closed up that nothing could grow'.[5] But Lily, unlike Plato's lover of male beauty, is terrified that the man 'will shrivel up her wings and drive her out into loneliness'. Believing the man 'the greatest of all worldly objects', she tries 'to crouch, and cower and fold the wings down flat on her back'. When, despite herself, her sense of her own competence returns, she feels like a 'naked wretch', realises that there are no sanctuaries or butterflies, that 'this civilization depends upon me'.

In a famous passage in *A Room of One's Own*, Woolf imagines for Shakespeare a sister Judith, as talented in mind and spirit as William, but unable to engage in his art. No matter how good a brother Shakespeare might have been, he could not have offered his world to his sister. He could (to change Woolf's story) have helped her to run away, supplemented her small change stolen from home, introduced her to his friends. Despite his efforts there would have been no place in his world for a person with a woman's body who wished to practise a man's art. Thoby was neither Bob Brinsley nor Shakespeare. He was a beautiful, good brother and his world was more welcoming to sisters than Shakespeare's had been. But the world was not welcoming enough, nor was Thoby's relation to it clear. In *A Room of One's Own*, Woolf articulated the exclusions and demeanings, implicit and explicit, which women suffered in Thoby's world. She could be so clear about that world's promises and evils because she had already wrestled with personal questions: Who was Thoby? What promises did he make to his sister? What promises would he have kept? Whose side was he on? These questions haunt *Jacob's Room*, the 'life' of a son and brother.

Introduced as a child by the seashore, Jacob Flanders grows into a beautiful though awkward young man, a Cambridge student who travels first to Cornwall, then to Greece and Turkey. Jacob plans to enter politics, perhaps become a judge. His mid-life ordinariness is hinted at and dreaded. But he dies in his twenties, during the First World War. Woolf sent the fair copy of *Jacob's Room* off to the typist in April 1922. As the novel neared completion, she exulted, 'There's no doubt in my mind that I have found out how to begin (at forty) to say something in my own voice' (*WD*, p. 46). That same summer, the following lines appear in her reading notes:[6]

> 'Atque in perpetuum, frater, ave atque vale'
> Julian Thoby Stephen
> [1881–1906]
> Atque in perpetuum, frater, ave atque vale

If we think of Thoby as presenting a 'problem' to his sister to be resolved, or at least transmuted, in her fiction, that problem was in part metaphysical. How do we live with the fact of death? What can we know about a person? What can we have of him when he is gone? Why, if we can know and have so little, do we care so much?

The epistemological reply is clear: knowledge of anyone is tentative and incomplete. 'It is no use trying to sum people up. One must follow hints, not exactly what is said, nor yet entirely what is done' (*JR*, p. 31). We are singular individuals, not 'ideal observers'. 'It seems that a profound, impartial, and absolutely just opinion of our fellow creatures is absolutely unknown' (*JR*, p. 71).

The epistemological modesty of *Jacob's Room* is conjoined with feelings of 'overpowering sorrow' at the impossibility of possessing either the living or the dead. Humans are insubstantial and fragile. Jacob himself is introduced to us as an absence. Three times his brother hollers the name 'Jacob, Ja-cob' before we see the child: 'The voice had an extraordinary sadness. Pure from all body, pure from all passion, going out into the world, solitary, unanswered, breaking against rocks – so it sounded' (*JR*, p. 8). At the end of the novel, Jacob is once again an absence, his tenuous presence in his empty room barely suggested by a creaking chair, his useless shoes in his mother's hand, perhaps by the wind which rustles the leaves outside the window.

Behind the questions 'What can I know?' and 'What can I have?' lie the questions 'How can I afford to care?', 'How caring can I bear the pain of insubstantiality and loss?' 'In any case life is a procession of shadows, and God knows why it is that we embrace them so eagerly, and see them depart with such anguish, being shadows' (*JR*, p. 72). The affirmation of the novel is clear: we are right to embrace the shadows. Occasionally we shall be rewarded with connection and solidity, with a 'vision of a young man who is of all things the most real, the most solid, the best known to us'. Yet, as we know and embrace, we must accept the conditions of our connection: 'the moment after we know nothing of him. Such is the manner of our seeing. Such the conditions of our love' (*JR*, p. 72).

The elegaic tone of *Jacob's Room* perfectly expresses its epistemological and moral restraint, the 'manner of our seeing' and the 'conditions of our love'. So powerful is the renunciation of knowledge and possession that we may lose sight of the life that is seen, however imperfectly, and loved, however painfully. Unlike Thoby's, Jacob's death is the avoidable outcome of institutionalised violence. When the 'overpowering sorrow', the atmosphere of *Jacob's Room*, is named, the name is history.

> What is this sorrow? It is brewed by the earth itself. It comes from the houses on the coast. We start transparent and then the cloud thickens. All history backs our pane of glass. To escape is vain. (*JR*, p. 49)

> When a child begins to read history one marvels, sorrow-fully, to hear him spell out in his new voice the ancient words. (*JR*, p. 98)

In history, Jacob is a boy–man of a particular society in a specifiable era. He is in a world governed by divisions of class and sex, a world on the verge of war. Jacob, like Thoby Stephen, is an inheritor. The world he inherits will destroy him.

In Jacob's world, as in Thoby's divisions of class and sex, the connection of both with violence, are evident. Mrs Flanders and her helper Rebecca, although 'conspirators plotting the eternal conspiracy of hush and clean bottles', are divided by class. Captain Barfoot, Mrs Flanders's proper but vaguely adulterous suitor, is separated by class from his 'servant' Dickens. Dickens looks after the estranged Mrs Barfoot while living vicariously through his 'master' the captain. Mrs Barfoot's formal orders to Dickens do not conceal the fact that she stares straight through him, making him as object-like as the chair he moves for her. Mrs Barfoot literally and spiritually invalided, is herself a 'prisoner of civilization'. Captain Barfoot, crippled in war, is taken by some women, including Betty Flanders, to be a symbol of law and order. But Mrs Jarvis, Mrs Flanders's clear-sighted friend, knows better: 'Yet I have a soul . . . and it's the man's stupidity that is a cause of all this, and the storm's my storm as well as his.' While Jacob's friend Timothy studies at Cambridge and sails to Cornwall, his sister Clara, who loves Jacob, waits at home encased in satin and propriety. Mrs Durrant, at once her daughter's ally, jailer and trainer, is, like Betty Flanders, divided from other women by class distinctions to which she is insensible. Imperiously visiting her Cornish neighbor Mrs Pascoe, whose nephew, 'immobile as stone', drives her horses, she expresses a sentimental respect for the countrywoman while commenting with supreme confidence on the defects and virtues of her garden. Woolf makes the divisiveness quite general: 'Nature and society between them have arranged a system of classification which is simplicity itself. . . . One has to choose . . .' (*JR*, p. 69).

Jacob chooses. He accepts the privileges of gender which, in turn, allow him the privileges of class: 'He looked satisfied; indeed masterly; . . . the sound of the clock conveying to him (it may be) a sense of old buildings and time; and himself the inheritor' (*JR*, p. 45). In exclusive Cambridge, where he sides with the excluders, the very stones seem to echo his right to belong: 'Back from the Chapel, back from the Hall, back from the library, came the sounds of his footsteps, as if the old stone echoed with magisterial authority. "The young man – the young man – the young man, back to his rooms"' (*JR*, p. 46).

In a diary written while she was twenty-one and waiting for her father to die, Woolf expressed a fantasy: 'I think I see for a moment how our minds are all threaded together – how any live mind today is of the very same stuff as Plato's and Euripides: It is only a continuation and development of the whole thing – it is this common mind that bends the whole world together and all the world is mind.'[7] In reading or discussion, and most clearly in writing, one is sharing in and enlarging a universal mind. This fantasy is three times suggested in *Jacob's Room*. On his sailing trip Jacob follows, then continues his friend's argument. 'Some people can follow every step of the way and even take a little one six inches long, by themselves at the end' (*JR*, pp. 49–50). The British Museum, in which he reads, is said to house an 'enormous mind'. The names of the great men who made that mind are ringed around the dome of the reading room. Jacob is quite at home there, looking regal and pompous to Julia Hedge, a feminist who reads near him. Later, Jacob reads Plato's *Phaedrus*, 'a very difficult dialogue'.

> One reads straight ahead, falling into step, marching on, becoming (so it seems) momentarily part of this rolling imperturbable energy which has driven darkness before it since Plato walked the Acropolis. . . . The dialogue draws to its close . . . and for five minutes Jacob's mind continues alone, onwards, into the darkness. (*JR*, p. 110)

In the same diary in which Virginia Woolf first recorded the compelling fantasy of a vast mind to which living individuals could contribute, she also noted that she found her own reading interrupted by the disturbing question, 'What right have I to read all the things that men have done? They would laugh if they saw me.' Who were the men in question? Whatever his other faults, Leslie Stephen did not laugh at his daughter's intellectual aspirations, and George was too 'stupid' to laugh effectively. It is likely, however, that from a distance Thoby and his witty, articulate friends could have made Virginia feel like an uninvited and inappropriate guest at their intellectual feasts. Later, when Virginia was able to join the charmed circle, she seemed acutely shy and fiercely defensive.[8]

In *Jacob's Room* Julia Hedge, reading around the dome of the British Museum Reading Room, laments the exclusive maleness of its honour roll: 'Why didn't they leave room for an Eliot or a Brontë?' Like the twenty-one-year-old Virginia, she is ill at ease in the dome of the enormous mind. While Julia composes what seems to be a draft of *A Room of One's Own*, self-serious Jacob, the inheritor, is collating editions of Marlowe in order to write an 'incredibly dull' literary essay which he will read to five young friends with whom he is building 'a better age'. Julia, riveted to her chair, writes with 'death and gall and bitter dust' on her pen, red in her cheek-bones, light in her eyes. Jacob, like the other young men, seems to her composed and unconcerned. He passes notes with a friend, comes and goes as he likes, with the insouciance of an insider. 'Unfortunate Julia.' Embittered and untidy, she is distracted from her 'gigantic labours' by the young men beside her, by all of the men who have preceded him. When Jacob walks out with his friend, she imagines them laughing aloud directly they were in the hall (*JR*, pp. 105–7); and, indeed, Jacob's laughter rings through *Jacob's Room*.

Jacob's unthinking assumption of male superiority is explicit. He thinks it as suitable for a dog as for a woman to be allowed into a Cambridge chapel, he charges 'damned women' for spoiling the ruins of Greece. With one exception, he is callous, condescending, possessive or self-preoccupied with the women he loves. The one exception, Sandra Wentworth Williams, is a married woman who 'floats from the particular to the universal', making no demands on Jacob during her brief flirtation with him. Fanny Elmer's remark 'Some people are real . . . women never' seems to express Jacob's own sure appreciation of the beauties of his male life. His horrified response to the economically struggling, ambitious academic family that lives outside Cambridge, his worries about 'his people', his enjoyment of Lady Rocksbier's invitations and Mrs Durrant's excursions, his desire to enter established politics – all suggest that he easily identifies with a class just above his own, within the natural reach of a young man with a Cambridge degree.

Jacob is killed in a war which Woolf believed to be the effect of institutionalised hierarchies of class, sex and intelligence; he is himself in part a killer. As a child he catches a crab and lets it die in his bucket. As a grown boy he hunts butterflies, a sport associated with death, the exclusion of women, and the mutilation of a soul.[9] As a young man he is shocked by the world of adults, thrown in black outline upon *his* 'reality' of Moors, Byron, sea and lighthouse. He has a sense of his own specialness for which 'there will be no form in the world unless Jacob makes one for himself'. However, when he sits in Hyde

Park shortly before he goes to war, he thinks of Rome, architecture and jurisprudence. He treats the ticket-collector with considerable contempt, and is oblivious to a woman who we know loves him and weeps for him. There is no suggestion that he is making for himself that special form which will allow him to live differently from the other young men of patriarchy.

In her memoirs and letters, Woolf shared the pleasures of butterfly-hunting and flattered Thoby, the leader of the hunters. Similarly, Woolf shares many of the values, appreciates the beauty, of Jacob's world. When Jacob, returning from a butterfly-hunt, bursts in upon and startles his worried mother, we feel that Woolf's sympathy is as much with the awkward Jacob in from the dark woods as with the concerned mother unable to control her son. Though the dons of Cambridge may provoke Woolf's satire, its beauty, friendship and respect for ideas do not. Clara, waiting for Jacob, her existence 'pinched and emasculated in a satin shoe', is an object of pity. Her quiet purity is not nearly so attractive as Jacob's eager, self-absorbed and callous adventurousness.

If the dominant mood of *Jacob's Room* is renunciatory and elegaic, its counterpoint is a bitterly loving protest against a destructive world whose beauty is never denied. Although awkward Jacob partakes of the beauty and becomes beautiful, he also partakes of the destruction to which he contributes by his indifference, ambition, insensitivity and sexual–social pride. Yet we do not respond to Jacob with the ambivalence his destructiveness warrants. His death is absolutely our loss. Woolf has managed, for this reader at least, to induce towards Jacob a condition of love and a suspension of judgement. This effect is, in part, the particularisation of Woolf's insistence on the universal requirements of love and knowledge which I have already mentioned. However, both as author and as sister, Woolf invents another technique for restraining judgement and inducing love. She feminises the perspective from which she reveals Jacob's life and the history of which it is a part. Jacob is shown to us both under the aspect of eternity and under the aspect of maternal care; his life is framed by the hopes, work, vision and losses of his mother. The 'impersonal', 'universal' voice speaks with the accents of a woman.

Jacob's Room opens with a mother writing. Betty Flanders's letters weave through the book. They are part of 'the unpublished works of women, written by the fireside in pale profusion' (*JR*, p. 91). Like all letters, they represent the attempt to 'lace our days together and make of life a perfect globe' (*JR*, p. 93). After Jacob's life is ended, Betty Flanders stands in his empty room, his shoes in her hand, the remains of her 'work' that was Jacob. Her gaze and love are powerful. When tears come to her eyes, the mast of a ship wobbles. Her mere letter lying outside the door where Jacob makes love becomes a living, suffering maternal presence.

The powerful gaze and powerful love are limited. Betty Flanders cannot bring herself to speak truthfully of what she feels when she writes to Jacob. She loses the garnet brooch Jacob bought for her with his own money. She does not hear the guns of a war she cannot comprehend, but thinks only of the life of her chickens, the comfort of her helper, Rebecca, the safety of her house. Her mind wanders, her pen blots, she forgets the meat.

Though her love is imperfect and her vision limited, it is upon them that the 'omniscient narrator' builds. The centrality of Betty Flanders to Jacob is clear at the outset when he is introduced as one of the children of an energetic woman with a life of her own. The mother's vision is both preordinate and limited. In a central episode, Mrs Page, Mrs Cranch and Mrs Garfit watch Betty Flanders climbing the town hill with her children. The women's names sound a litany choiring Mrs Flanders on her way to the vantage point which dominates the village. From that point, Mrs Flanders *could* have seen the entire life of the village and the lay of the varied land as it changed throughout the seasons. In fact, she sees next to nothing, because, busy mother that she is, she is patching Jacob's breeches while playing 'tea' with John, the youngest, and worrying over the sleeplessness of Arthur, the eldest. If Mrs Flanders, for good reasons, does not see, no one else sees further. We move to the impersonal narrator, who tells us what Betty Flanders *could* have seen. The narrator's vision is the natural extension of that of Betty Flanders, to whose occupations we return after our excursions into the transpersonal.

That there is no 'omniscient' narrator is the epistemological point of the novel. No one sees, just as no one prevents, the coming of the stupid war which will claim Jacob's life. When Betty Flanders cannot hear the guns of war, she does hear the 'dull sound' that she takes to be the sea and likens to nocturnal women beating great carpets. Turning from the great sounds, she hears the small sounds, has the small worries of a woman keeping her house in order. When her son is killed, Betty Flanders does not 'break up her lines to weep'.[10] She too is a nocturnal women who will continue to beat her particular carpets.

Earlier, Betty Flanders had walked out on the moor with her confidante, Mrs Jarvis, the clear-sighted, unpopular, melancholy clergyman's wife with a special fondness for Jacob. They go as far as the Roman camp where Betty Flanders had lost Jacob's brooch and many knitting needles. Mrs Flanders is at home there, the place of ancient history: 'If all the ghosts flocked thick and rubbed shoulders with Mrs. Flanders in the circle, would she not have seemed perfectly in her place, a live English matron, growing stout?' (*JR*, p. 132). The moor at midnight is the place of preservation, of a history that lies beneath the history of wars. 'The moonlight destroyed nothing. The moor accepted everything.' At midday, in sunshine, the moor seems to hoard human treasures 'like a nurse'. Yet the sceptic, not the mother goddess, has the final word: 'At midnight when no one speaks or gallops, and the thorn tree is perfectly still, it would be foolish to vex the moor with questions – what? and why?' (*JR*, p. 134). Scepticism, silence, restraint are the deepest responses to Jacob's life. But, when silence is broken, the speech we hear is not genderless, 'human', but uttered in female accents and images. When restraint gives way, the first connection and the best of imperfect visions is achieved in a mother's caring work.

The device of showing a son and brother through his mother's eyes is a shaping determinant of *Jacob's Room*. *The Waves*, begun seven years after *Jacob's Room*, is essentially a post-mother book in which children must see each other through their own eyes.

In the interval, Woolf wrote *To the Lighthouse*, exploring and coming to peace with the power of the mother's vision. Sisters often become motherly with brother rivals or aggressors, as Woolf herself did with Adrian and even George ('Take care of yourself and come back fatter'). The adoption in art of a mother's perspective is a deeper political and more differentiated psychological act. In *To the Lighthouse*, Woolf makes explicit what was implicit in *Jacob's Room*, the priority of the mother's vision. 'If she wanted to be serious about him, she had to help herself to Mrs. Ramsay's sayings, to look at him through her eyes' (*TTL*, p. 293). Lily, the artist, speaks here of the woman taunting Charles Tansley, her surrogate brother and rival. But the reference could be generalised. Mrs Ramsay's vision is necessary to understand *lives*; for this reason, the artist daughter must connect to and make use of the maternal mind. However, as Woolf insists, affirming maternal value does not require merging with a particular mother, living a mother's life, or accepting oppressive social conditions of mothering. Lily, the artist, need not *be* Mrs Ramsay, nor need she idealise Mrs Ramsay, in order to appropriate her sayings and her vision. As *The Waves* shows, a maternal perspective can survive independent of a maternal presence.

While she was revising *To the Lighthouse*, Woolf found herself 'haunted by some semi-mystical, very profound life of a woman, which shall be all told on one occasion'. In a fascinating essay,[11] J. W. Graham argues that *The Waves*, begun three years later, indeed articulates the vision of an omnipercipient, androgynous yet recognisably female narrator. In the early parts of the first holograph draft, the narrator explicitly identifies herself: 'I am the seer. I am the force that arranges.˙I am the thing in which all this exists. Certainly without me it would perish. I can give it order. I perceive what is bound to happen' (HD, 39 and *passim*). According to Graham, even 'when the narrator becomes so attenuated that few readers suspect her existence, her bardic voice continues to deliver the book'. As Graham himself notes, the literal sex of the narrator is explicitly disguised: 'The lonely mind, man's or woman's, it does not matter which . . . ' (HD, 9 and *passim*). Yet I would follow Graham in continuing to call that androgyne a woman. Her counterpart in the finished novel is a successor to Mrs Ramsay, 'the lady [who] sits between two long windows writing'. Nameless, she is now the teller rather than the object of the tale. She has human representatives in the novel: Mrs Constable 'baptises' the children by squeezing a wet sponge on their spines; Mrs

Moffat sweeps up the litter of Bernard's life. Nature also wears its motherly garments. The sun is a woman or a girl. The waves themselves were, in the early holograph, 'many mothers, and again many mothers, and behind them many more, endlessly sinking and falling, and each held up as it raised its crest and flung itself upon the shore, a child' (HD, pp. 9, 63).

Yet, whatever the status of the metaphysical and literary hovering mother, *The Waves*, like the two novels which follow it, relinquishes a privileged, powerful maternal presence. Though the universe may be mother-haunted, Susan, the representative mother, is prey to a particular passion, 'the bestial and beautiful passion of maternity', which gives rise to life-attachments and perspectives in no way privileged. The children of *The Waves* are described in almost total isolation from parents. Indeed, Susan's father, a headmaster and headmistress, Mrs Constable and Mrs Moffat and one glimpse of Bernard's parents are all we see of any adults. As the children grow up, they have lovers, some a spouse, some children. Yet we still meet them as they meet each other, a group of age-mates, a sibling-like group.

There are seven children. Percival appears only after the earliest childhood of the others, when the boys have been separated from their 'sisters' (*W*, p. 196). Often taken to be modelled after Thoby, he is beautiful, 'natural', and the prototype of the brother leader. His proper setting is in the institutionalised brotherhood typified by school and college, with its atmosphere of sport and homoerotic passion. Susan, the woman he is said to love, is a quintessential 'female', identified with nature, maternity and love of father. Jinny is another type of female, whose imagination, whose being, is bodily and who lives by 'dazzling', charming and seducing. She appreciates Percival's importance, but neither loves nor is loved by him. Neville, an ambitious poet and academic success, is as sensual and, in his way, as 'unnatural' as Jinny. A fastidious homosexual, he is passionately in love with Percival. Louis, like Percival, is quintessentially male. He thrives by manipulating organised power. Unlike Percival, his power is neither natural nor beautiful, but grows out of a need to compensate for an initial sense of inferiority and unseemliness. Louis the tycoon is also solitary and anguished. His lover

Rhoda is entirely solitary. She is directly opposed to Percival, as faceless and as lacking in identity as he is chock-full of being. Bernard is Jacob's successor, the inheritor, the continuer. Relatively untouched by Percival as a boy, he mourns him as an adult, reposseses him as a hero when he is old and confronting death.

No one of the seven characters represents Thoby. Although Percival is the brother-figure *par excellence*, his traits are only occasionally reminiscent of Thoby's. Woolf did not, in *The Waves*, even attempt to repossess the *individual* brother as she did in *Jacob's Room* and moments of *To the Lighthouse*. Rather she portrayed different forms and resolutions of a *relationship*, that of a vulnerable person to the beauty, power and privilege of a male guide and hero. That her living brother possessed beauty and privilege whose power increased under the spell of his early death provides only one of the many autobiographical resonances of the novel.

It is impossible to do justice even to the single theme of sister–brotherhood in such a complex, ambitious novel. I shall barely touch upon possible sexual responses to the brother leader or, more generally, to male power. For Susan, the young alluring male plays a conventional and unthreatening role as the facilitator of maternity. She dreams of a hot midday when her lover will come. 'To his one word I shall answer my one word. What has formed in me I shall give him.' But she adds immediately, 'I shall have children.' Her lover becomes a snoring husband, a fate Woolf envisions as dreadfully possible for Jacob and Percival, and Thoby. Neville suffers from a 'violent and absurd passion' for Percival, who is the very image of the schoolboy object of homoerotic love. After death, Percival becomes a type of warrior lover who returns again and again in Neville's later passions. Like Neville, Rhoda finds in Percival a sexual lover. But her sexual desire is released and named only after Percival's death. I shall consider Rhoda's sexual longing again as one aspect of her relation to Percival's power. Otherwise, I shall ignore sexuality, admitting that any treatment of *The Waves* which omits it is seriously limited. To explore Woolf's sexuality – i.e. her experience and her artistic expression of sexual politics and desire – would require a separate essay. Postponing a discussion of sexuality, I shall examine Woolf's imaginative construction of male power in the character of Percival and three possible responses to that power: the envy and reactive self-assertion of Louis, the isolation and self-effacement of Rhoda, and the realistic affection of Bernard.

Percival is the symbolic centre of *The Waves*. He is the silent presence and vacuum-like absence which draws to itself the other characters' fantasies of their brother/leader/opposite. His death from a fall while riding is the most important event in the novel. Like Thoby's death, it is apolitical, accidental. Again like Thoby's death, it casts over the life a mythological light with its attendant dangers of falsification. Although after death Percival becomes, even for Bernard, a knight and warrior confronting the great enemy, the moral character of his life is ambiguous.

Percival is once explicitly identified with 'boasting boys' (*W*, p. 220) of 'majestic order' and 'beautiful obedience' who, none the less, 'leave butterflies trembling with their wings pinched off' and 'make little boys sob in passages' (*W*, p. 207). These boasting boys are the future soldiers, the cricketers and volunteers. They march about in troops of four following the orders of their general. Percival is usually set apart from them as that general. His distinction does not make him the less fearful to those 'trooping after him, his faithful servants, to be shot like sheep' (*W*, p. 200).

Percival is as conventional as he is heroic. We are several times reminded that he is not 'precocious', reads or studies little, yet, like the romantic heroine, understands everything. His guffaw sanctions the other boys' laughter, his gestures and inflections are imitated by the epigone. He would have become a judge. His 'oddly inexpressive eyes', 'pagan indifference' and absolute self-possession which 'defends itself from any caress' make him awesome. He might have 'ridden alone at the head of troops and denounced some monstrous tyranny' (*W*, p. 281). For Neville, he is a pagan deity who can replace the 'stricken Christ' and his 'trembling mother'. Such an awesome boy is dangerous. Percival, in his magnificence, destroys Bernard's story, Louis's poetry, Neville's confidence in his love.

In her great pacifist essay, *The Iliad, Poem of Force*,[12] Simone Weil describes the 'mighty warrior' in terms reminiscent of Percival. Believing himself to be 'exempt from the misery that is the common human lot', the warrior's 'prestige is first of all made up of that superb indifference which the powerful have for the weak, an indifference so contagious that it is communicated even to those who are its object'. 'Other men do not impose upon [his] acts that moment for pausing from which alone our consideration of our fellow proceeds.' '[The warrior] who possesses strength moves in an atmosphere which offers him no resistance. Nothing in the human element surrounding him is of the nature to induce, between the intention and the act, that brief interval where thought may lodge.' It would be foolish to push too closely the analogy between the mighty of the *Iliad* and Percival, the English schoolboy hero and future colonialist. At most we can say that Percival represents the common longing for and fear of the warrior; the unanswerably, indifferently strong. His presence in *The Waves* requires the others to confront the allure of the silent and beautiful mighty.

Among the characters in *The Waves*, only Bernard responds to Percival in a way that humanises and utilises his strength. Louis and Rhoda respond respectively, with envy and self-negation. Both are aspects of Woolf's own response to alluring strength, aspects which she expresses but does not endorse.

Louis hates Percival, a hatred born of envy. His character, more than any other in *The Waves*, combines political and psychological acuity with autobiographical significance.[13]

Early in the holograph draft of *The Waves*, Woolf describes a 'plan of the soul' (*HD*, p. 23 and *passim*). The soul is a little figure, whose roots go 'deep, so deep' into 'an unfathomable pit in the centre'. The figure is liable to be sucked and drawn into the darkness. To avoid oblivion it must have 'tentacles' which attach to the world. The most obvious of these 'far stretching filaments' is love of self. The soul is soft and tender. When brought to the surface, the light of individual existence is painful for it. It must secrete a hard shell to cover itself, replacing the wax around the spine which was melted by the hot water of baptism. Because the shell is fragile, individuals meet as antagonists, cowering to preserve privacy or comparing and competing to preserve identity. Self-love is fraught and requires continuous effort.

This plan describes the soul of each of the six children in

some of its moments. It is embodied by Louis, who, even in the earliest holograph, inspired it.

Louis transcends sex and time. He is the seer of the history which Jacob learned to spell; his 'roots go down to the depths of the world'. Personal worldly identity here and now is painful for him. Rather than be Louis, he would be, 'now a duke, now Plato'; rather than live his own life he would have existed a thousand years. Brought to the surface, awakened, his soul is 'shivering', 'tender', 'unprotected', 'infinitely young'. This vulnerability is born from the union of his poetical, semi-mystical intuiton of history with his acute sense of the injuries of class from which he suffers in a particular society.

Louis, the seer, the 'best scholar in the school', the child most fit to appreciate and contribute to the 'great mind' to which even the unscholarly Jacob has access, is 'excluded': first excluded by the fact of his class origins (revealed by an Australian accent and a banker father in Brisbane), he compounds initial exclusion by his defensive sensitivity. Mincing, affected, ironic, Louis lives by hatred and scorn in a world dominated by Percival and his boasting boys. Knowing himself intellectually superior, he despises Percival with his 'slovenly accents' and troop of 'small fry' who 'trot subserviently after him'. By studying, by reading, by writing, he continually and vainly knocks at the 'grained oak door' which locks him out of his master's study and all possible Cambridge rooms. Deprived of university education, to which Bernard, Neville, Percival and the boasting boys are entitled by birth, consigned to an office, Louis is sickened by envy. 'Hence my pursed lips, my sickly pallor; my distasteful and uninviting aspect as I turn my face with hatred and bitterness upon Bernard and Neville, who saunter under yew trees; who inherit arm chairs; and draw their curtains close so the lamplight falls on their books' (*W*, p. 241).

Even as a schoolboy, Louis cannot be indifferent to Percival. He 'adores' his beauty and magnificence; takes them to be the necessary inspiration of his poetry. Loving and depending upon a power he scorns and is scorned by, his 'heart turns rough; it abrades [his] side like a file with two edges' (*W*, p. 200). Later, unprotected by established institutions while acutely sensitive to the seemliness and judgement of those inside them, Louis must make for himself a hard shell to cover his soft soul. He does so by developing a power and a persona which is conformist, 'masculine' and proto-fascist. He imposes on the world his mark: I, I, I.

'Half in love with the typewriter and telephone', Louis inherits a mahogany desk from which he sends luxury steamers around the world. In contrast to Betty Flanders's letters, which 'lace our days together', Louis has 'laced the world together with [his] ships'. *His* letters command, and are distinguished by his *signature*: 'I have signed my name already twenty times. I, and again I, and I and again I . . . . Here is the pen and the paper; on the letters in the wire basket I sign my name, I, I, and again I' (*W*, pp. 291, 294). If Betty Flanders's letters are part of the 'unpublished works of women', Louis's epitomise male power.

The adult Louis who fears that without the appurtenances and appointments of power he would 'fall like snow and be wasted' is continuous with the child who could lose his painful identity only in the dimly lit, authority-ridden ritual of his school chapel service. It may seem proleptic to call him proto-fascist. It would be some years before Woolf made explicit the connection between professional and sexual possessiveness and the growing tyrannies of Europe. Yet Louis, longing for community, raging to 'reduce' everything to order (*W*, pp. 241 and *passim*), 'stiff from force of will' (*JR*, p. 156 – the words suit Louis), reminds us of the fascist men and women to come. Indeed, in Louis Woolf created a figure who embodied those personal and political characteristics she most feared: envious hatred, frantic egocentricity, and a dangerous, compulsive will to dominate. It is most remarkable, then, that the portrait, in sum, is so largely sympathetic. Though Louis is a worthy target of anger and fear, Woolf seems largely to identify with him in his envy.

It would have been appropriate and 'sane' for Virginia Stephen bitterly and deeply to envy her conventional beautiful brother who moved so easily in the world behind 'grained oak doors' from which she was excluded. The exclusion Woolf suffered, by virtue of gender, she also perpetrated (and despite hard-won political clarity, knew she continued to perpetrate) by virtue of her class. Both oppressor and oppressed, she had reason to fear from others the very hating envy she herself suffered. In expressing through Louis – a powerful quintessentially 'male' businessman – the 'female' envy she herself suffered, in allowing her social 'inferior' the sense of injury she herself inflicted, she achieved in her art a psychological richness the implications of which are as political as they are therapeutic.

Louis is portrayed empathetically throughout *The Waves*. In the end he is allowed the fruits of his particular struggle. Although Woolf may scorn his earned 'inheritance' – the power that lies behind his mahogany desk – she allows him his poetry, his place in the 'great mind'. Though he may live in Surrey and own two cars, he returns to his attic to resume in solitude 'that curious attempt I have made ever since I brought down my fist on my master's grained oak door'. Though his efforts may be inflated by ego and embittered by envy, the attempt is one with which Woolf identifies and sympathises. 'My destiny has been that I remember and must weave together, must plait into one cable the many threads, the thin, the thick, the broken, the enduring of our long history, of our tumultuous and varied day' (*W*, p. 316).

Once Woolf explicitly links the exclusion she felt as a sister to that which Louis feels, because of his class. In a London restaurant, Louis feels different from 'the average men', who can include the waitress's rhythms in their own. Louis is 'not included' in this rhythm, this sibling circle. 'She [the waitress] deals you your apricots and custard unhesitatingly, like a sister. You are her brothers' (*W*, p. 241). Neither Woolf nor Louis can be among the brothers. It is that common exclusion which unites them as 'outsiders'.

It is fitting that Louis loves Rhoda, the solitary spirit. It is fitting too that Rhoda, the only one who understands the poetry Louis loves, should leave him. Rhoda's sole defence against a society always abrasive is solitary fantasy. 'Faceless', 'invisible', 'horrified', 'terrified', she cannot love. There is nothing natural or easy about Rhoda's relation to her friends, to the physical world, even to her own body. She must look to others to see how to laugh or what to feel. She hides from her face in the mirror, bangs her hand against some hard door to call herself back to her body, cannot carry a message across a puddle because 'identity fails her'. Totally isolated, she longs to give, but there is some check in the flow of her being. In imagery explicitly sexual, she describes the 'thawing' and unsealing of her body and her overwhelming desire to return all that flows through her (*W*, p. 213). But she can give only to Percival and only to him after his death. While Percival lived, there was no suggestion of a sexual or any other connection between him and Rhoda. The death of the male hero releases Rhoda's capacity for mourning love: 'The figure that was robed in beauty is now clothed in ruin' (*W*, p. 285). It also consigns her to a world which is terrifyingly ugly without the hero's shaping beauty. 'I am alone in a hostile world. The human face is hideous. . . . Percival by his death has made me this present, has revealed this terror, has left me to undergo this humiliation' (*W*, p. 286). Rhoda escapes this world with a Percival she resurrects in fantasy. The two deny the fact of his death as they consummate their union, allowing Rhoda finally to give her flowers, her gift.

> Now I will at last free the checked, the jerked back desire to be spent, to be consumed. We will gallop together over forest hills where the swallow dips her wings in dark pools and the pillars stand entire. Into the wave that dashes upon the shore, into the wave that flings its white foam to the uttermost corners of the earth I throw my violets, my offering to Percival.   (*W*, p. 289)

The union, sadly, has the emptiness of fantasy. It does not last. Later, in her wanderings, shortly before her suicide, Rhoda laments, 'the wave has broken; the bunch is withered. I seldom think of Percival now' (*W*, p. 319). Once again she is weaving flowers into a garland – a gift for which there is no imaginable recipient.

Rhoda is a poet. In imagery usually exquisite, occasionally pungent, she expresses the isolation of human living, the despair and disgust of human company, the allure of the landscapes of fantasy. She finds in the creations of music one of the principal consolations for the meaninglessness of living and for gratuitous death. Three times (*W*, pp. 288, 318, 335) she affirms the triumph of art in a world where no metaphysical triumph is possible, where we ourselves must construct our 'dwelling place'. 'The structure is now visible, what is inchoate is here stated; we are not so various or so mean, we have made oblongs and stood them upon squares. This is our triumph; this our consolation' (*W*, p. 288). Rhoda might be taken to state the moral and metaphysical aesthetics of *The Waves*. But her own poetry is abortive. She is too 'afraid of the door opening and the leap of the tiger to make even one sentence'. Alone she is 'mistress of [a] fleet of ships' – fantasy ships, the counterpart of Louis's luxury liners. In company, she 'breaks into pieces'. She is her dead lover's true opposite. Faceless, where Percival is beautiful; lacking identity, where he is full of natural being: she leaps to her death, a suicide. Her willed, frightened death is the counterpart to Percival's accidental and lamented fall.

Rhoda reminds us in her experiences, images, fears and gifts of Woolf herself.[14] But the abortive poet who cannot complete a sentence or tolerate human company, who fears the embraces of the living and can love only the dead, is an entirely different person from the active participant in an extensive social, literary and political circle, the woman who wrote *The Waves*, sustained a marriage, started the Hogarth Press, and completed sentence upon sentence in novel, pamphlet, diary, essay and letter. Woolf felt, like Rhoda, that Thoby's death revealed a hard reality and that the revelation was a gift she was fortunate to receive (*MB*, p. 118). But she did not escape to fantasy. In her life she fought despair and comforted others. In her art, she re-created her brother in personae and relations which are political, compassionate and realistic. When in *The Waves* she articulates the deep fantasies of desire, fear and loss that cluster around the brother-figure, she does so from a position of strength.

Although Rhoda undoubtedly expresses a dark current of Woolf's being, Woolf, in the words of Bernard, explicitly repudiates her fearful isolation.

I went into the Strand, and evoked to serve as opposite to myself the figure of Rhoda always so furtive, always with fear in her eyes, always seeking some pillar in the desert, to find which she had gone; she had killed herself. 'Wait', I said, putting my arm in imagination (thus we consort with our friends) through her arm. 'Wait until these omnibuses have gone by. Do not cross so dangerously. These men are your brothers.' In persuading her I was also persuading my own soul. (*W*, pp. 371–2)

Rhoda's fantasy-crazed isolation is one possible response to the very real pain of death, the very real danger of 'male' will and indifferent might. Percival represents that pain and danger made beautiful. Rhoda responds to frightening might with beautiful words, to strength with a garland of flowers, to death with violets of sexual fantasy. We are inevitably moved by her sufferings and her exquisite imaginings. Yet it is Bernard, Rhoda's would-be comforter, who shows the way to tame and to live with the experience of Percival.

Bernard has a realistic, even humorous view of Percival. While Louis anxiously opposed himself to Percival and Rhoda was faceless in his presence, Bernard is simply and self-confidently different. Their difference is captured in Bernard's repeated remarks that though Percival would have been a leader who dispensed justice and pronounced verdicts, he, Bernard, is 'not a judge', 'not a moralist', 'not called upon to give [his] opinion' (*W*, p. 339), too aware of 'the shortness of life and its temptations to rule red lines' (*W*, p. 327). Bernard humorously perceives for Percival a future when, riding a 'flea-bitten mare' and wearing a sun helmet, he will 'settle the Oriental problem' 'by applying the standards of the West, by using the violent language that is natural to him' (*W*, p. 269). After Percival's death, Bernard resists the temptation to sentimentalise: 'Furthermore, this is important; that I should be able to place him in ridiculous situations, so that he may not feel himself absurd, perched on a great horse' (*W*, p. 282).

At the 'last supper' before Percival's departure, the seven friends enjoy a communion, create 'a globe whose walls', according to Jinny, 'are made of Percival'. Percival's part in the dinner – a god-like hero-presence who makes the moment possible – is analogous to Mrs Ramsay's at her dinner in *To the Lighthouse*. Bernard needs no god. Though he appreciates the importance of the 'moment created by us from Percival' (*W*, p. 146) ('he sat there in the centre') he finds Percival 'too small a mark' to bear the 'width and breadth' of the feelings of communion. For Bernard, Percival is only one petal of a seven-sided flower, 'a whole flower to which every eye brings its contribution' (*W*, p. 263). When Bernard later mourns for Percival, he misses neither hero nor leader, but a companion with whom he could 'walk off arm-in-arm together laughing' (*W*, p. 367), someone natural, truthful, calm, *almost* indifferent but compassionate (*W*, p. 284). This realistic affection in no way dilutes Bernard's mourning, nor does it prevent his final identification with Percival, the knight, the half-mythical creature, who rather than falling flings himself against the great enemy, death.

Bernard's role in *The Waves* is analogous to Lily's in *To the Lighthouse*. Like Lily in her painting, Bernard in his phrase-making 'sums up', makes of lives something whole, reduces relations without irreverence. Like Lily, he is neither ambitious nor successful in a conventional way. Like her, he is suspicious of the uses and fate of his work, his phrases. It is to Bernard, more than to the four other writers of *The Waves* (i.e. the woman writing in the window, Louis, Neville and Rhoda), that Woolf assigns the human functions of the craft. Bernard's writing began when he dropped his knife and ran to comfort Susan. His writer's creed is a moral one. He will not use words to falsify or sentimentalise. 'Let us commit any blasphemy of laughter and criticism rather than exude this lily-sweet glue; and cover him with phrases' (*W*, p. 360) he exclaims after Percival's death. He realises the incompleteness of his understanding and refuses to 'reduce to order' (*W*, pp. 354 and *passim*), as Louis would, the complexities and nuances of lives. He knows that words can work against understanding, that 'at every crisis, some phrase which does not fit insists upon coming to the rescue' (*W*, p. 303). Sometimes he, like the natural Susan, comes close to Percival's silence. It is not the silence of the warrior or the schoolboy hero that 'defends itself from any caress'. It is silence in search of 'some little language that lovers use, broken words, inarticulate words, like the shuffling of feet upon the pavement (*W*, p. 342).

The great last section of the novel is Bernard's summing up. Using the capacity for sympathy which is the basis of his craft, he rehearses, relives and subsumes the spiritual lives of all the characters. He, the most natural man, speaks with the accents of the goddess seer. 'For this is not one life; nor do I always know if I am man or woman' (*W*, p. 342).

It is impossible, finally, to distinguish between Woolf and her *male* creation, between either of them and the mother seer. Having adopted maternal vision while refusing a motherly identity or life, Woolf freed herself both to give birth to and to appropriate a benign maleness – a protective brotherliness, a realistic cameraderie. In Bernard, Woolf has given *herself* a voice which is that of a male inheritor who is trustworthy and moral, a voice which is qualified to speak on behalf of fraternity: 'these men are your brothers'. Listening to that voice as she herself creates it, she is free to mourn her dead brother with the absolute purity of wholeheartedness.

> Here in the few minutes that remain, I must record, heaven be praised, the end of *The Waves*. I wrote the words O Death fifteen minutes ago, having reeled across the last ten pages with some moments of such intensity and intoxication that I seemed only to stumble after my own voice, or almost, after some sort of speaker (as when I was mad) I was almost afraid, remembering the voices that used to fly ahead. Anyhow, it is done; and I have been sitting these 15 minutes in a state of glory, and calm, and some tears, thinking of Thoby and if I could write Julian Thoby Stephen 1881–1906 on the first page.   (*WD*, p. 165)

Bernard represents the best aspects of brotherliness while matter-of-factly disassociating himself from judgement and alluring might. With such a man a sister 'could walk . . . not alone anymore but arm in arm',[15] as Bernard imagines he would walk with Rhoda. With such a private brother, she need not fear the public world.

'Do not cross so dangerously. These men are your brothers.' In allowing Bernard to persuade Rhoda, she was 'also persuading [my] own soul'.

Even as I write this testimony to Woolf's spiritual progress I can hear my own doubts. I have written as if art disposes while life proposes, as if experience is transformed in word and symbol, enabling new experience, which in turn requires further transformations. I do believe this to be part of the truth about the uses of art in the service of spiritual progress. But, of course, life itself does its share of disposing while the transformations of art may be more stably helpful for us the beneficiaries than they were for their creators.

It is well known that in 'real life' Virginia Woolf enjoyed relations to men in some way brother-like to her: Clive Bell, E. M. Forster, Duncan Grant and many others. Her nephew Julian Bell seemed to her both a reincarnation and an inferior version of Thoby. Her husband, Leonard Woolf, a friend of Thoby's, even in love with him before he met Virginia, was the most crucial of her brother friends. Woolf's loving life and struggles with these men surely affected her reconciliation with her brothers, both in life and in art.

It is, of course, often life which disposes what earliest fantasy, earlier art and life itself has proposed. Conversely, the disposition of art has its clear and mysterious limits. Despite the hard-won political and psychological insights of her art, Virginia Woolf continued to suffer intermittently from an intense anxiety for which she had developed ill-suited or ineffective defences. Her suicide, prompted by 'madness' and the fear of more madness, puts the lie to any simple story of *therapeutic* progress.

Therapeutic progress, like its relative happiness, is quite distinct from spiritual progress or wisdom. I believe that in her adult life Woolf became increasingly wise, that her capacities for indignation, charity and political acuity steadily grew. This political, moral and spiritual progress is, I believe, evident to any common reader who looks for it. By contrast, even the specially trained know little about the causes, less about the experience of madness. Yet we often take it upon ourselves to diagnose the malady we do not understand, to enumerate the defects of the afflicted psyche at the cost of appreciating its virtues. Untrained myself, I ask only that we know how much we do not know. With our ignorance before us, we can avoid some prevalent confusions between a therapist's assessment of mental health and the common reader's assessment of political and moral strength. In her writing, as in much of her art, Woolf was among the sanest, the strongest, the most joyful of women. If we are to learn, as she advises, 'to think back through our mothers', we must matter-of-factly endure their weaknesses so that we may concentrate our energies on their strengths.

NOTES

I am grateful to Margaret Comstock, Evelyn Fox Keller, Jane Marcus and Marilyn Blatt Young for helpful comments on an earlier draft of this paper and to Jane Marcus for suggesting it in the first place.

HD   First holograph draft of *The Waves*, in the Berg Collection of the
       New York Public Library.

1. From Adrienne Rich, 'Natural Resources', in *The Dream of a Common
   Language* (New York: W. W. Norton, 1978):

> It was never the rapist:
> It was the brother, lost,
>
> the comrade–twin whose palm
> would bear a life-line like our own: . . .
>
> merely a fellow-creature
> with natural resources equal to our own.

2. Woolf's relations to Adrian and to the Duckworth brothers are
   interesting in their own right. I discuss them in some detail in the larger
   paper of which this is a part. Briefly: Woolf's relation with Adrian and
   her literary recreation of that relation in *To the Lighthouse* are explicable
   in psychoanalytic terms. Her relation to the Duckworth brothers and its
   consequences *should* be expressed in moral–political rather than
   psychological language. However, as we are learning, politics and
   psychology are inseparable. Woolf's relation to Adrian is finally
   comprehensible only if we understand the familial and social institutions in which that relation occurred. As many critics have pointed out,
   Woolf's relation with the Duckworth brothers had profound
   psychological consequences in her life.
3. According to one standard interpretation, this 'shock' comes from a
   disguised sexual connection of brother/lover/father combined with an
   unconscious fantasy of the male violence of sexual intercourse. According to this interpretation, Woolf suddenly 'sees' that she is allowing
   herself to be loved/beaten by her brother and cannot tolerate either the
   fear or the wish of that perception. I believe that this may in fact be one
   element of the memory, and I treat it differently when discussing
   Woolf's sexuality. However, in assessing the allegedly standard childhood fantasies, we must discuss the 'politics' of their origin and their
   persistence, must explore connections between actual male dominance,
   violence and sexuality which a child of either sex may involuntarily 'see',
   may fear, and may wish to emulate.
4. Virginia Woolf, 'The Introduction', in *Mrs Dalloway's Party*, ed. Stella
   McNichol (London: Hogarth Press, 1973).
5. Plato, *Phaedrus*, trs. R. Hackforth (Cambridge: Cambridge University
   Press, 1972) p. 96.
6. Brenda Silver, who is preparing an invaluable edition of Woolf's
   reading notes, sent me these lines and dated them for me.
7. I first became aware of the 1903 diary and this particular quotation
   from it in Brenda Silver's 'The House, the Playhouse, and *Between the
   Acts*: A Study of Community in Virginia Woolf'. A very much shorter
   version of this paper appears in *Women's Studies*, IV (1977) pp. 291–8.
8. See, *inter alia*, Duncan Grant's memoir in *Recollections of Virginia Woolf*,
   ed. Joan Russell Noble (London: Peter Owen, 1972).

9. The connections are clearest in Jacob's daydream which occurs during the Cambridge chapel service. 'Death in the forest', insects knocking against their lantern aimlessly, a besotted toad forcing his way in, pistol shots (the sound of a fallen tree) – we recognise Jacob's associations to the earlier experience of the butterfly hunt, described in many of the same words. His reverie is immediately followed by the thought that a dog is as eligible for entrance to the chapel as a woman (*JR*, p. 32).

10. The line – from Yeats's 'Lapis Lazuli' – seems to epitomise a virtue of many Woolfian characters, particularly her central women characters.

11. J. W. Graham, 'Point of View in *The Waves*: Some Services of the Style', in *Virginia Woolf*, ed. Thomas S. W. Lewis (New York: McGraw-Hill, 1975).

12. Simone Weil, *The Iliad or the Poem of Force*, Pendle Hill Pamphlet (Wallingford, Penn.). I am amending some of the phrases in the light of the translation used in the *Simone Weil Reader*, ed. George A. Panichas (New York: McKay, 1977).

13. Doris Eder has argued that Louis is 'modelled' on Eliot: 'Louis Unmasked: T. S. Eliot in *The Waves*', *Virginia Woolf Quarterly*, II, nos 1 and 2. Though Louis sometimes reminds me of Leonard Woolf, Eder's arguments are convincing.

14. In *Moments of Being*, Woolf remembers being unable to cross a puddle, an experience which, in *The Waves*, she diagnoses. Rhoda cannot carry a message, cannot embrace or communicate, because she has no 'identity'. In Woolf's characters, identity fails because of too-ready merging (low ego boundaries) of a self which is so divided, frightened and ashamed that it has no natural centre. Both the capacity to merge in acute empathy and the willingness to suffer the divisions and feelings endemic to selfhood have their positive aspects. Rhoda and Woolf share many other experiences recorded in the diaries and memoirs – propensity to fantasy, appreciation of beautiful language, fitful disgust with the physical nature of human beings, fear of sexuality, obsession with mirrors, a sense of the body as unnatural and emotions as learned, and, of course, suicide. I do not wish to deny these in insisting on the disidentity so evident in Woolf's ability to create, to understand, and to disavow the terror and isolation which mar Rhoda's beauty.

15. This phrase, reminiscent of Bernard's expression when he misses Percival, comes from *To the Lighthouse*. Lily, in the presence of a scientist, William Bankes, relives a night-time visit in which she tested out and resisted her temptation to merge with Mrs Ramsay, becoming 'like waters poured into one jar, inextricably the same, one with the object one adored'. Subsequent to this separation, she achieves intimacy with Bankes with whom she shares her painting: 'one could walk . . . not alone anymore but arm in arm with somebody'. Bankes is a hybrid figure. For Mrs Ramsay, he is Lily's suitor and would-be husband. Although Lily knows this, she considers Bankes a comrade and older brother, even avuncular, with none of the powerful, beautiful allure of the male hero whom Woolf treats in *The Waves*.

10 The Politics of City Space in *The Years*: Street Love, Pillar Boxes and Bridges

SUSAN SQUIER

I

In *The Years*, as in so many of her novels, Virginia Woolf presents a politics of space. Focusing on the urban experience, she guides her readers to an awareness of the female experience, both as it is and as it may be. The speech she gave in January 1931 to the London National Society for Women's Service reveals her keen understanding of the difficulty a woman writer encounters if she tries to tell the truth about her experiences.[1] In order to practise her profession, she points out, the woman writer has to give in to some impulses and to deny others. She must kill the Angel in the House, who coaxes her to flatter and to defer to men, and she must let 'her imagination sweep unchecked round every rock and cranny of the world that lies submerged in our unconscious being' (*P*, p. xxxviii). Yet those fishing trips of the creative imagination are often disrupted, Woolf tells us, to the fisherwoman's dismay. Either the line of her imagination floats 'limply and dully and lifelessly upon the surface' of her mind, for want of experience, or the reason reels it in, because 'men would be shocked' by the 'very queer knowledge' it has hooked 'about womens [*sic*] bodies ... their passions' (*P*, pp. xxxviii–xxxix). Not only the more common problem of a limited experience

216

hampers the woman novelist. The male taboo against free speech concerning sexuality, which women have internalised, also checks the free movement of the female writer's mind. What Woolf described, in her speech to the London/ National Society for Women's Service, is the allegorical 'watcher at the gates' that Friedrich Schiller playfully evoked in his letter to a friend suffering from writer's block:

> In isolation, an idea may be quite insignificant, and venturesome in the extreme, but it may acquire importance from an idea which follows it. . . . In the case of a creative mind, it seems to me, the intellect has withdrawn its watchers from the gates, and the ideas rush in pell-mell, and only then does it review and inspect the multitudes. . . . You are ashamed or afraid of the momentary and passing madness which is found in all real creators, the longer or shorter duration of which distinguishes the thinking artist from the dreamer. . . . You reject too soon and discriminate too severely.[2]

Schiller understood that, although an excessively strict watcher at the gates could curtail a writer's creativity by inhibiting promising ideas, at the proper time and place the watcher played a useful role. In contrast, Woolf's watcher quite literally barred the gate to the outside world for women writers. To outwit the watcher, she wrote 'at a rapid and haphazard gallop' in her diary; she also wrote at unexpected times and in unexpected places.[3] For her, as for all women writers, the watcher was on the alert for more than bad art. As the protector of the patriarchal castle, he was on the alert for subversive material as well: for shocking sexual candour or that partisan anger and special pleading which, Woolf felt, were more threatening to the castle of the traditional canon even than candour about female sexuality.[4]

Woolf outwitted her watcher by modifying not just where and when she wrote, but also what she wrote: she learned to use a modern descendant of the patriarchal castle to disguise and to embody the truth of her experience as a woman. For this, she turned to London, which 'takes up the private life and carries it on, without any effort' (*WD*, p. 61). The watcher, surveying the view from the castle gates, would fail to recognise subversive topics because they were mingled with their urban surroundings, the tune of a barrel organ or the puzzle of a street crowd. An examination of the image and experience of the city in *The Years* reveals both the process and the product of Woolf's vision of woman's experience, then: not just what that truth was that she fought the watcher at the gates to express, but what the creative strategies were that enabled her to achieve that expression.

II

Woolf's working title for the early drafts of *The Years* was *The Pargiters*. Published in 1977 by the New York Public Library, *The Pargiters* reveals Woolf's awareness of the woman novelist's difficulty in writing about her experience. Since Jane Marcus's exciting finding of the resemblance between the book's title (and surname of the novel's family of protagonists) and 'pargeters', an entry in Joseph Wright's *English Dialect Dictionary* meaning to cover up, whitewash or lie, and to patch up, build and beautify, critics have explored the ways in which the word 'Pargiter' evokes the creative struggle of *The Years*.[5] The negative and positive connotations of 'pargeter' echo the tension Woolf struggled with in her work. Concerned to tell the truth about 'the sexual life of women' (*WD*, pp. 161–2), a truth which reflected their political and social oppression, she turned to the technique of 'pargeting' to express her vision. Both meanings of 'pargeter' are thus crucial to an understanding of *The Years*. Woolf built up her picture of women's lives in the experience of the city itself. Thus, she used the constructive technique of the 'pargeter' to convey the destructive truth, that male oppression causes women to cover up, whitewash, or lie about the truth of the female experience in order to avoid alienating their male audience. 'Pargeting', building the truth of women's experience into the setting itself, she used the city to embody her ideological perspective.

Woolf had first intended to combine fact and vision in the 'novel–essay' *The Pargiters*. As she envisioned it, the essay part of the book would explore the sexual, economic and social forces affecting the lives of those characters whose experiences she would dramatise in the fictional sections. Her fear that anger could distort a work of art was marked in her approach to fiction. However, both *A Room of One's Own* and *Three Guineas* use the essay form strongly to express Woolf's feminism.[6] Therefore it is not surprising that she was able to express her vision of woman's experience more fully in the essay chapters of *The Pargiters* than in the later, fully fictional manuscript of *The Years*. In those essay sections, Woolf connects the urban and the female experiences: the war for sexual equality is fought in the battlefield of London, where men and women struggle with each other for control of the streets. She shows us a city 'artificially partitioned off' into sex-linked zones, each with its own form of 'love' (*P*, p. 36).[7] To women and children belongs the drawing room, with its varied forms of open and concealed love. The largely male force Woolf calls in contrast, street love, which seems 'different from all the other loves inside the drawing room', controls the streets, and besieges the private home 'on all sides' (*P*, pp. 35, 37). In her discussion of street love, Woolf focuses on the question central to the novel as she first envisioned it: 'I have this moment, while having my bath, conceived an entire new book – a sequel to *A Room of One's Own* – about the sexual life of women' (*WD*, pp. 161–2). Woolf did not produce the exposé one might expect from such a description of her subject, however. Instead, she turned the topic inside out, to show how the sexual life of women, or rather their lack of sexual freedom, was a result of the restrictive structure of their lives. Woolf's analysis of street love uncovers the powerless situation of the Pargiter women in 1880; the politics of city space suggests the underlying sexual politics which was the novel's theme.

The fact of street love, Woolf tells us, had a far greater influence upon the women of the time than upon the men. Although it affected women in all areas of life, the social effects of street love were undoubtedly the most blatant, for by street love Woolf meant the frank, aggressive, in many cases hostile, display of male sexuality, like that which Rose Pargiter experiences one evening when she disobeys the rules and ventures out to Lamley's. As she hurries to the shop to buy a box of ducks and swans for her bath, she passes a man whose face frightens her. '"The enemy – the enemy!" Rose cried to

220   *New Feminist Essays on Virginia Woolf*

herself, ... playing the game'(*P*, p. 42). On her return trip, there is nothing playful about the encounter. 'When she reached the pillar box there was the man again. He was leaning against it, as if he were ill, Rose thought.... There was nobody else anywhere in sight. As she ran past him, he gibbered some nonsense at her, sucking his lips in & out, & began to undo his clothes ...' (*P*, p. 43).

Because of the threat of such incidents, Rose Pargiter and her sisters were virtually confined to their home in Abercorn Terrace. They could not go for a walk alone except in the streets right around their house, and then only during the daylight hours. Expeditions to other parts of London were impossible unless they had a brother or a matron to chaperone them. Street love made the simplest form of meeting impossible for the Pargiter girls: they could not move freely from one part of London to another.

The social limitations which street love enforced upon the Pargiter girls had psychological effects as well, Woolf explains, for, since they were spirited children, they did not always obey the rules. Occasionally they did the forbidden; went to Bond Street or the Burlington Arcade alone, and then, to make matters worse, lied about it to their father. The restrictions on their physical and social liberty thus resulted in limitations upon their psychological freedom as well, manifest in the need to cover up, to lie to others about their activities. So Rose was unable to tell Eleanor what she had seen that had frightened her so much, following her confrontation with the man at the pillar box.

Not only was communication between siblings, or between parent and child, affected. Soon the self could not communicate with itself, with the discouraging effects which Woolf described in her speech to the the London/National Society for Women's Service. In fact, the interruption of self-awareness which street love created was far more damaging than the frightening incidents which resulted from it: 'not only did it restrict their lives, [but] to some extent it [poisoned] their minds – lies of all sorts undoubtedly having a crippling and distorting effect, and none the less if the liar feels that his lie is justified' (*P*, p. 52). The guilt and confused pleasure which the girls felt when they saw one of the taboo scenes of street love woke them in the night with strange feelings and disturbing dreams, reactions to the cloistered, sexually straitened atmosphere in which they lived. The shock and guilt provoked in Rose by the man's frightening act of exhibitionism at the pillar box was accompanied, Woolf explains, by her sudden awareness of an untapped fund of feeling inside her which the experience identified and even seemed to elicit. Woolf calls it 'a rage of emotion',[8] and the ambivalence of the term is appropriate, for Rose finds now that her sexuality, like her anger, is difficult to express. Both emotions were taboo for women in a patriarchal society, as Woolf pointed out in 'Women and Fiction' (1929) and her speech of 21 January 1931.

City experience and female experience are interrelated in *The Pargiters*. The effect of the restrictions street love placed on the Pargiter girls was to alienate them from two of their fundamental experiences as human beings: to turn to ugliness their own sexual feelings by overlaying them with guilt, and to defuse anger at their oppression by confusing it with guilt and hence robbing it of legitimacy. Such repression in the mind of a child could have lasting effects on the adult as well. Kitty Malone, for instance, who was sexually sheltered throughout adolescence, lost contact not only with the outer world from which she had to be protected to preserve her innocence, but with her inner world as well, with her feelings as a woman. Since restraint was the first lesson she had been taught, she felt little, even when proposed to. Like many Victorian women, Woolf explains, Kitty's sexual response had been muted by the restrictions placed upon it.

Since sexual response is dependent upon that escape into freedom which each longed to make, the women in *The Years* paradoxically directed their sexual energy towards those qualities of life which would liberate it. '[They] are drawn to women who (erroneously) seemed to have escaped the tyrannies and repressions endured by most of their sex and whose lives as a consequence seem more romantic, less constricted, more autonomous, freer, and bolder than their own.[9] Thus Kitty Malone loves Lucy Craddock's passion for knowledge, for 'things in themselves' (*P*, p. 112). Her love expresses her mingled longing to break free of all her oppressions: free play of the mind is at least as important, if not more, as sexual freedom in motivating her love. The women of *The Years* eroticise liberty because for them liberty *is* sexuality. The oppression of the former results in the denial of the latter.

Cut off both from the outer world of the city streets and from the inner world of their female experience, the Pargiter girls also suffered from a diminished sense of life's possibilities. Because they had to be protected from street love, they could not go to parties or even visit friends without a chaperone. Thus their chance for enjoyment or occupation was reduced to finding the one socially acceptable route out of their father's home into a less straitened existence: marriage. Woolf's comments in the interpolated essays shed more light on the hostility Eleanor senses between Delia and Milly in '1881', when Colonel Pargiter mentions that he 'met old Burke at the Club', who asked him to bring 'one of them to dinner because his son Robin was "back on leave"'.[10] Rivalry between sisters inevitably resulted from such a restricted, competitive social environment: the economics of marriage settlements and dowries added a further complication. So later, in *The Years*, North Pargiters considers Eleanor's spinsterhood. 'She had never married. Why not? he wondered. Sacrificed to the family, he supposed – Old Grandpapa without any fingers' (*Y*, p. 372).

Since in most cases women were unable to earn a living wage, a single life posed a grim threat to a woman. Competition in the marriage market was intense. Quentin Bell seems to miss the point of the conversation to which he alludes in his biography. As Woolf described the conversation in her essay 'Leslie Stephen', Lady Ritchie's tendency to exaggerate was provoked by Stephen's own 'sobriety'. ' "There are 40,000,000 unmarried women in London alone!" Lady Ritchie once informed him. "Oh, Annie, Annie!" my father exclaimed in tones of horrified but affectionate rebuke.'[11] Bell overlooks Lady Ritchie's playfulness, revealed in this scene; instead, he calls her 'hardly aware' of facts and 'unabashedly sentimental'.[12] His view of her conflicts markedly with Woolf's description in her essay 'The Enchanted Organ' (1924). There, Lady Ritchie is neither sentimental nor dreamily vague. Although 'she said things that no human being could possibly mean; yet she meant them' (*M*, p. 195). Her instinct for truth was profound: 'if her random ways were charming, who, on the other hand, could be more practical, or see things, when she liked, precisely as they were' (ibid.). That irrepressible honest ability to see things as they were and to express what she saw was captured for Woolf in a scene from Lady Ritchie's childhood, a scene which provides a surprising analogue to Rose Pargiter's night-time escapade, yet which, unlike the episode of exhibitionism at the pillar box, has a happy ending.

> The enormous respectability of Bloomsbury was broken one fine morning about 1840 by the sound of an organ and by the sight of a little girl, who had escaped from her nurse and was dancing to the music. The child was Thackeray's elder daughter, Anne. For the rest of her long life, through war and peace, calamity and prosperity, Miss Thackeray, or Mrs. Ritchmond Ritchie, or Lady Ritchie, was always escaping from the Victorian gloom and dancing to the strains of her own enchanted organ.   (*M*, p. 193)

Woolf's description of Lady Ritchie's moment of freedom from the respectable Victorian home has a curiously fitting *double-entendre* which reveals the true extent and significance of such an escape. In freeing herself from the 'Victorian gloom' which Woolf described so thoroughly in the interpolated essays of *The Pargiters*, woman frees her sexuality from repression as well. Lady Ritchie's dance seems to celebrate her female sexuality itself, 'her own enchanted organ' to which she dances.

The free celebration of female sexuality which Lady Ritchie's dance suggests was also disbarred by street love.

> The question of chastity was therefore complicated in the extreme, since it was influenced by so many feelings that could not be discussed and by so many facts that might be resented but could not possibly be altered. Had not the demand for the vote, which might ultimately lead to some right to earn one's living, been again defeated in the House of Commons?   (*P*, p. 53)

The effect of that dismissal was maddeningly circular. The vote was denied women, Woolf implies, to protect their chastity: female chastity was essential because women did not have the vote, and hence could not change the law which disabled them from earning enough money to support the children which might result from sexual freedom. The ultimate effect of street love in the 1880s, Woolf argues, was to keep from women economic, social and legal equality. Women were denied the vote, and hence denied the opportunity for education and a profession, because their chastity must be protected. And from what? From assertive male sexuality: street love. And so street love reveals the relationship between the urban experience and the female experience, a relationship Woolf went on to explore, implicitly rather than explicitly, in *The Years*.

III

Woolf revised the manuscript of *The Pargiters* in 1933, and the revision was sweeping. 'Today I finished – rather more completely than usual – revising the first chapter. I am leaving out the interchapters – compacting them in the text . . . .'[13] Abandoned along with the essay portions of the novel was Woolf's explicit consideration of the experience of women, contained in her analysis of street love. Instead, Woolf presented her vision implicitly, moving towards 'that aesthetic tension which is generated from documented vision in union with poeticised truth'.[14] Two urban objects, the pillar box and the bridge, suggest in microcosm how Woolf uses the whole city experience implicitly to convey the truth of woman's experience in *The Years*. The pillar box appears in Woolf's speech to the London/National Society for Women's Service, which was the origin of *The Years*.[15] There, it marks the boundary between the private and public worlds, between the dependence of a woman in the patriarchal home and the freedom of money and a room of one's own. To the difficulty that many women, among them the composer Dame Ethel Smyth, faced in finding a place in the professions, Woolf contrasts her own relative ease at becoming a writer: the result, she claims with tongue in cheek, of 'the cheapness of writing materials' (*P*, p. xxviii). All a woman need do to become a writer, she tells her audience, is to follow the example of the girl in the story, who is, of course, Virginia Woolf herself.

my story is compared with Dame Ethel's a very tame one. You have only got to figure to yourselves a girl [sitting and writing] ⟨in a bed-room with a pen in her hand⟩ a girl who had plenty of pens and paper at command. Then it occurred to her to do what again only costs a penny stamp – to [send] ⟨slip⟩ an article [on to a news-paper ⟨into a pillar box⟩ ; and to suggest to the editor of that newspaper that she might be allowed to try her hand at reviewing . . . a book. (*D*, p. xxix)

'Hence I became a reviewer', Woolf tells her audience. Yet in her speech she goes on to describe how something which seems so simple, that walk to the pillar box with envelope in hand, is actually fraught with difficulties for women. The pillar box is first associated with work, and with the oppression which makes work so difficult for women.

In *The Years*, the pillar box besides marking the boundary between the private home and the professional world, marks other thematic boundaries. 'That red box at the corner' first teaches Rose Pargiter the distinction between male and female sexuality.[16] In *The Years*, as in *The Pargiters*, Rose eludes her nurse and sneaks out of the house one night in 1880, drawn to Lamley's shop by the box of toy ducks in the window. The forbidden jaunt is an adventure to Rose at first; in a strikingly militaristic and masculine fantasy, she imagines herself a brave rescuer of besieged British troops. Yet, when the mewing, pock-marked man by the pillar box exposes himself to her, her fantasy world is shattered and she flees for home. Even when she is safely in bed, the experience continues to affect her, troubling her sleep with fear and guilt.

The exhibitionist episode links the pillar box to the social oppression of women which Woolf saw was a product of street love. As she rode down Melrose Avenue with the dash of a man, imagining herself to be 'Pargiter of Pargiter's Horse' (*Y*, p. 27), and enjoying therein feelings of competence and adventure, Rose was confronted by an experience which sharply redefined her sexual role and limited her appropriate feelings. 'She was herself again, a little girl who had disobeyed her sister, in her house shoes, flying for safety to Lamley's shop' (*Y*, p. 28). The man's exhibitionism drove Rose from the streets back to the nursery in the private home. So the pillar box also marks the boundary between the world of sexuality, which men have annexed for themselves despite Rose's heroic attempt to liberate it, and the world of the private home, where women live in cloistered, pre-sexual retreat. The experience at the pillar box also cloisters off certain areas of Rose's mind. She cannot tell Eleanor what she saw – the man's genitals, presumably. Woolf has now added another association to the pillar box. While in her talk of 21 January 1931 it was an emblem of woman's freedom of speech, in *The Years* it is associated with prohibitions against speech, especially speech about sexuality. In fact, Rose herself lives in the 'besieged garrison' of her fantasy. The man at the pillar box, whom she rightly knows to be 'the enemy', now not only holds her captive at home, but has invaded her mind. The consequences for Rose can be disastrous, for it is 'hard to fight an enemy with outposts in your head'.[17]

To the pillar box's two associations of work and sexuality, Woolf adds a third: education. That theme is embodied in a ritual which Eleanor remembers, the night her life changes forever with the death of her mother. She writes a letter to her brother Edward about her mother's condition, and Morris offers to post it for her.

> He got up as if he were glad to have something to do. Eleanor went to the front door with him and stood holding it open while he went to the pillar box.... Morris disappeared under the shadows round the corner. She remembered how she used to stand at the door when he was a small boy and went to a day school with a satchel in his hand. She used to wave to him and when he got to the corner he always turned and waved back. It was a curious little ceremony dropped now that they were both grown up. (*Y*, p. 41)

One wonders if the ceremony has been dropped because it has served its purpose. After years of training, Eleanor has accepted her place in the private home; that night, with her mother's death, she will take on the role of housekeeper for her father. The 'suppressed emotion' which Morris feels 'cooped up with all these women' is the product of that obsolete little ceremony (*Y*, p. 44). That ceremony is responsible, too, for the distance which has grown up between

Eleanor and Morris. Here the pillar box marks another barrier, between the education available to women and that given to men. Eleanor's sketchy self-education prevents her from communicating with Morris; she no longer asks questions about his work, for fear of seeming silly, and he, in turn, no longer shares his thoughts with her.

> Ought she not to have said Lord Chief Justice? She never could remember which was which; and that was why he would not discuss Evans v. Carter with her.
>   She never told him about the Levys, either, except by way of a joke. That was the worst of growing up, she thought; they couldn't share things as they used to share them. When they met they never had time to talk as they used to talk – about things in general – they always talked about facts – little facts. (*Y*, p. 34)

When Morris disappears under the shadows round the corner, he crosses another boundary marked by the pillar box, the boundary of education. Morris receives the education of a man – Eleanor, of a woman. As Woolf writes of this distinction in *Three Guineas*, it is a 'precipice, a gulf so deeply cut' between the female and the male that she wonders whether 'it is any use trying to speak across it' (*TG*, p. 4). Education permits Morris to enter the world of the Bar; without it, Eleanor must stay in the home or do volunteer work with the Levys. The gulf which separates them affects communication; it discourages the speaker and lessens the receptivity of the listener. So the pillar box embodies the demarcation Woolf deplored between the male, public world (where educational and sexual experiences are allowed men) and the female, private world (where both educational and sexual experiences are strictly controlled, by rationing money and interactions).

The triple associations of the pillar box, then, characterise the Victorian era's oppression of women. Woolf does not express her subversive vision directly. Instead, she conveys it through the image of the pillar box, which embodies and connects the different episodes of oppression (societal, sexual, psychological) she presents. So, in 'Present Day', Eleanor and Peggy Pargiter pass Abercorn Terrace as they take a taxi to a family party. As they both look at the 'imposing unbroken avenue with its succession of pale pillars and steps' Eleanor thinks of her childhood. ' "Abercorn Terrace", said Eleanor. "The pillar box." ' Peggy wonders why Eleanor makes the association, but soon she seems to have made the same one. 'Was it that you were suppressed when you were young?' she asks Eleanor. In an image which combines the three associations of the pillar box, Eleanor remembers 'a picture – another picture – [which] had swum to the surface': 'There was Delia standing in the middle of the room; Oh my God! she was saying; a hansom cab had stopped at the house next door; and she herself was watching Morris – was it Morris? – going down the street to post a letter' (*Y*, pp. 335–6).

Although Eleanor had no way of knowing the pillar box's associations for her sister Rose, the picture of her repression as a young girl includes those limitations which the division of social life into male and female zones, the boundary marked by the pillar box, places upon women.[18] Woolf elaborated upon Delia's feelings during this scene in *The Pargiters*. There, sexual, social and psychological freedom are linked. Delia, despairing, says 'Oh, my God!' because she sees a woman wheeling a baby carriage; that image of her own probable future makes her realise she will never be allowed to travel to Germany to study music. Eleanor's memory of watching Morris post the letter recalls the same triad of restrictions which settled upon her with the death of her mother. While that event freed Delia and her sisters from the private home, as Eleanor promised it would, it left Eleanor as the spinster housekeeper for her father.

IV

While the picture of London which Woolf's use of the pillar box paints in *The Years* is a grim one, it is important to emphasise that Woolf is not suggesting that the oppression of women is a result of the urban environment. Far from it; in fact, here as in her other works, Woolf's treatment of the city setting stresses the interaction of urban environment and the structure of human society. In her use of the pillar box she explores the way in which oppressive human societies shape, even distort, the urban environment; she uses the bridge image in *The Years* to explore the opposite interaction: the city's effect on human behaviour. The bridge image, which Woolf drew on to suggest her sense of the positive future for women, is deeply rooted in the past – both in the history of the Pargiter family within the novel, and in the history of the novel itself. In fact, the two histories are mingled; an understanding of their interrelationship illuminates the significance of the bridge image in the novel. *The Years* grew out of the speech which Woolf gave to Pippa Strachey's society, the London/National Society for Women's Service. There, she analysed the obstructions to a career as a writer which she had faced as a young woman. Woolf celebrated the accomplishments of Dame Ethel Smyth, the preceding speaker, who 'built bridges and thus made a way for those who came after her' (*P*, p. xxviii):

> we honour her not merely as a musician and a writer, but also as a blaster of rocks and the maker of bridges. It seems sometimes a pity that a woman who only wished to write music should have been forced also to make bridges, but that was part of her job and she did it. (Ibid.)

As in her talk, so in *The Years* Woolf analyses woman's situation in society; yet she uses the novel's background, both physical (the city setting) and historical (the characters' memories) to present her message. Woman's talent – and her job – is 'bridge building'.

A memory of Eleanor Pargiter's, of a curious little song her nursemaid Pippy used to sing her, possesses significance which radiates throughout the novel's thematic exploration of oppression. 'Sur le point d'Avignon', Pippy sang; as the song continues, 'l'on y danse, tout en ronde' (*Y*, p. 91). Metaphorically, that bridge presents the experience of the women in *The Years*. There, on the bridge between the private home and the professions, the women dance – sometimes a dance of liberated sexuality, like Rose's lesbianism or Maggie's happy marriage, and sometimes a dance of death. That such an important image of woman's future should appear in the nursery rhyme Pippy sings prompts a re-examination of those songs to uncover the primal self-definitions they instil.

Just as the novel was nursed to life by *Pippa* Strachey's request for a talk by Woolf, so the vision which the novel explores, that complex interaction between women, men, and the space in which they live, is revealed through memories of the songs sung by the Pargiters' nurse, *Pippy*. Although several critics have mentioned the evocative quality of those songs Pippy sang to her small charges, no critic has realised that Pippy sings a different tune depending upon the sex of her listener.[19] Pippy is, in fact, something of a sociological oracle. To Martin Pargiter, who will grow up to be a wealthy businessman, Pippy sings, 'The King of Spain's daughter came to visit me/All for the sake of my silver nutmeg tree' (*Y*, p. 227). The song suggests Martin's role of sexual and economic superiority; in it he commands the attention of the King of Spain's daughter because of his wealth, embodied by a silver nutmeg tree. The curious image is revealing: the nutmeg tree, called the pasha of spices, grew in rows like a harem, one male tree for every ten female trees. Male sexual and political domination are both associated with the nutmeg tree, for many (male) wars were fought for possession of lands planted with those valuable spice harems.[20] While Martin's exotic possession thus defines his economic, political and sexual dominion, the woman in the nursery rhyme is defined by her powerful male relative, the King of Spain. In the fantasy world of the nursery rhyme, as in reality, the role of the woman is ancillary; the excitement of being visited by the King of Spain's daughter, one assumes, lies in the political implications of such a visit.

Pippy may be an oracle, but she is not Fate herself; we see Martin's own influence shape the meaning of the song, and of his life. In his youth, the song was part of a ritual of release in which Martin, unafraid, abandoned his sense of safe continuity to an exciting discontinuity. 'She used to take him on her knee and croak out in her wheezy rattle of a voice, "The King of Spain's daughter came to visit me, all for the sake of . . ." and then suddenly her knee gave and down he was tumbled onto the floor' (*Y*, p. 226). However, as he grows up, Martin comes to use the song for an opposite purpose, to support his ego when he feels threatened. Martin has turned his song into a private incantation, a type of personal hymn to money and power.

While the song Pippy sings Martin evolves from a celebration of exciting discontinuity to a retreat into stability and stasis, the song she sings Eleanor instead emphasises the qualities of discontinuity, change and movement.[21] The bridge image of that song is developed further in *Three Guineas*, where it takes on an ironically pessimistic tone:

> We, daughters of educated men, are between the devil and the deep blue sea. Behind us lies the patriarchal system; the private house, with its nullity, its immorality, its hypocrisy, its servility. Before us lies the public world, the professional system, with its possessiveness, its jealousy, its pugnacity, its greed. The one shuts us up like slaves in a harem; the other forces us to circle, like caterpillars head to tail, round and round the mulberry tree, the sacred tree, of property. It is a choice of evils. Each is bad. Had we not better plunge off the bridge into the river; give up the game; declare that the whole of human life is a mistake and so end it? (*TG*, p. 74)

Woolf's angry, ironic tone emphasises the difficulties of change. If the professional system oppresses women through jealousy, pugnacity and greed, that transition from the private to the public world may well seem like a move from one form of stasis to another. Then, instead of dancing on the bridge, women will be tempted to plunge from it into the river.

What Woolf states directly in *Three Guineas*, she expresses through her use of the urban setting in *The Years*. If human life is not all to seem 'a mistake', the oppression of women must cease; human beings must learn to respond positively to people and experiences which are alien to them. That single quality of otherness is central to urban experience, of course; it gives the city that exciting sensation of change and discontinuity anatomised by writers and social theorists.[22] Woolf's striking insight lies in her awareness that in responding to the urban experience, whose main quality is otherness, men are suggesting the way they respond to women as well – women, who have cross-culturally and throughout history been seen as the 'Other'.[23] Martin Pargiter's transformation of his song from a celebration of discontinuity to a reinforcing personal hymn echoes that sultan-like sexual, political and economic dominion he establishes as part of the patriarchal system. That system is threatened by otherness, change, discontinuity: all qualities which Woolf knew were characteristic both of the urban and the female experiences. The pillar box and the bridge represent two responses to that experience of otherness which *The Years* explores; the former, denial and retreat; the latter, affirmation and connection.

V

As *The Years* moves from 1880 to 1937, the novel shows a changing city and a change in the situation of women. The fellowship enjoyed by women in 1880, brought about by street love, is the fellowship of oppression, of what Lillian Robinson has called the 'sexualization of women's experience'. Robinson evokes that fellowship in her essay 'Who's Afraid of a Room of One's Own?': 'It occurred to me that even Virginia Woolf on an omnibus was exposed to the same possibility of insult, the same hint of danger. She could not be "just" a brilliant novelist observing a segment of London life; she was also a piece of female flesh experiencing it.'[24] We can accept Robinson's description of the oppression of women – even famous and creative women – in the patriarchal city. In *The Years*, as in Robinson's New York, the city streets reflect both woman's role and her potential for the future. Either her surroundings allow her an identity which transcends her physical capabilities – allow her to dance across that bridge between the private and the public realms – or they relegate her to immanence as a 'piece of female flesh', restricted from the world beyond the pillar box by the masculine tyranny of street love.

Yet, when we accept Robinson's insight, we do so with an understanding that the city she describes is a patriarchal one, an identity Woolf showed changing in *The Years*. If we reflect on the interaction between self or society and city revealed there, we see that Woolf would be unlikely to affirm or advocate a role as serene, uninvolved and static as that of a 'brilliant novelist' and observer. Rather, in *The Years* Woolf used the changing city to affirm a more engaged, active relationship to the urban environment. She used the image and the experience of the city to make a point implicitly which she felt she could not make explicitly, and so to outwit the watcher at the gate. In her use of pillar box and bridge imagery, she incorporated both the positive and negative connotations of 'pargeter', she both covered up and built up the truth of female experience.

Virginia Woolf created a politics of space in *The Years*. In her use of those two urban objects she showed two responses to otherness, whether it be the otherness of the woman or the otherness of the city. The pillar box embodies the first response: denial and retreat, and an attempt to protect the *status quo*. The phenomenon of street love is an aspect of that response to otherness; it limits the woman's freedom geographically and socially. The spatial enactment of the other response to otherness is embodied by the bridge image; like a bridge itself, it affirms and unifies.

Finally, like Robinson's New York, the London of *The Years* mirrors the 'sexualization of women's experience', the oppression which Woolf saw as characteristic of the 'sexual lives of women' (*WD*, pp. 161–2). Women do find their treatment as women embodied in the geography of the city. However, Woolf moves beyond that view of the city as image for the political and social situation of women at present to consider its role in affecting the future. Vivid and vital embodiment of otherness and change, by the end of *The Years* the city confronts the characters with an experience to which they must respond. As Woolf shows, their response will determine not just the way the sexes will live together, but the possibility of international coexistence as well. Discontinuity and otherness are the challenges the city presents in *The Years*. The response of the pillar box, that impulse to retreat and deny those threatening alien qualities, will result in what Woolf called 'subconscious Hitlerism', totalitarianism at home and abroad.[25] Woolf explores that totalitarian response fully in the novel through her use of the urban setting.

Yet she conducts an equally thorough exploration of the other response in *The Years* as well – of that bridging impulse which affirms change and unifies the discontinuous. We see that affirmative response to otherness in one striking episode at the end of the novel. Two Cockney children, representatives of the inscrutable, alien future generation of city dwellers, sing their discordant and jarring song to the gathered Pargiter family. 'The grown-up people did not know whether to laugh or cry. . . . Nobody knew what to say. There was something horrible in the noise they made. It was so shrill, so discordant, and so meaningless' (Y, p. 430). Patrick acts the privileged and removed spectator, thanking them genially; Martin slips coins into their hands. But Eleanor takes neither the stance of the removed observer nor of the powerful patron. Humble and interested, Eleanor responds affirmatively: she asks a question. ' "Beautiful?" she said, with a note of interrogation' (Y, p. 431). The Years ends there, having presented both a model of woman's situation at present and a vision of the possibilities for men and women in the future – a vision of an affirmative response to otherness and change enacted by Eleanor Pargiter's final words to her brother Morris. ' "And now?" she asked, holding out her hands to him' (Y, p. 435).

NOTES

1. Virginia Woolf, 'Speech Before the London/National Society for Women's Service, 21 January, 1931', in 'The Pargiters': The Novel–Essay Portion of 'The Years', ed. Mitchell A. Leaska (New York: New York Public Library and Readex Books, 1977) pp. xxvii–xxxxiv. Further references (to The Pargiters proper and to the speech) are to this edition, cited as P.
2. Friedrich Schiller, cited in Sigmund Freud, The Interpretation of Dreams (New York: Avon Books, 1965) p. 135.
3. Virginia Woolf, A Writer's Diary, ed. Leonard Woolf (New York: Harcourt, Brace, 1965) p. 7. Further references are to this edition, cited as WD.
4. In 'Women and Fiction', Woolf argued that such partisan anger and special pleading in the works of George Eliot and Charlotte Brontë resulted in the 'consciousness of a woman's presence', which by her aesthetic standards, distorted the work's style and point of view – 'Women and Fiction', Granite and Rainbow (New York: Harcourt, Brace and World, 1958) p. 79.
5. Jane Marcus, 'The Years as Greek Drama, Domestic Novel, and Götterdämmerung', Bulletin of the New York Public Library, Winter 1977, pp. 280–1. See also Mitchell A. Leaska, 'Virginia Woolf, the Pargiter: A Reading of The Years', ibid., pp. 172–210.
6. Virginia Woolf, A Room of One's Own (New York: Harcourt, Brace and World, 1957), and Three Guineas (New York; Harcourt, Brace and

World, 1966). Further references to the latter are to this edition, cited as *TG*.

7. 'Love, then, whether of the drawing room or of the street variety, affected the lives of the Pargiter sisters profoundly ... it restricted them to certain quarters of London, and was perpetually impeding their freedom of movement' (*P*, p. 52).

8. I disagree with Mitchell Leaska's transcription of this phrase in his edition of *The Pargiters*. He transcribes it as 'a range of emotion', which, while it captures the same sense of untapped and unrecognised feelings, neither has the lovely metaphoric sweep of Woolf's phrase nor, more practically speaking, seems to be what Woolf actually wrote. Repeated readings of the holograph manuscript of *The Pargiters* have convinced me that there is no 'n' in the word Woolf wrote. The phrase appears at *P*, p. 50.

9. Sallie Sears, 'Notes on Sexuality: *The Years* and *Three Guineas*', *Bulletin of the New York Public Library*, Winter 1977, p. 217.

10. Virginia Woolf, *The Years* (New York: Harcourt, Brace and World, 1965) p. 15. Further references are to this edition, cited as *Y*.

11. Virginia Woolf, 'Leslie Stephen', *The Captain's Death Bed and Other Essays* (New York: Harcourt, Brace and World, 1950) p. 71. Woolf also writes of Lady Ritchie in 'The Enchanted Organ', *The Moment and Other Essays* (New York: Harcourt, Brace, Jovanovich, 1974). Further references are to this edition, cited as *M*.

12. Quentin Bell, *Virginia Woolf: A Biography*, 2 vols (New York: Harcourt, Brace, Jovanovich, 1977) vol. i, p. 63.

13. Mitchell A. Leaska, Introduction, *P*, p. xvii.

14. *P*, p. xviii.

15. *P*, p. xv.

16. The phallic overtones of the pillar box are inescapable. The *Bulletin of the New York Public Library*, Winter 1977, p. 251, has a picture of an unmistakably phallic pillar box. Jane Marcus points out that not all pillar boxes were so distinctly phallic, however: 'they were red and, in shape, ambivalently male/female; they bore the King's [or Queen's] initials'. Yet, if the suffragists saw the pillar boxes they blew up as 'symbols of the state', we might assume they were not unconscious of the pillar boxes' equal role as symbols of the phallic power which Woolf called 'street love' (ibid., p. 284).

17. Sally Kempton, 'Cutting Loose', *Liberation Now* (New York: Dell, 1971) p. 55.

18. Here I disagree with Mitchell Leaska, who sees it this way: 'They pass Abercorn Terrace, . . . and Eleanor murmurs " . . . the pillar box" . . . ; and again we are in 1880 recalling Rose's horrifying experience which Eleanor has somehow assimilated' – in *Bulletin of the New York Public Library*, Winter 1977, p. 192.

19. In Woolf's essay 'A Sketch of the Past', we learn that the model for Pippy was Justine Nonon. Unlike Pippy, however, Justine Nonon sang both the 'male' and the 'female' songs to her young charge, Virginia Stephen. 'I used to sit on her knee; and her knee jugged up and down; and she sang in a hoarse cracked voice "Ron ron ron et plon plon plon" – and

then her knee gave way and I was tumbled onto the floor.' Woolf's memory unifies Eleanor's song ('Sur le pont d'Avignon') and the tumbling game Pippy played with Martin (*Y*, p. 226). See *Moments of Being, Unpublished Autobiographical Writings of Virginia Woolf*, ed. Jeanne Schulkind (New York: Harcourt, Brace, Jovanovich, 1976) p. 74.

20. I am grateful to Jane Marcus for this information. The sultan theme also appears in the episodes excluded from *The Years* during the final revision; there, Kitty Lasswade's retreat from the new freedom of her widowhood is 'chaperoned' by her big dog, Sultan. Oppressed by the patriarchal property laws which have evicted her from the home and the land she loves, Kitty has responded by identifying with her oppressors. So, in her response to the city, she resembles the sultan-like Martin Pargiter. Overwhelmed by disappointment and pessimism, Kitty can only imagine one option for her own life, a regression to the past and an identification with the sex and class which is responsible for her present powerlessness. So, she adopts mannish gestures, eats 'like a school boy', and stands 'in front of the fire with her arms behind her like a country gentleman'. With her dog, Sultan, she will retreat to a 'Tudor manor house' in the north of England to live the life of feudal isolation which befits her nickname, 'The Grenadier'. See Grace Radin (ed.), '"Two Enormous Chunks"; Episodes Excluded During the Final Revisions of *The Years*', *Bulletin of the New York Public Library*, Winter 1977, pp. 221–51.

21. The nursery rhyme may even contain a concealed allusion to a change in the locus of power, appropriate to the unifying, affirmative response to otherness Woolf anticipates in the 'New World' of the future (*Y*, p. 297). Avignon was the papal residence from 1309 to 1377; then the seat of spiritual power shifted to Rome. We can imagine Woolf's ironic enjoyment of such an undercurrent to her subversive vision of the future, embodied in the 'innocent' nursery rhyme.

22. See, for example, Paul J. Tillich, 'The Metropolis in Modern Times: Spiritual Aspects', in *The Metropolis in Modern Life*, ed. Robert Moore Fisher (New York: Russell and Russell, 1955) pp. 346–8; Richard Sennett, *The Uses of Disorder: Personal Identity and City Life* (New York: Knopf, 1970); Virginia Woolf, *The London Scene* (New York: Frank Hallman, 1975); and Walter Benjamin, 'On Some Motifs in Baudelaire', *Illuminations*, ed. Hannah Arendt (New York: Schocken Books, 1969) pp. 154–200.

23. Simone de Beauvoir, *The Second Sex*, trs. H. M. Parshley (New York: Vintage Books, 1974) p. xix.

24. Lillian D. Robinson, 'Who's Afraid of a Room of One's Own?', in *The Politics of Literature: Dissenting Essays in the Teaching of English*, ed. Louis Kampf and Paul Lauter (New York: Random House, 1973) pp. 354–409; cited in Madeline Moore, 'Virginia Woolf's *The Years* and Years of Adverse Male Reviewers', *Women's Studies*, IV (1977) p. 249.

25. For a further discussion of this phenomenon, see Virginia Woolf, 'Thoughts on Peace in an Air Raid', *The Death of the Moth and Other Essays* (New York: Harcourt, Brace, Jovanovich, 1970) pp. 243–8; and Margaret Comstock, 'The Loudspeaker and the Human Voice: Politics

and the Form of *The Years*', *Bulletin of the New York Public Library*, Winter 1977, pp. 252–75. For an analysis of the relationship between subconscious Hitlerism and woman-only mothering in the works of Woolf, see my 'Mirroring and Mothering: Reflections on the Mirror Encounter Metaphor in Virginia Woolf's Works', *Twentieth Century Literature*, forthcoming.

11 What is to Console Us?: the Politics of Deception in Woolf's Short Stories

SELMA MEYEROWITZ

Virginia Woolf's short stories have frequently been viewed as lyrical fiction that is experimental in form and concerned with a quest for reality.[1] This approach, however, denies a political vision which shapes most of the short fiction just as it does Woolf's feminist essays and her novels. As in *A Room of One's Own* and *Three Guineas*, Woolf's political analysis of social experience in the short stories is presented through female characters whom she considers a society of outsiders. Because they are denied social and class privilege, women reveal the destructive nature of a classbound society and its effects on individual consciousness and interpersonal relationships.

When readers have not ignored Woolf's social criticism or political vision in the short stories, they have reacted negatively. This is clear with Woolf's story 'A Society', which appeared in her first volume of short fiction, *Monday or Tuesday*. Jean Guiguet, for example, commented that in 'A Society' Woolf was extreme in her social criticism, and, as a result, the work was 'a failed venture into militant literature which Virginia Woolf had the good taste to cast aside'.[2] Guiguet also criticised technical aspects of the work, stating that 'the general design is uncertain, the irony often clumsy'.[3] Woolf seems to have anticipated negative public reaction to this story, for in her diary she wrote, 'And as for "A Society"' though spirited it is too one-sided.'[4] At this point, relatively early in her literary career, she may have been reluctant to offend her reading public; thus, according to Leonard Woolf, she decided not to republish the work.[5]

In 'A Society', Virginia Woolf's sense of social criticism is developed through a feminist vision of the role of women in society. At the beginning of her story, her female characters are portrayed as conventional upper-middle-class ladies; they focus on the 'scarlet feathers and golden slippers'[6] in a milliner's window and spend their energies 'building little towers of sugar upon the edge of the tea tray' (*MT*, p. 9). Their attitude towards men is also determined by the sex roles typical of their class: they admire and praise the male sex and consider marriage their highest priority, indeed, their life's goal. Yet Woolf's spirit of social iconoclasm, her desire to destroy meaningless conventions of a patriarchal, classbound society, emerges in the character of Poll who has been devoting all her time to reading, only to discover that the literature created by men is 'unutterably bad': for example, in what passes for history, 'not a word . . . seemed to be true and the style in which it was written was execrable' (*MT*, p. 11); similarly, poetry contains 'verbose sentimental foolery' (ibid.). Woolf's female characters are now determined to judge the civilisation created by men. As they form their society for asking questions and come in contact with the institutions of society, Woolf ridicules the professional men: the Navy captain who believes that 'six light taps upon the behind . . . avenge the honour of the King's Navy' (*MT*, p. 15); the Law Court judges who 'were either made of wood or were impersonated by large animals resembling man . . . trained to move with extreme dignity, mumble and nod their heads' (*MT*, p. 17); the Royal Academicians, whose standard of literature is 'gibberish' (*MT*, p. 18); and the prestigious university professors who use 'prodigious ingenuity' to dispute 'the use of some implement which looked . . . for all the world like a hairpin' (*MT*, p. 20). The women investigate male-dominated social institutions and professions with the serious purpose of evaluating whether or not the achievements of men justify the continuation of the human race and having women 'sacrifice' their youth to bear sons (*MT*, p. 27). They begin to suspect that perhaps women should not have 'taken it for granted that it was a woman's duty to spend her youth in bearing children' (*MT*, pp. 12 –13).

Woolf's female characters in 'A Society' conclude that a belief in the superiority of male intellect is a fallacy; not only does it deny women a role in social and political life, but it also distorts the male ego and the emotional and sexual relationship between men and women. They comment on the male sex:

> Soon he cannot come into a room without making us all feel uncomfortable; he condescends to every woman he meets, and dares not tell the truth even to his own wife; instead of rejoicing our eyes we have to shut them if we are to take him in our arms. True, they console themselves with stars of all shapes, ribbons of all shades, and incomes of all sizes – but what is to console us? (*MT*, pp. 38–9)

As the women discuss the destructive effects of male supremacy on the professions and on social institutions, particularly marriage and the family, the war years (1914 –18) are drawing to a close. The military and political developments of the First World War destroyed man's hope for social progress as advances in science and knowledge were used for destructive purposes. Woolf implies that male domination in a patriarchal, class society can be as deadly as war. For there to be peace, for civilisation to survive and progress, men must share in a commitment to preserve the human race and to grant equality to women. The rejection of male supremacy is presented as the first step in the salvation of humanity; thus, Woolf's women characters exclaim:

> Let us devise a method by which men may bear children! It is our only chance! For unless we provide them with some innocent occupation we shall get neither good people nor good books; we shall perish beneath the fruits of their unbridled activity; and not a human being will survive to know that there was once a Shakespeare. (*MT*, p. 39)

In 'A Society', Woolf's political vision evaluates the relationship between the individual and the social, political and economic structures of society. In addition to criticising social

institutions, Woolf offers a perspective for social change.
Women must assume the responsibility of re-educating themselves in order to reassess the social structure and its effects on
individual life, and to examine the role of men in society. To do
this, women must no longer believe in the superiority of men;
instead, each women must realise that she should teach her
daughter, the woman of the future,.that 'there's only one
thing . . . to believe in – and that is herself' (*MT*, p. 40).

Virginia Woolf's political understanding of sex-role divisions and social conventions and institutions is developed
further in several other short stories which analyse the
relationship between the social structure and individual
psychology. Through her women characters, Woolf portrays
a struggle to achieve fulfilment and continuity of self, either
through or despite social conventions and institutions determined by the class and patriarchal structure of society. As the
mental and emotional states of Woolf's characters are developed in relation to such social institutions as marriage, the
family, the professions and the society world, they reveal the
class nature of individual psychology and interpersonal relationships.

The women in Woolf's short stories are often portrayed as
insecure, unsatisfied, and uncertain about their role in society.
As a result, their attempts to establish emotional and
psychological security and social acceptance become a dominant concern. When her female characters fail to achieve
fulfilment, Woolf suggests it is because their inner life is
distorted by social influences, particularly class conflict, social
snobbery, and the destructive nature of social institutions in a
patriarchal and class society. Four short stories, 'Lappin and
Lappinova', 'The Legacy', 'The New Dress' and 'The Introduction', reveal the role of deception in the lives of women. Sex
and class oppression cause women to deceive themselves and
others, or to use deception as a protection from reality. Woolf
presents the struggles of her women characters to overcome
deception as a measure of the possibility for psychological and
physical survival in a classbound society.

In 'Lappin and Lappinova' and 'The Legacy', the conflict
between the public and private self is explored through the
social institution of marriage which is examined in relation to
class position. Although there are some strains of sentimental-

ity, 'Lappin and Lappinova' comments on an intense struggle to achive self-fulfilment despite social conventions;[7] it also reveals the futility of an escape from reality which involves retreating into the imagination. Likewise, in 'The Legacy', a rather typical plot involving an extramarital love relationship is transformed into a perceptive statement about the destructive effects of class and status on human values and interpersonal communication.

Rosalind of 'Lappin and Lappinova' is clearly in rebellion against the upper-class life-style to which her husband, Ernest Thorburn, belongs. After a conventional marriage ceremony, Rosalind avoids a realistic appraisal of her husband's nature. By transforming him into a creature of her imagination, she hopes to disguise the fact that he is a typical upper-class Englishman, 'born at Portchester Terrace, educated at Rugby; now a clerk in Her Majesty's Civil Service' (*HH*, p. 69). This reaction is part of her inability to adjust to her new social position and role: 'Rosalind had still to get used to the fact that she was now Mrs. Ernest Thornurn. Perhaps she would never get used to the fact that she was Mrs. Ernest Anybody' (*HH*, p. 68). She senses a surrender of individuality in marriage; she is no longer a separate identity, but the wife of someone else. Rosalind, moreover, wishes to rebel against some English conventions, particularly 'the Albert Memorial, mahogany sideboards, steel engravings of the Prince Consort with his family – her mother-in-law's dining-room in Portchester Terrace in short' (ibid.). Yet she accepts traditional class and sex roles. When Ernest's physical characteristics remind Rosalind of a pet rabbit, she transforms that image into one appropriate to Ernest's physical appearance and temperament. He is 'A hunting rabbit; a King Rabbit; a rabbit that makes laws for all the other rabbits' (*HH*, p. 69). Ernest thereby preserves his ruling-class status, as well as his dignity and domination. As this animal fantasy builds, it is clear that Rosalind and Ernest each embody the qualities conventionally associated with the male and female sexes respectively:

> They were the opposite of each other; he was bold and determined; she wary and undependable. He ruled over the busy world of rabbits; her world was a desolate, mysterious place, which she ranged mostly by moonlight.

All the same, their territories touched; they were King and Queen. (*HH*, p. 71)

Rosalind's imaginary world is both destructive and nurturing: it prevents her from developing communication with Ernest; at the same time, it ensures her survival by providing a shelter from everyday reality, for 'without that world, how, Rosalind wondered, that winter could she have lived at all?' (*HH*, p. 72) Rosalind needs fantasy to compensate for her insecurities, especially when faced with the upper-class world of Ernest's family, which makes her feel insignificant, 'an only child and an orphan at that; a mere drop among all those Thorburns' (ibid.). At the fiftieth wedding anniversary of Ernest's parents, the irony underlying Rosalind's rabbit world is apparent. The sexuality of rabbits is implicitly a parallel to the 'fruitful' union of Ernest's parents, which 'produced nine other sons and daughters into the bargain, many themselves married and also fruitful' (ibid.). In contrast, Rosalind's white wedding dress suggests her virginal nature and non-procreative state.

The wealth, social status and self-possession of the Thorburns overwhelm Rosalind, threatening her sense of security and individuality: 'She was half hidden by the great chrysanthemums. . . . She felt she was being melted; dispersed; dissolved into nothing; and would soon faint' (*HH*, p. 73). She also loses her sense of contact with Ernest. When she sees him, he seems completely a part of his family, 'straight as a ramrod with a nose like all the noses in the family portaits; a nose that never twitched at all' (ibid.). Soon, however, she is saved when Ernest's nose twitches and her rabbit fantasy revives. Through fantasy, Rosalind avoids being destroyed by the Thorburn world, which she feels she can never enter as an equal.

Virginia Woolf reveals that an imaginative retreat from reality is but a feeble and temporary attempt to achieve emotional fulfilment or to create communication with others. Rosalind's fantasy rabbit world does not survive. When Ernest can no longer participate in their imaginative game, Rosalind feels her life becoming a replica of the Thorburns' pattern of living: 'A vision of her mother-in-law's dining-room came before her; and there they sat, she and Ernest, grown old, under the engravings, in front of the sideboard. It was, their golden-wedding day. She could not bear it' (*HH*, p. 76)

Although saved from psychic destruction two years earlier when she became Mrs Ernest Thorburn, Rosalind now faces the death of her rabbit world and the sterility of her marriage. Woolf clearly leaves no illusions alive at the end of the story, as she comments, 'that was the end of that marriage' (*HH*, p. 78).

Although Rosalind in 'Lappin and Lapinova' rejects the social conventions of the class into which she marries, she cannot establish viable conventions outside that class's life-style. She accepts the typical role of a submissive wife, remaining sheltered from contact with the outside world and exalting her husband's status. Her position in her marriage and in society does not allow her to develop a sense of identity or the resources necessary for a continuing emotional relationship. As a result, her fantasy world proves ineffectual and destructive. Sadly, Rosalind's awakening to the truth is painful, yet Woolf implies that her fantasy retreat ensured her immaturity and fruitlessness, as well as her inability to communicate and achieve emotional fulfilment in her marriage.

'The Legacy' presents another picture of the failure of emotional commitment and communication in marriage. Angela Clandon has led a life of deception by maintaining the façade of her conventional upper-class marriage. After her death, however, Angela's diary reveals the truth to her husband, as it records the alienation which grew between them and destroyed their marriage. Again, Virginia Woolf links the destruction of personal happiness and interpersonal relationships to class status and social conventions, primarily through the characterisation of Gilbert Clandon, which develops as his wife's diary reveals her role in their marriage. Clandon seems isolated in his own world of upper-class social status and public esteem that is characteristic of a moderately successful politician, a type Virginia Woolf portrays in several of her works.[8] Consequently, he is insensitive to what has happened to his marriage and to his wife.

Gilbert Clandon's insensitivity to others is related to upper-class snobbishness. This is first evident in his thoughts about Sissy Miller, his wife's secretary: 'She was scarcely distinguishable from any other woman of her kind. There were thousands of Sissy Millers – drab little women in black carrying attaché cases' (*HH*, p. 127). His thoughts contrast with his wife's evaluation of Sissy: 'But Angela, with her genius for sympathy, had discovered all sorts of qualities in Sissy Miller. She was the soul of discretion; so silent; so trustworthy, one could tell her anything, and so on' (ibid.). Clandon, prominent politican though he is, certainly lacks his wife's sensitivity to people, her 'genius for sympathy'. Perhaps his political success, or his upper-class position, has made him scornful of others and has filled him with a sense of self-importance. Clandon thinks of himself as magnanimous, although his generosity seems to be primarily a sense of *noblesse oblige* when he offers assistance to Sissy Miller, and then regards her offer of help in return as a sign that she is romantically interested in him. His vanity thus allows him to interpret her words as a sexual compliment: 'He caught his own reflection in the glass as he passed. He was over fifty; but he could not help admitting that he was still, as the looking-glass showed him, a very distinguished-looking man' (*HH*, p. 129). Clandon's vanity is not completely unfounded, since the early sections of his wife's diary are full of Angela's admiring comments about him. Perhaps Angela had acted like a flattering looking-glass for her husband, bolstering his ego and reinforcing his vanity, a role Virginia Woolf claimed women often performed.[9] Similarly, Clandon remembers how Angela would confess to her limited experience and knowledge (*HH*, p. 130); he feels masculine pride when he thinks of that trait as one of her charms, since her impressionable nature and eagerness to learn made her dependent upon him and ready to accept a subordinate role in their marriage.

Clandon emerges as thoroughly self-centred. Unaware that he neglected his wife in his efforts for political success, he is surprised to read about Angela's regret at not having a son: 'Oddly enough he had never much regretted that himself. Life had been so full, so rich as it was. That year he had been given a minor post in the government' (*HH*, p. 131). For Clandon, personal fulfilment and the richness of life lay in a government position, not in personal relationships or parenthood. Moreover, he obviously had no respect for his wife's individuality, but saw her mostly as a beautiful object, of which he was proud, and as someone to minister to his needs. When Angela claimed she wanted to help others, Clandon reflected, 'Hadn't she enough to do looking after him, after her home?

Still if it amused her, of course he had no objection' (ibid.).
Thus, Clandon cannot relate to the sections of Angela's diary
which reveal her involvement in social activities: 'His own
name occurred less frequently. His interest slackened. Some
of the entries conveyed nothing to him' (*HH*, p. 132).
Nevertheless, her references to BM raise his curiosity. Since
BM is of the lower classes, Clandon is supercilious:

> So B.M was a man – no doubt one of those 'intellectuals' as
> they call themselves, who are so violent, as Angela said, and
> so narrow-minded. Gilbert knew the type and had no liking
> for this particular specimen.... He could see him quite
> distinctly – a stubby little man, with a rough beard, red tie,
> dressed as they always did in tweeds, who had never done an
> honest day's work in his life. (Ibid.).

Clandon's thoughts reveal a typical upper-class attitude towards social reformers which associates them with violence
and a lack of manners and aesthetic taste.

Clandon's attitude toward his wife is patronising. He feels
Angela was intellectually immature, perhaps even unable to
comprehend the complex social questions BM raised. Similarly, he cannot imagine that she was dissatisfied with their
marriage or that she found emotional fulfilment with another
man. His limited understanding of his wife makes his final
realisation that her suicide was a rejection of him a surprise:
'She had told the truth. She had stepped off the kerb to rejoin
her lover ... to escape from him' (*HH*, p. 135). While his
self-satisfaction and insensitivity to others make him a less
than admirable character, Clandon's final understanding of
the illusions he maintained about his wife and his marriage
renders him somewhat pathetic.

In contrast to Clandon, Angela had overcome the emptiness of her marriage by using deception as a means to achieve
freedom and pursue fulfilment outside her relationship to her
husband. While social prestige and vanity have left Clandon
without emotional fulfilment and have contributed to the
self-destruction of others, namely Angela and BM, Angela's
diary, a record of her inner life, becomes the source of truth
and self-revelation for her husband – a veritable gift or
legacy. Thus, through her characters in 'The Legacy', Woolf

suggests that people can find emotional fulfilment only through intimate communication and selfless caring. The world of social conventions, embodied in upper-class status and conventional political aspirations, creates vanity, self-centredness, and insensitivity to others. Under these circumstances, a marriage relationship becomes meaningless.

Social and class discrimination again destroy emotional fulfilment in 'The New Dress', as seen in the character of Mabel Waring. Mabel is of the lower class, part of a family of ten 'never having money enough, always skimping and paring' (*HH*, p. 56). At Mrs Dalloway's party, she thinks of 'her own drawing-room so shabby' (ibid.) and of her inability to dress fashionably because it is too costly. Mabel's anxiety about her appearance, her manners, and her values is provoked by her encounter with the society world of the Dalloways; however, her insecurity is more pervasive: 'At once the misery which she always tried to hide, the profound dissatisfaction – the sense that she had had, ever since she was a child, of being inferior to other people – set upon her, relentlessly, remorselessly, with an intensity which she could not beat off' (ibid.). When she imagines that everyone is judging her appearance, Mabel's painful self-consciousness turns to self-hatred. Sensing her ineffectuality, she expresses her low self-esteem through an animal image, 'We are all like flies trying to crawl over the edge of the saucer' (*HH*, p. 57); she also expresses a similar sense of alienation from others: 'She was a fly – but the others were dragonflies, butterflies, beautiful insects' (*HH*, p. 58). Her need for assurance makes her attempt to communicate with another guest, Robert Haydon, whose polite but insincere comments leave her even more disillusioned and unhappy with herself and her social interactions.

Virginia Woolf suggests that society's conventions destroy Mabel's inner resources, since she implies that there are moments when Mabel has self-confidence and experiences pleasure. At the dressmaker's, for example, she was happy about the originality of her dress: 'Just for a second . . . there looked at her . . . a . . . mysteriously smiling, charming girl, the core of herself, the soul of herself; and it was not vanity only, not only self-love that made her think it good, tender, and true' (*HH*, p. 59). Her peace with herself allows her to recognise goodness in others:

> She felt, suddenly, honestly, full of love for Miss Milan . . . that one human being should be doing this for another, and she saw them all as human beings merely . . . and the thought of it, of this side of human nature and its patience and its endurance . . . filled her eyes with tears.   (Ibid.)

In Mrs Dalloway's drawing-room, however, she feels only painful emotions about human nature and relationships with others, and self-conscious shame about herself. She visualises the fly in the saucer unable to get out because 'the milk is sticking its wings together' (*HH*, p. 60). She thus cannot consistently maintain a positive self-image.

Mabel's sense of alienation also exists because her insecurity makes her self-centred and unable to respond to others. She sees herself and another guest, Mrs Holman, as a yellow dot and a black dot, both detached; therefore, 'it was impossible that the black dot . . . should make the yellow dot, sitting solitary, self-centred, feel what the black dot was feeling, yet they pretended!' (*HH*, p. 62). Neither Mabel nor Mrs Holman understands what the other feels, because each demands sympathy for herself: 'Ah, it was tragic, this greed, this clamour of human beings . . . for sympathy – it was tragic, could one have felt it and not merely pretended to feel it!' (ibid.). To Mabel, and to Virginia Woolf, who presumably uses the above comment by the narrator to imply her own view, pretence and lies are more despicable and more destructive to interpersonal communication than a self-centred demand for sympathy.

Woolf does suggest positive values in this story. Again, although Mabel feels only distress from social interactions, she can at least remember moments of spontaneous joy, either in nature, where social competition and alienation do not exist, or in everyday activities:

> Now and then, there did come to her delicious moments, reading the other night in bed, for instance, or down by the sea on the sand in the sun, at Easter . . . and then the melody

of the waves . . . and the children's shouts . . . yes, it was a divine moment. . . . And also with Hubert sometimes she had quite unexpectedly . . . divine moments, when she said to herself . . . 'This is it. This has happened. This is it.' (*HH*, pp. 63–4)

Mabel's sense of the meaning and peace of life gives her a momentary determination to reject dissatisfying social relationships and strive for a way of life which provides 'divine moments'. She decides to leave Mrs Dalloway's party, but she is again caught in the trap of social intercourse. Exclaiming, 'I have enjoyed myself' (*HH*, p. 65) to Mr and Mrs Dalloway, she realises that she is back 'right in the saucer' (ibid.). Her struggle to rise above superficial social amenities and painful social interactions is thus largely unsuccessful. Mabel cannot develop a consistently independent sense of values necessary for security. Instead, she is vulnerable to social status and social pretences.

In 'The Introduction', Virginia Woolf provides an alternative female character to Mabel Waring, while still focusing on the position of women in society and on aspects of male-female relationships as set against the society world and a patriarchal and hierarchical social structure. Lily Everit, a young woman in Academia, struggles to preserve her sense of self while surrounded by the guests at Mrs Dalloway's party. She desperately clings to her sole source of strength, her literary work, an 'essay on the character of Dean Swift . . . marked with three stars: First rate' (*HH*, p. 37). In the presence of upper-class society, however, the essay 'wobbled, began wilting . . . and all her being . . . turned to a mist of alarm, apprehension and defence. . . . This was the famous place: the world' (*HH*, p. 38). Thus, Mrs Dalloway, coming to introduce Lily to the other guests, seems to be 'bearing down on her' (*HH*, p. 37), like an animal after its prey, and people seem 'to menace and mount over her, to turn everything to water' (*HH*, p. 38).

The social situation is awkward physically and emotionally for Lily. She senses that her movements and appearance are being observed and that she is expected to behave accordingly: 'Lily accepted the part which was now laid on her, and, naturally, overdid it a little . . . accentuating the delicacy, the artificiality of her bearing' (*HH*, p. 39). Lily also senses the formality of the new world she enters; it is regulated and orderly, like 'the towers of Westminster; the high and formal building; the talk; this civilisation' (*HH*, p. 40). This world is foreign to her and contrasts with her usual terrain, the countryside:

> [To] come in the hearts of woods or wide lonely moors upon little ceremonies which had no audience, private rites, pure beauty offered by beetles and lilies of the valley and dead leaves and still pools, without any care whatever what human beings thought of them, which filled her mind with rapture and wonder – all this was, until tonight, her ordinary being, by which she knew and liked herself and crept into the heart of mother and father and brothers and sisters.   (Ibid.)

By identifying Lily with a love of nature and close family relationships, Woolf indicates the contrast between the world of personal fulfilment and the world of social and professional status.

Civilisation appears to Lily to be a 'massive masculine achievement' (ibid.), thus indicating her awareness of the patriarchal nature of society. Similarly, she views the academic world as a masculine preserve. When she wonders what she can offer of her own to this male-dominated realm of society, she thinks of her essay. Yet her security and sense of academic accomplishment are soon challenged by Bob Brinsley: 'With his great forehead, and his look of self-assurance . . . and direct descent from Shakespeare, what could she do but lay her essay, oh and the whole of her being, on the floor as a cloak for him to trample on, as a rose for him to rifle' (ibid.). Here Woolf aptly links masculine domination in intellectual and social matters with sexual oppression and dehumanisation. There is a brutal, destructive aspect to Brinsley, as if he is tearing off the wings of a fly. Lily sees herself as the fly, fighting not to let 'this terror, this suspicion of something different, get hold of her and shrivel up her wings and drive her out into loneliness' (ibid. p. 42). To assert herself against the male world, Lily must risk the destruction of her wings which she would need to escape from the typical isolation of

the non-professional woman who stays at home. The choices
are clear: Lily can be an object of beauty, admired and
protected by men – 'She wanted to have her handkerchief
picked up on the staircase and be a butterfly' (ibid.); or she can
be the source of flattery and the moral and emotional support
of a man – 'Why not, since this is the greatest of all worldly
objects? And to worship, to adorn, to embellish was her task,
her wings were for that' (ibid); or, as the last choice, she can
gain independence and respect through professional,
academic accomplishment, despite the domination of men.

Although Lily does assert her right to be a professional
woman, her instincts have been distorted by the male supremacy inherent in a patriarchal society:

> Her essay upon the character of Swift became more and
> more obtrusive . . . only with a terrible lustre, no longer
> clear and brilliant, but troubled and bloodstained, as if this
> man, this great Mr. Brinsley, had just by pulling the wings
> off a fly as he talked . . . confused her for ever and ever and
> shrivelled the wings on her back. (*HH*, pp. 42–3)

Male achievements, male self-assertion, and male domination
of women in social, intellectual, and economic areas make Lily
think of 'civilisation with horror' (*HH*, p. 43). Yet she is
determined that the accomplishments of men must be rejected because they are destructive. It is a woman's duty to
preserve the life-sustaining qualities upon which civilised
instincts are based: 'This civilisation, said Lily Everit to
herself . . . depends on me' (ibid.).

Virginia Woolf's short stories thus portray social and
interpersonal relationships as painful and unfulfilling.
Through her female characters she reveals the effects of class
discrimination and alienation on individual psychology.
Rosalind in 'Lappin and Lapinova' demonstrates the destructive nature of an escape into a fantasy world, while Mabel
Waring in 'The New Dress' portrays the negative effects of
social pretences and class divisions. Through the contrast
between Gilbert and Angela Clandon in 'The Legacy', and
through the personal and professional struggles of Lily Everit
in 'The Introduction', Woolf also demonstrates how devotion
to social prestige and political power can destroy possibilities

for emotional commitment and interpersonal communication. As her characters attempt to overcome deception and class alienation in order to achieve fulfilment, she affirms love and social responsibility as necessary to emotional satisfaction. Class conflict, social divisions, and meaningless social institutions must be rejected for the characters in her short stories to establish personal and social survival. The commitment to social criticism and the political vision so evident in Woolf's early story 'A Society' pervades her later short fiction which examines the effects of social and class reality on individual consciousness.

NOTES

1. Jean Guiguet, *Virginia Woolf and Her Works*, trs. Jean Stewart (London: Hogarth Press, 1965) p. 343.
2. Ibid., p. 341.
3. Ibid.
4. Virginia Woolf, *A Writer's Diary*, ed. Leonard Woolf (New York: Harcourt, Brace and World, 1953) p. 30.
5. Virginia Woolf, *A Haunted House and Other Short Stories* (New York: Harcourt, Brace and World, 1944) p. v. Further references are to this edition, cited as *HH*.
6. Virginia Woolf,*Monday or Tuesday* (New York: Harcourt, Brace, 1921) p. 9. Further references are to this edition, cited as *MT*.
7. In *A Writer's Diary*, pp. 296–7 (Tuesday, 22 Nov 1938), Virginia Woolf refers to 'Lappin and Lappinova' as being written when she was writing *Night and Day*, which has the same focus on class factors in relation to marriage and self-fulfilment. Also, the story was revised in April 1939; thus, it was written contemporarily with *The Years* and *Three Guineas*.
8. Other political figures in the short stories and the novels are Hugh Whitbread and Richard Dalloway.
9. Virginia Woolf, *A Room of One's Own* (New York: Harcourt, Brace and World, 1929).

12 Virginia Woolf's Last Words on Words: *Between the Acts* and 'Anon'

NORA EISENBERG

While writing *Between the Acts*, her last novel, Virginia Woolf also wrote the essay 'Anon', which has never been published and which has received little critical attention.[1] Essay and novel, I hope to show, are companion pieces, sharing a single hero and theme. In both, Woolf, with the aid of her hero (La Trobe of the novel, Anon of the essay), imagines an old world in which a communal life flourished free from conventional language, which she thought a male dominion, ruling and often ruining her world.

The old world dug up in *Between the Acts*, it has been suggested, is the rich old world presided over by the ancient mother goddess. La Trobe, we have been told, bears the maiden aspect of the ancient two-faced (mother–maid) deity.[2] Anon too, though like La Trobe not a mother, seems attendant to the old mother-world and its fertile old chants, chants which Woolf suggests we have forgotten how to sing. In both novel and essay Woolf points to such an old 'language' – that is not quite language – to cure modern words and woes, patriarchal words and woes.

Woolf's relations with language were always complex. Both delight and doubt about the medium of words weave through her life and art. The delight came easily to the born writer for whom words were the 'natural means of expression'.[3] But the doubts came as well with the recurring sense that language

253

was an artificial convention – 'inadequate to its experience',[4] 'an impure medium',[5]'slow and deluding'.[6] For language was rigid, Woolf often feared, dividing a world that was, or should be, unified. In much of her fiction, in *The Waves* most emphatically, she suggests that language emerges to mark and serve our individual as opposed to our communal and united selves.

But there was, Woolf indicates in *The Waves* and elsewhere, another language – 'the little language'. Composed of small or broken words, brief or unfinished sentences, cries, calls, songs, silences, and even sights and gestures, 'the little language' marks and fosters our common life, not the single life, the single self that wars with others. 'The little language', we learn in *The Waves*, encourages the union of separate selves, is indeed the 'language lovers use'[7]; it is, we read in 'Anon' and its sequel, 'The Reader', 'brief', 'colloquial', 'intimate'.[8]

Not surprisingly, Woolf associated 'the little language' and the maintenance of the common life with women, conventional language and the maintenance of the single life with men. For language often seemed to Woolf a male convention: in life she saw language used largely by men to serve men; in books she saw it used often to spread the insistent 'I' of the manly writer far and wide.[9] If not in total collusion, language often seemed at least guilty by association with the ego she mistrusted and identified with exclusive masculinity. In contrast, 'the little language' was the speciality of women, who traditionally worked, Woolf thought, to smooth over the divisions and rifts caused by men.

As early as *The Voyage Out*, Woolf lets her heroine's music – a prototype of 'the little language' – stand as an alternative to the words of the manly Hirsts and Hewets. Music, not words, Rachel Vinrace thinks at the novel's start, expresses in its rhythms and counterpoints the deep, fluid world of feeling that she wishes to share with others. Though, in the course of the novel, the inarticulate heroine voyages into a world of words, she returns in the end to her beloved sounds and silences. But, forsaking language utterly, Rachel also forsakes her self and finally her life. Thus, even in her earliest fiction, Woolf points not only to the virtues but also to the dangers of the 'language' of selflessness – 'the little language'. For like the waves, which flow through her works, we are, Woolf knew, not just one, floating together, but separate as we break into selfhood. In her fiction from *The Voyage Out* to *The Waves*, she cautions us to acknowledge our complexity – our uniqueness and unity alike. And to express such complexity, we must all – men and women – learn to speak both language and 'the little language'.

Towards the end of her life, however, as fascists – the manliest of men[10] – threatened to bomb her and all else to bits, Woolf seems to have reassessed her relations with language. Manly men made wars and talk that divided, if not totally destroyed. More than ever Woolf longed for the communal life, and more than ever she seems to have despaired of language. *The Years* communicates this sense of conventional language failing. Characters feel so great 'a gap, a dislocation, between the word and the reality',[11] that they forsake language and leave speeches unspoken.[12] In this next to last novel, conventional language seems ineffective, and viable expression emerges more in 'silence' (*Y*, p. 424), songs with 'unintelligible words' (*Y*, p. 430) but intelligible rhythms, drawings of 'little holes from which spokes radiated' (*Y*, p. 367), 'broken sentences, single words' (*Y*, p. 411) – versions of 'the little language'.

In *Between the Acts* Woolf exposes more than ever the limitations of language as such and the virtues of different communicative forms that might better pull life together. Similarly, in the essay 'Anon', she hails the common 'little language', which, she imagines, flourished once upon a time before men and their words came to rule; once upon a time when classes and sexes and even species were not severely demarcated; a time, therefore, when people, like Anon – the anonymous, androgynous artist, whose career of many centuries she traces in her essay – could be 'sometimes man; sometimes woman',[13] and be sometimes, like birds, singing among the trees. The golden age that Woolf imagines, the age of Anon, was not 'word conscious';[14] people and creatures and things were not thus labelled and bound. Anon's was the era before division between artist and audience, between writer and reader. In Anon's world there was no country gentleman's library, the value of which Woolf questions in *Between the Acts*.[15] There was only Anon – 'the common voice, singing out of doors'.[16]

And Anon, we find, is reborn in *Between the Acts*. Tired of language with its 'larding, stuffing, or cant' (*BA*, p. 187), Miss La Trobe, the novel's hero, takes up Anon's part, urging her audience to shed their habitual names and words and anonymously join in a life together. To this end, her pageant displays the false distinctions created by names. During the historical time presented in the pageant, disguises – costume and name – change, but the people beneath remain the same. The same woman, Mr Streatfield notes, plays Lady Harraden and a Canterbury pilgrim; only her costume and name have been altered. Mr Streatfield asks to be excused 'if I get the names wrong' (*BA*, p. 192). Such confusion of names, however, seems calculated by La Trobe for her audience and Woolf for hers. Like the viewing audience, the reading audience can find it difficult to distinguish characters and names. Easily, we can confuse 'Lady H. H.' and 'Mrs. H.', Carinthia, Ferdinando, and Flavinda. Both audiences are encouraged to see that 'we are all one', and that variations in names, variations we have conjured up to distinguish ourselves, do not work. We blend together. All are encouraged by the pageant to see that there never 'were such people' as the Victorians, 'only you and me and William dressed differently', as Lucy Swithin puts it (*BA*, pp. 174–5).

But individual names are not the only labels fixing and separating us. The plays within the pageant suggest the falsity and weakness of speech itself. Like Lady Harraden, the audience is urged to see that 'words' are 'tinsel wrapped round a Christmas cracker' (*BA*, p. 146) – mere disguises like names. Thus words separate more than connect. For example, the words of Phyllis Jones, the first performer, 'peppered the audience as with a shower of hard little stones', so that a 'vast vacancy' exists between her and the audience (*BA*, p. 78).

The choral interludes provided by the 'digging and delving' villagers continue to stress the insignificance of appearances marked by names and speech, the strength and significance of the common life existing beneath such costume and cover:

> *Digging and delving*, the villagers sang passing in single file in and out between the trees, *for the earth is always the same, summer and winter and spring; and spring and winter again; ploughing and sowing, eating and growing; time passes....*

The wind blew the words away.   (*BA*, p. 125)

The diggers and delvers attend to a world that is 'always the same', a timeless world that has no need of language with its suggestions of distinctions and change. Their words, therefore, can blow away, for their words 'didn't matter' (*BA*, p. 94). The long line of villagers discards words for simple dance and senseless song suggestive of their changeless, eternal lives together.

Plays and interludes alike shake the viewer's belief in his individuality and the words and names used to protect this identity. As we would expect, the viewers between scenes feel an exciting anonymity, feel not quite 'here or there . . . as if what I call myself was still floating unattached, and didn't settle. Not quite themselves, they felt' (*BA*, p. 149). At the pageant's end they feel more united than usual and fear that words and labels will force them back to their separate selves. 'Must I be Thomas, you Jane?' they wonder (*BA*, p. 190). 'Protect and preserve us from words the defiler from words the impure', that would divide us again (*BA*, p. 190).

Conventional language, the audience is asked to see, is not capable of rendering a unified existence. And so La Trobe, desiring unity, must present in her pageant more than just words; she must have the players, chorus, and even the audience, 'act; dance; sing; a little bit of everything' (*BA*, p. 58).

Music particularly is considered here a more vital and unifying medium than words. The words of the villagers' song 'Didn't matter'; most important is the 'intoxicating' music that lasts long after their words have blown away. Similarly, the words and plots of the plays get muddled, but the sounds, Isa thinks, 'beget emotion' (*BA*, p. 90). More specifically, La Trobe uses gramophone music to create in her audience a sense of unity. Between the acts of her pageant, she lets simple melodies work to hold together the dispersing audience. The wandering audience is much affected:

For I hear music, they were saying. Music wakes us. Music makes us see the hidden, join the broken. Look and listen. See the flowers, how they ray their redness, whiteness, silverness and blue. And the trees with their many-tongued much syllabling, their green and yellow leaves hustle us and shuffle us, and bid us, like the starlings, and the rooks, come together, crowd together, to chatter and make merry while the red cow moves forward and the black cow stands still. (*BA*, p. 120)

Music, then, encourages a recognition of the unity of all things. People under music's spell feel closer not only to each other, but to the trees, the birds, the cows. Even the trees and birds, we see, are 'called out of their private lives' by music, called 'out of their separate avocation, and made to take part' (*BA*, p. 117). Indeed, La Trobe's tunes call all so clearly from 'private lives' towards a common one that Isa feels they could absorb and express her: 'The little twist of sound could have the whole of her' (*BA*, p. 181).

La Trobe's music stresses the need to create unity from diversity:

Like quicksilver sliding, filings magnetized, the distracted united. The tune began; the first note meant a second; the second a third. Then down beneath a force was born in opposition; then another. On different levels ourselves went forward; flower gathering some on the surface; others descending to wrestle with the meaning; but all comprehending; all enlisted. The whole population of the mind's immeasurable profundity came flocking; from the unprotected, the unskinned; and dawn rose; and azure; from chaos and cacophony measure; but not the melody of surface sound alone controlled it; but also the warring battle-plumed warriors straining asunder: To part? No. Compelled from the ends of the horizon; recalled from the edge of appalling crevasses; they crashed; solved; united.
                                                                (*BA*, p. 189).

La Trobe's tunes seem to the audience 'somebody speaking', a powerful voice telling of overwhelming unity, a refreshing alternative to the voice of words telling mostly of division (*BA*, p. 188).

Gramophone music is not the only music playing a part in the pageant. The villagers sing; the actors speak melodiously, if not always sensibly. And, as the words of the pageant 'die away', the music of a cow who has lost her calf takes over:

> In the very nick of time she lifted her great moon-eyed head
> and bellowed. All the great moon-eyed heads laid them-
> selves back. From cow after cow came the same yearning
> bellow. The whole world was filled with dumb yearning. It
> was the primeval voice sounding loud in the ear of the
> present moment. Then the whole herd caught the infec-
> tion. Lashing their tails, blobbed like pokers, they tossed
> their heads high, plunged and bellowed, as if Eros had
> planted his dart in their flanks and goaded them to fury.
> The cows annihilated the gap; bridged the distance; filled
> the emptiness and continued the emotion.
>
> (*BA*, pp. 140–1)

The 'emptiness', the 'vast vacancy' left by the failing words of
the pageant, is filled by natural music.

In *Between the Acts*, music comes to stand for a variety of
non-verbal forms which Woolf hopes might supplement a
failing language. As the audience awaits a scene to be played, a
melody is heard, and then we are told of the 'melody' of the
view, the 'melody' of cows not now as they bellow, but as they
move about in silence:

> And the tune repeated itself once more.
> The view repeated it its own way what the tune was
> saying. The sun was sinking; the colours were merging; and
> the view was saying how after toil men rest from their
> labours; how coolness comes; reason prevails; and having
> unharnessed the team from the plough, neighbours dig in
> cottage gardens and lean over cottage gates.
> The cows, making a step forward, then standing still,
> were saying the same thing to perfection.
> Folded in this triple melody, the audience sat gaz-
> ing. (*BA*, p. 134)

Sounds, sights, movements are all part of an orderly whole,
harmonious in a way Woolf associated with the finest
harmony – that provided by music.

La Trobe's gramophone music, then, provides only one
instance of music and opportunity for harmony and unity.

When this music is missing, other kinds of music take over. In presenting the 'Present Time', La Trobe at first offers no music from the gramophone but just the 'music' of the 'cow, the meadow, and the view' (*BA*, p. 177) and the unexpected, unifying music of rain. 'Nature once more has taken her part', adding to the harmony. La Trobe marks this exquisite fusion with a simple gramophone tune, and all join in the harmonious play of sound, sight and motion: 'And Lord! The jangle and the din! The very cows joined in. Walloping, tail lashing, the reticence of nature was undone, and the barriers which should divide Man the Master from the Brute were dissolved. Then the dogs joined in' (*BA*, p. 184).

Neither 'Man the Master' nor his language, then, is very masterful. Human talk can be seen essentially and simply as part of the glorious 'jangle and ... din' contributed to by fellow creatures as well. If we humans dig beneath the cover of civilised, conventional language, we find our true identity, which we share with 'the Brute' – the cow, the dog, the bird.

La Trobe, like her line of villagers, digs and delves in her art toward this old anonymous existence. Her pageant includes 'a primeval voice sounding loud in the ear of the present moment' (*BA*, p. 140), 'the other voice ... that was no one's voice' (*BA*, p. 181). So eager is La Trobe to blend all that, when she finally speaks to the audience, no one can be sure that it is she: 'It came from the bushes – a megaphonic, anonymous, loudspeaking affirmation', insisting, as the tunes and bellows have, 'O we're all the same' (*BA*, pp. 186–7). She 'wishes it seems to remain anonymous' (*BA*, p. 194), not to distinguish herself from the human and non-human actors or from her audience. In both manuscript and novel the audience wonders about her name.[17] Often she is simply 'Whatsername'.

And Whatsername, La Trobe, as I have suggested, is Anon of the essay. Like its companion novel, 'Anon' stresses the importance of song, and indeed opens with birds singing on 'matted boughs', strikingly echoing the birds singing on 'matted branches' in the book Woolf crafts for Lucy Swithin to read in *Between the Acts*:[18] '"For many centuries after Britain became an island" the historian says, "the untamed forest was king." On the matted boughs of that forest innumerable birds sang ....'[19]

Thus essay, like novel, hearkens back to ancient song. For

music in 'Anon', as in *Between the Acts*, is shown to be a great, vital force, preceding and overpowering language. And Anon is 'for the most part a simple singer'[20] who has learned his art in the forest from his fellow singing birds, much as La Trobe learns from the starlings the beautiful sounds for her next play. For Anon, as for La Trobe, it is the song that is most important: 'To enjoy singing, to enjoy hearing the song, must be the most deep rooted, the toughest of human instincts comparable for persistence with the instinct of self-preservation.[21] Anon's art, like La Trobe's, depends on music, which joins all, including author and audience. For 'the audience', Woolf writes, 'was itself the singer; "Terly terlow" they sang; and "By, by lullay", filling in the pauses, helping out with a chorus. Every body shared in the emotion of Anon's song . . . '[22] So too in *Between the Acts* 'The chorus' of villagers fills in for Anon's old audience. And the actual audience on the lawn at Pointz Hall helps out as well, singing in the jangle and din of 'Present Time', humming, murmuring, sharing in the emotion. The warm, anonymous, singing world offers hope to a world stiffly bound with names and words.

Indeed, it was the printed word that killed the intimate, old world of Anon. 'Anon died around 1477' with Caxton's press, Woolf writes. 'It was the printed books with the authors' names that killed him.' She continues, 'After that the audience was separate from the singer. And with Anon died that part of the song that the audience sang, the voice that supplied the story, filled in the pauses and added sometimes a nonsensical chorus. . . . Time has drawn its blue hand over the horizon.'[23] With the printed book, Anon is lost, and his audience is transformed from an active, united chorus into relatively passive and isolated readers. And so the song is lost. For the reader's ear, Woolf writes in 'The Reader', 'lost its acuteness'.[24] The printed words dulled life, as they 'Cover[ed] over the original song'.[25]

In *Between the Acts* Woolf asks that our ears be awakened once more to life's song. Indeed, in an early draft of the novel she presents a 'Prayer to the Night Bird', asking that our dulled hearing be sharpened. The prayer, in playful scorn of high literary tradition, begins, 'Not to the nightingale . . . do we turn; praying to be released from the herring and the council houses . . . but to some little anonymous bird of

daylight, who thinking to sleep has woken; a sociable fowl'.
Woolf's prayer continues,

> Come and twitch and free our long ears clutted (*sic*) up with
> fur; in which dust that no housemaid can broom away has
> lodged, tweak us awake this jocund night of early summer
> and remind us of the fun under our feet; of how the sole of
> the foot and all of the skin is bare; and the hairs are still
> capable of sensation; while our tongues shape the smoke in
> our brains into talk.[26]

And on the opening page of the published novel we have a
later version of this friendly bird, chuckling now, even in his
sleep, in counterpoint to the talk about cesspools (*BA*, p. 3).
We need the friendly 'anonymous bird', 'the chuckling bird',
the nameless song-bearer, to revive us with music from dead
and deadening talk. In short, we need Anon once more.

And we need, Woolf suggests in *Between the Acts* and 'Anon',
all of Anon's talents and creations to help us. Though Anon
was principally a 'simple singer', he contributed and encouraged more than song. In his prime, Anon led the folk to dress
in green leaves and dance about – 'enacting their ancient
parts'.[27]

Even in his last years, after Caxton's press dealt the fatal
blow, Anon miraculously lingered on to keep the world
together. In the Elizabethan age, Woolf thinks, Anon lived to
unite people of all classes in the playhouse. The playhouse,
dominated by his spirit, connected not only person to person,
but people to nature. For the playhouses were 'open to the air',
and 'the sun beat or the rain poured upon the common
people'.[28] The play itself was everyone's. The early
Elizabethan plays bear no name, for 'the play was a common
product, written by one hand, but so moulded in transition
from the written to the spoken that the author had no sense of
property in it. It was half the work of the audience'.[29] And,
though these plays still exist in printed form, much has been
lost in the process. In the printed plays, Woolf writes, much is
'sunk' and gone:

> We have lost the sound of the spoken word; all that the sight
> of the actor's body gives through the eye to the mind. We

have lost too the sense of being part of the audience. We miss a thousand shades that the dramatist conveyed by inflection of voice, by gesture, by the placing of the actors' bodies.[30]

Between the Acts encourages the recapturing not only of Anon's lost song, but also of the rest of Anon's lost world. Anon once provoked the playing of 'ancient parts', and so La Trobe in her pageant provokes, as Lucy Swithin says, our 'unacted part' (*BA*, p. 153). Anon once brought all classes together in the playhouse, and so La Trobe joins gentry and common folk, peer and cowman. And La Trobe's theatre, like the Elizabethan playhouse, is 'open to the air', poured on by sun and rain alike. And La Trobe's pageant, like the early Elizabethan dramas, is anonymous, belonging not only to La Trobe but also to the actors, the villagers, the audience, cows, trees, and even rain. The pageant, moreover, digs up the 'sunk' part of Anon's Elizabethan plays. The audience sees the actors' bodies, their gestures and arrangements. The audience hears the sound of the actors' voices. And we, the reading audience, along with the audience on the lawn, are asked to imagine and thus resurrect the world that has been sunk – the world of Anon.

Though the age is printed and bound with words, Woolf insists, Anon's world can nevertheless be recaptured. In her essay, she notes that Anon's world can still be seen 'in some parts of England': 'Now and then by choosing a view carefully to shut out a chimney or a bungalow, we can still see a flat fen, reed whispering, waterlogged; or a down, covered still with turf only. But on the down lies a green scar along which the travellers [Anon and his friends] came....'[31] With Pointz Hall, it seems, Woolf offers us Anon's world. Certainly the 'view' from Pointz Hall includes no 'chimney' or 'bungalow'. For Pointz Hall 'commanded a fine view of the surrounding country', we read. 'No house had been built; no town had sprung up.' And 'Hogben's Folly was still eminent; the very flat, field parcelled land . . .' (*BA*, p. 52). Striking too at Pointz Hall are 'the scars' which, Bart claims, can be seen 'from an aeroplane', scars made by the trek of Romans, Britons, Elizabethans, who, we can imagine, travelled with Anon, singing, dancing, putting on a show (*BA*, p. 4). No wonder La

Trobe exclaims, 'the very place.... That's the place for the pageant', upon being shown the ground of Pointz Hall (*BA*, p. 57). For La Trobe, the modern day Anon, recognises her old world.

Between the Acts and 'Anon', then, both point to a remedy for the failing of words and worlds in the ancient cures of song, dance, pictures, gesture, the simplest of utterances, and the drama which includes them all. In a world made ill by the exclusive rule of male conventions – not least of all conventional language – Woolf prescribes as an antidote the traditionally selfless ways of women, prescribes a selfless speech – 'the little language'. But for Woolf this extreme too is dangerous. Once we have taken the cures of La Trobe, the cures of Anon, the curtain can rise and we can speak anew, in a language that is neither male nor female, but both – enriched by the healthy union.

NOTES

1. Since this was written, Brenda Silver has edited 'Anon' and 'The Reader'. See *Twentieth-Century Literature*, Autumn 1979.
2. For a discussion of fertility ritual in *Between the Acts*, see Jane Marcus's 'Some Sources for *Between the Acts*', *Virginia Woolf Miscellany*, Winter 1977; and Judy Little, 'Festive Comedy in Woolf's *Between the Acts*', *Women and Literature*, Spring 1977, pp. 26–37.
3. *The Flight of the Mind: The Letters of Virginia Woolf*, vol. I: *1882–1912*, ed. Nigel Nicolson and Joanne Trautmann (New York: Harcourt, Brace, Jovanovich, 1975) p. 144.
4. Virginia Woolf, 'Notes on an Elizabethan Play', *Collected Essays*, 4 vols (London: Hogarth Press, 1966–7) vol. I, p. 59.
5. Virginia Woolf, 'Walter Sickert', ibid., vol. II, p. 237.
6. Virginia Woolf, *A Writer's Diary*, ed. Leonard Woolf (New York: New American Library, 1953) p. 96. See Charlotte Walker Mondez, 'I Need a Little Language', *Virginia Woolf Quarterly*, Fall 1972, pp. 87–105.
7. Virginia Woolf, '*Jacob's Room*' and '*The Waves*': *Two Complete Novels* (New York: Harcourt, Brace and World, 1959) p. 381.
8. 'Anon', typescript fragment, with the author's manuscript corrections, unsigned, dated 24 Nov 1940, 26 pp. (Berg Collection, folder 9) p. 13 (crossed out); 'The Reader', typescript fragments, with the author's manuscript corrections, unsigned and undated (Berg Collection, folder 5) p. 13. I wish to thank Professor Quentin Bell and the Berg Collection, Astor, Lenox and Tilden Foundation, New York Public Library, for their permission to quote from Virginia Woolf's unpublished manuscripts. To Dr Lola Szladits, curator of the Berg Collection, I am grateful for assistance.

9. See, for example, her comments on the writing of the manly 'Mr. A' in *A Room of One's Own* (New York: Harcourt, Brace and World, 1929) pp. 103–4.

10. For Woolf's consideration of the relationship between patriarchy and fascism, see *Three Guineas* (New York: Harcourt, Brace and World, 1938) pp. 52–3. For a discussion of Woolf's intense concern with fascism while writing *Between the Acts*, see Alex Zwerdling's 'Between the Acts and the Coming War', *Novel*, Spring 1977, pp. 220–36.

11. Virginia Woolf, *The Years* (New York: Harcourt, Brace and World, 1937) p. 405. Further references are to this edition, cited as *Y*.

12. North, for example, has difficulty making sentences (*Y*, p. 410); Nicholas cannot finish his speech (*Y*, p. 420).

13. 'Anon', typescript fragment, with the author's manuscript corrections, unsigned and undated, 9 pp. (Berg Collection, folder 6) p. 1.

14. Until Spenser appeared on the scene, Woolf reflects, England was not 'word conscious'. Even early Elizabethan lyrics sustained Anon's world: 'Music moved beneath the words. No grammar bound them tightly together. They could be read aloud; danced to or sung to . . .' (Berg, folder 9, 'Anon', p. 14).

15. Virginia Woolf, *Between the Acts* (New York: Harcourt, Brace and World, 1941) p. 16. Further references are to this edition, cited as *BA*.

16. Berg, folder 9, 'Anon', p. 2.

17. In the published novel, people wonder, 'but where did she spring from? With that name she wasn't presumably pure English' (*BA*, p. 57). In the typescript in the Berg Collection, La Trobe is at one point 'Tracy', who is really a 'Trot' (Typescript, with the author's manuscript corrections, unsigned, dated throughout from 2 Apr 1938 to 30 July 1939, 186 pp., p. 80).

18. Mrs Swithin's 'Outline of History', recalling an ancient England, reads, 'on top of their matted branches birds sang' (*BA*, p. 218).

19. Berg, folder 9, 'Anon', p. 1. Woolf here credits G. M. Trevelyan as her historian. As Woolf indicates, only the first sentence is a direct quote from Trevelyan. Her second sentence is an imaginative and concise adaptation of Trevelyan's next sentence, which reads,

For many centuries after Britain became an island the untamed forest was king. Its moist and mossy floor was hidden from heaven's eye by a close-drawn curtain woven of innumerable tree tops, which shivered in the breezes of summer dawn and broke into wild music of millions upon millions of waking birds; the concert was prolonged from bough to bough with scarcely a break for hundred of miles over hill and plain and mountain, unheard by man save where, at rarest intervals, a troop of skin clad hunters, stone axe in hand, moved furtively upon an island, not dreaming that there could be other parts of the world besides this damp green woodland with its meres and marshes, wherein they hunted, a terror to its four-footed inhabitants and themselves afraid.

G. M. Trevelyan, *History of England* (New York: Longmans, Green,

    1926) p. 3. In other manuscript versions Woolf quotes an additional line
    from Trevelyan.
20. Berg, folder 9, 'Anon', p. 2.
21. 'Anon', typescript fragment, with the author's manuscript corrections,
    unsigned and undated, 8 pp. (Berg Collection, folder 5) p. 3.
22. Berg, folder 6, 'Anon', p. 1.
23. Berg, folder 9, 'Anon', p. 3.
24. Berg, folder 3, 'The Reader', p. 32.
25. Berg, folder 5, 'Anon', p. 3.
26. Berg, *Between the Acts* typescript, p. 3.
27. Berg, folder 6, 'Anon', p. 4.
28. Berg, folder 9, 'Anon', pp. 20–1.
29. Ibid., p. 24.
30. Berg, folder 3, 'The Reader', p. 31.
31. Berg, folder 9, 'Anon', pp. 1–2.

Index